LEON

BY REBECCA SEAL, CHANTAL SYMONS & JOHN VINCENT

conran OCTOPUS

CONTENTS

ABOUT THE AUTHORS

Rebecca Seal

Rebecca has written about food and drink for the *Financial Times*, *Evening Standard*, the *Observer*, the *Guardian*, *Red* and *The Sunday Times*. Her cookbooks include *Istanbul: Recipes from the heart of Turkey* and *Lisbon: Recipes from the heart of Portugal*, as well as *LEON Happy Soups*, which she co-authored with John Vincent. She is one of the food and drink experts on Channel 4's *Sunday Brunch*. She believes that with the right skills, and just a bit of knowledge, everyone can eat well and hopes that her writing goes a little way towards helping that happen. She lives in London with her husband and two small daughters.

John Vincent

John Vincent is Co-founder of LEON, which now has more than 55 restaurants (including restaurants in Amsterdam, Utrecht, Oslo and Washington, D.C.). He wrote *LEON Naturally Fast Food* with Henry Dimbleby, *LEON Family & Friends* with Kay Plunkett-Hogge, *LEON Happy Salads* and *LEON Fast & Free* with Jane Baxter, and *LEON Happy Soups* and *LEON Happy One-Pot Cooking* with Rebecca Seal. He believes food has the power to delight, invigorate and bring people together – like him, Rebecca and Chantal.

Chantal Symons

Chantal's passion for cooking was ignited when, as a teenager, she was diagnosed as allergic to dairy, eggs and wheat. She believes everyone should take joy and satisfaction from food and so she specializes in free-from cooking. Chantal has worked as a personal chef, caterer, restaurateur and in food product development. She is also a champion barbecuer, and has won several competitions including Jamie Oliver's 'Big Feastival'.

NO MEAT, ONLY PLANTS

We started Leon because we want to make it easier for everyone to eat and live well. This book is for all of you: vegans, those who want to eat more plants and those who just want some tasty recipes irrespective of whether they are made with plants or not.

Leon is built on five themes – food that tastes great, is remarkably good for you, leaves you feeling great after you have eaten it, is kind to the planet, and is affordable. Plants are key to all five. Since we opened in Carnaby Street in 2004 we have created recipes that used fresh herbs and spices to bring flavours alive. As for the role that vegetables play in wellbeing, while government orthodoxies have traditionally held that the basis of your plate should be built from grain-based carbohydrates (bread, pasta, potatoes etc), many organizations (including Harvard University in the US and Alliance for Natural Health in the UK) are increasingly challenging this. Both organizations advocate for making vegetables the food group we should be eating most of and most often. Plants of all sizes, colours, types and heritage – not just wheat and starchy carbs – are finally gaining their place in the sun.

Here are the ten things we believe to be true:

1. We all benefit from eating plants with every meal.

2. Plants provide the dietary fibre that is at the heart of our wellbeing.

3. By eating a wide variety of plants (think rainbow) we are not only getting a good broad spectrum of nutrients for our own cells, we are also diversifying our gut bacteria /microbiome because different bacteria are fed by different plants.

4. It's best not to eat raw plants too often in the evening – our digestive system will cope much better with them during the day.

5. We do well to eat our plants (all our food in fact) slowly, and if we can do so, with love. If you eat stressed or in anger even the best ingredients will turn rogue.

6. Yes, chewing thirty times really is good for us.

7. For those who still want to eat meat, treat it as a side dish, the way we used to think about veg.

8. We can all learn from cultures who are good at making vegetables taste good – the Mediterranean, the Middle East and southern India (especially Kerela).

9. We need to respect and honour the relatively thin layer of soil that we rely on to feed us (and to feed all animals) and maintain or even increase the genetic diversity of the plants we grow – at the very least this will help them be more resilient to climate change.

10. Oh, and lastly, we believe that we will see a return to the use of herbs to prevent and even treat illnesses. This won't please everyone and there will be many attempts to prevent this.

From our inception in 2004 we have made it our mission to make vegetables taste good. We wrote *Fast Vegetarian* in 2014 and our big focus in 2016 was 'The Power of Plants'. Since then even the mainstream has become obsessed with plants. This book is the result of our fifteen-year love affair with veg, not the product of a recent holiday fling. We have loved writing it. It has tested our creativity and at times our resilience. But most of the recipes are new, and pretty good actually.

We can't wait to hear what you think.

John, LEON Co-founder & CEO

NUTRITION

*A VEGAN OR PLANT-BASED
DIET CAN BE EXTREMELY
HEALTHY, BUT MAY
NEED PLANNING.*

Some vegans choose to take supplements, while others reckon they get everything they need from the food they eat. Whichever you choose, here are a few things to think about. (Consult a registered healthcare practitioner about supplements, and do consider taking some if you are pregnant or breastfeeding.)

PROTEIN: good sources of protein for vegans include pulses like chickpeas, lentils and beans, peanuts, tofu, tempeh and seitan (a wheat-based meat replacement). Try and eat a couple of portions a day. Since the jury is still out on whether soya is healthy or not, we tend to be conservative in our consumption, and we mostly stick to traditional soya products like tofu, tempeh and soy sauce, which have been around for hundreds of years, rather than eating soya as a dairy alternative. Try and buy organic soya products if you can, as they are less likely to contain genetically modified soya; choose soya from companies who do not use soya grown on land cleared from rainforests (Alpro and Provamel are good examples).

CALCIUM: the Western diet relies heavily on dairy for calcium, so it is worth seeking out plant milks that have been fortified with calcium and vegan vitamin D as well as eating green leafy vegetables and almonds.

VITAMIN D: in the UK, we don't get enough sunshine from September to April to make our own vitamin D, so it is recommended that everyone takes a supplement. Look out for vitamin D2, which is always vegan, and vegan versions of D3, which is often made from animal sources.

VITAMIN B12 AND IODINE: these are really hard to find in a vegan diet, so make an extra effort to eat fortified foods, or add plenty of nutritional yeast and seaweed into your diet.

FATS: we all need fat in our diet – for energy, to maintain a healthy weight and to allow our bodies and brains to complete vital functions. Some nutrients are fat soluble (vitamins A, D, E and K), so we need fat to help us absorb them. Even more importantly, we need to eat a range of fats, including omega 6, which is found in pumpkin seeds, hemp seeds, sunflower seeds and walnuts, and the harder-to-find omega 3. Vegans can either take an omega 3 microalgae-based supplement, or

help your body convert alpha-linoleic acid into other essential forms of omega 3 by eating about a tablespoon of chia seeds or ground flaxseeds, 2 tablespoons of hemp seeds or 3 walnuts every day (according to the Vegan Society). Too much omega 6 inhibits the body's use of omega 3, so be careful not to overdo it by using sunflower or corn oil for cooking – choose rapeseed oil instead.

IRON: this is essential and low iron levels can lead to a lack of energy or even serious illness. Vegan foods rich in iron include pulses, cashew nuts and almonds, quinoa, tofu, tempeh, soya, green leafy vegetables, sprouted seeds, dried apricots, raisins and dates, and fortified breakfast cereal. Iron is best absorbed when you eat it with something containing vitamin C, like citrus.

If you are eating a good amount of all the foods mentioned above, then the chances are you are also getting plenty of vitamin K and zinc. Add a few Brazil nuts to your diet for an extra hit of selenium. The vegan diet is almost always full of fibre (as long as you don't eat nothing but chips!). Eating a wide spectrum of multicoloured fruit and vegetables, along with wholegrains and complex carbohydrates, means you will get the full range of trace elements and nutrients that we all need to thrive.

KEY

Suitable for Freezing

Family Friendly

Lunchbox Friendly

Gluten Free

Wheat Free

Nut Free

Soy Free

	MONDAY	**TUESDAY**
BREAKFAST	OVERNIGHT OATS WITH FRUIT	FRENCH TOAST WITH POACHED RHUBARB
LUNCH	SPANISH OMELETTE	FREEKEH SALAD WITH ALMOND FETA
SNACK	ROASTED CHICKPEAS	LEFTOVER SPANISH OMELETTE
DINNER	LEMON, PEA & BASIL RISOTTO	CHILLI CON THREE BEANS OR JACKFRUIT

YOUR WEEK-LONG MENU PLAN

CAREFUL PLANNING CAN MAKE VEGAN COOKING A LOT SIMPLER.

Having the fridge or freezer full of leftovers, ready to be zapped into a quick meal or turned into something new, is very helpful so we've included a symbol (see page 9) where a dish can be frozen.Check out our list of fridge raiders on page 119 – we like to keep a stash of ready-made quick and filling snacky things, like arancini, croquetas and fritters, as well as a jar of crunchy roasted chickpeas (see page 242), so that we aren't always reaching for the biscuits…although we do love biscuits too! Many of the recipes in this book will work in a sandwich or wrap – have a look at the lists on page 118 and page 103 for some inspiration.

It's a cliché, but a good breakfast will set you up, even on rushed weekday mornings. Batching things like our savoury breakfast muffins (see page 28), blueberry muffins (see page 26) or granola (see page 25) can mean a happier start to the day, while weekends are made for leisurely brunches and our fluffy pancakes (see page 20) or vegan scrambles (see pages 36 and 38).

WEEK

MENU

LONG

PLAN

SATURDAY

SUNDAY

FLUFFY AMERICAN-STYLE PANCAKES

HAVE A LIE-IN & SWITCH BREAKFAST FOR BRUNCH

PHO VIETNAMESE NOODLE SOUP

CARROT SMOKED 'SALMON' BAGELS

MISO BUTTER CARAMEL POPCORN

SCONES WITH JAM & VEGAN CREAM

PIZZA, FOLLOWED BY CHOCOLATE SORBET

MR BAO'S SESAME & AUBERGINE BAO

11

WEDNESDAY	THURSDAY	FRIDAY
BLUEBERRY POPPY SEED MUFFINS	GRANOLA WITH CHIA SEED YOGHURT	FENNEL, RADISH & DILL AVOCADO TOAST
LEFTOVER CHILLI WRAPS WITH MEXICAN SLAW OR SALAD	VEGAN POKE, WITH A BLUEBERRY MUFFIN	PARSNIP, KALE & BEETROOT SALAD, WITH A BLUEBERRY MUFFIN
NUT BUTTER JAM COOKIES	LEFTOVER SPANISH CHICKPEA FRITTERS	NUT BUTTER JAM COOKIES
SPANISH CHICKPEA FRITTERS WITH ROMESCO & A GREEN SALAD	SUPER-GREEN GREEN CURRY WITH RICE	MAISIE'S 'FISH' & CHIPS

SWITCHES & SWAPS

Figuring out how to make vegan versions of your favourite recipes is great fun. If you are using any pre-prepared (shop bought) ingredients, always check the label to ensure they are vegan and work for you or your guests if you are catering for allergies, to ensure that they don't contain the ingredients that you would like to avoid. Many seemingly innocuous items (including stock cubes, flat breads, burger buns and condiments containing wine) sometimes contain meat or dairy products so make sure you always read the label carefully. Here are our top discoveries for some great vegan switches.

AQUAFABA: the fancy name for the water from a tin of chickpeas (aquafaba means 'bean water'). You can use other cooked beans (experiment with beans like haricot), but chickpeas are the most reliable (you can also use the liquid from jarred chickpeas). It's a miraculous ingredient – and we usually throw it away. It behaves just like egg white – in many ways it is even better as you can't over-beat it – and it can be used almost anywhere you might use egg whites, from cloud-like white meringues and chewy cookies, to pancakes and even cocktails and mayo. Save it whenever you cook with chickpeas; one 400g tin will yield 150–200ml aquafaba and it keeps for up to 5 days in the fridge. Some brands work better than others: choose chickpeas in unsalted water, shake the tin well before opening and when you've drained it into a bowl, look for thick, gloopy liquid. If it seems thin, reduce it in a pan to thicken, then cool before using.

FLAXSEEDS & CHIA SEEDS: as well as **bananas**, and occasionally **apple sauce**, we use ground (also known as milled) flaxseeds (linseeds) or chia seeds to make 'eggs', which help bind baked goods. Both keep well if kept in a sealed container, in a cool dark place. To replace 1 egg, mix 1 tablespoon ground flaxseeds (whole seeds won't work) or 1 tablespoon chia seeds, with 3 tablespoons water, then set aside. After 5–10 minutes, the mixture will turn into a gel. (Don't try and use the seeds without soaking first.) Don't try the gel in an omelette! If you want an omelette, go for **gram flour** (see page 150). And if you want scramble, use **soft tofu**, or **ackee**, with a pinch of eggy **black salt** (see page 38).

NUTRITIONAL YEAST: also known as 'nooch', this sounds weird and looks like flaky fish food, but is a brilliant (and cheap) replacement for Parmesan. The yeast is deactivated, and it adds savoury, nutty, umami-ness to foods. We use it to make 'cheese' and cheesy sauces and to sprinkle over pasta dishes. It is rich in hard-to-find B vitamins.

MISO: **white** or **yellow miso paste**, used sparingly, replicates the tang and funk of mature cheeses, and can be delicious in broths, sauces and even vegan 'butter' (see page 229). If you need to avoid soya, non-soya miso is available online (we use Tideford Organics). Similarly, we love using an occasional splash of old-fashioned **pickle brine**, as proper cultured pickles contain lactic acid, just like cheese and butter.

SEAWEED POWDER: seaweed is a brilliant addition to a vegan diet as it is rich in iodine, otherwise found in dairy and seafood. **Kelp powder** is sold as a health food, but its seaside tang makes it good at replacing fish sauce, anchovies and even Worcestershire sauce. (You can also use dried and rehydrated leafy seaweeds, like **hijiki** or **wakame**, in salads, as well as **nori** sheets to wrap up sushi rolls.)

SMOKE: **liquid smoke** is now easy to find online and in large supermarkets; made from concentrated smoked water, it absolutely is worth getting hold of if you want to make carrot smoked 'salmon' (see page

34) or vegan bacon (see pages 40–1). **Sweet smoked paprika** is a good second choice though, especially in sauces. Both keep almost forever.

SOY SAUCE:
soy sauce is a fantastic source of savoury umami. Use it to replace the roasty flavours you get from dark stocks and browned meats. If you need to avoid wheat, choose tamari soy sauce (but check the label). Rebecca can't eat soya, so often replaces soy sauce with a little bit of **Maggi liquid seasoning**. However, Maggi is made from wheat, and Chantal can't eat gluten, so when we eat together, we use a dash of **coconut aminos** instead.

COCONUT OIL:
because of its relatively high saturated fat content, coconut oil is very good at replacing butter when baking, and anywhere you need extra help to bind things, like 'meatballs' or burgers. We much prefer using it to processed vegan margarine, where possible, which is often made with palm oil. **Refined coconut oil** is flavourless, so is best used when you don't want the strong flavour of **extra virgin coconut oil** to come through. Find it with the cooking oils in the supermarket – it is excellent for cooking with in general and we use it all over the place, instead of dairy butter. If you are making a straight swap with butter, use 80% coconut oil and 20% water, which is the make-up of butter, plus a pinch of salt and ¼–½ teaspoon vegan cider vinegar. Coconut oil is not suitable to use in dressings and mayonnaise, however – for these you need to choose an oil that is liquid at room temperature.

MARGARINE:
if you have found a vegan margarine (sometimes called vegan butter) that you like, check the packet to see if it is suitable for frying or baking as well as spreading.

SUGAR:
in some countries, certain sugars are refined using bone char, which makes them unsuitable for vegans. In the UK, most sugar is vegan, and if you are concerned about sustainability and the well-being of workers, you can even buy sugar made from British sugar beets. Be cautious when it comes to swapping a sugar or sweetener in a recipe, as different sugars do different jobs. **Icing sugar** and **caster sugar** are very dry, fine sugars, and add to the structure of a dish or cake without adding liquid. Less refined brown sugars like **muscovado** and **palm sugar** contain more moisture, with dark and toffee-flavoured sugars like **molasses** being very wet, and so may change how something like a cake behaves as well as tastes. Be sure that the sugars you are swapping have the same texture – chunky palm sugar nuggets often can't replace fine caster. You can swap between liquid sugars more easily – **maple syrup**, **agave nectar** and **golden syrup** all work the same way, and can be used to replace honey, which isn't vegan. There is no such thing as a healthy sugar – it doesn't matter which you choose, in the end, they all do the same thing inside the body.

ACIDS:
we use a lot of **vegan cider vinegar** for several reasons. One is that it helps activate some raising agents, which is especially useful in recipes that need to rise, but don't contain eggs. Another is because it helps to replicate the tangy flavour you get from dairy products. Used sparingly, you won't taste the vinegar at all (we like Natural Umber organic vinegar, which has a really delicate flavour). There are dozens of folk remedy and health claims about cider vinegar – whether any are true or not is still up for debate. **Cream of tartar** is a powdered acid, found in the baking aisle at the supermarket, and very helpful when whipping aquafaba into meringues, or for making any kind of plant-based whipped cream.

YOUR STORECUPBOARD

TINS, JARS & BOTTLES

Refined coconut oil
Extra virgin coconut oil
Full-fat coconut milk
Coconut cream
Vegan cider vinegar
Pomegranate molasses
Fermented tofu
Vegan bouillon powder
Red pepper paste
Artichokes in oil or brine
Olives
Pickled cabbage
Kimchi
Capers
Harissa
Preserved lemons
Tamarind paste
Maple syrup
Sesame oil
Olive oil
Vegan sherry vinegar
Ackee
Banana blossom
Unripe green jackfruit
   in brine
Vegan chipotle paste
Sriracha chilli sauce
American hot sauce
Tamari soy sauce
Maggi liquid seasoning
Vegan Dijon mustard
Vegan rice wine or mirin
Vegan rice vinegar
Tahini
White or yellow miso paste
Vegan wine
Vegan beer
Vegan sherry

VEGETABLES & FRUIT

Avocados
Wild mushrooms
Large mushrooms
Garlic
Onions
Spring onions
Shallots
Peppers
Kale
Unwaxed lemons
Limes
Plantains
Chillies
Cauliflower
Squash
Sweet potatoes
Aubergine
Pomegranate
Pumpkin
Cucumber
Radishes
Celeriac

DRIED

Basmati rice
Wild rice
Thai sticky rice
Risotto rice
Pasta
Oats
Dried mushrooms
Panko breadcrumbs
Polenta

BAKING

Dairy-free dark chocolate
Ground arrowroot

Tapioca flour
Probiotic powder
   or capsules
Plain or gluten-free plain
   flour
Vital wheat gluten flour
Cream of tartar
Gram (chickpea) flour
Dates
Unsweetened cocoa powder
   or cacao powder
Dried fruit
Ground almonds
Rice flour
Cornflour
Caster sugar
Soft brown sugar
Icing sugar
Palm sugar
Maple sugar
Golden syrup
Agave
Nut butters

NUTS & SEEDS

Cashew nuts
Almonds
Hazelnuts
Pine nuts
Ground flaxseeds
Chia seeds
Pistachios
Pumpkin seeds
Sesame seeds
Sunflower seeds
Peanuts
Walnuts

PULSES

Tinned chickpeas
Haricot beans
Puy lentils
Red lentils
Black beans
Kidney beans

NATURAL FLAVOURS

Black salt
Kelp or seaweed powder
Dried seaweed
Nutritional yeast
Mustard powder
Liquid smoke
Sweet smoked paprika
Cumin
Coriander
Flaky sea salt
Fine sea salt
Vanilla extract or vanilla
    bean paste
Garlic powder
Onion powder
Fennel seeds
Cayenne pepper
Chilli flakes
Garam masala
Cardamom
Turmeric
Fresh ginger
Nutmeg
Saffron
Curry leaves
Lime leaves
Dried edible rose petals
Paprika
Lemongrass

FRIDGE

Extra-firm tofu
Silken tofu
Non-dairy full-fat plain
    yoghurt
Plant milk
Vegan margarine or butter
Fresh herbs
Vegan cream
Vegan cream cheese

FREEZER

Sweetcorn
Peas
Spinach
Berries
Vegan shortcrust pastry
Vegan puff pastry
Flat breads
Wheat and corn tortillas

HOW TO COOK *FAST*

Vegan food is notorious for being, let's say, a little time-consuming to prepare. We have included plenty of easy speedy recipes here, as well as some more ambitious ones, but you will be able to hustle through your mealtime prep even faster with these tips.

- Keep your knives and peelers sharp. Learn how to care for them yourself, or get them professionally sharpened. This will speed up your chopping no end.

- Watch a few online videos about how to chop vegetables efficiently. Life. Changing.

- A high-speed blender is a great investment, but can be pricy. Get the best that you can afford (Rebecca swears by her Vitamix).

- If you want to get really nerdy (and we are definitely kitchen nerds) arrange your cupboards and shelves so the most-used things are at the front (salt, sugar, vinegar, flour) and the least used (dried rose petals, nutmeg) are at the back.

- When ready to cook, read the recipe in full. Then read it again. Then cook.

- Get all the ingredients out before you start cooking, so you're not rummaging about in the cupboard for pine nuts to toast when everything else is ready and waiting.

- Line up your tools. Realizing the blender is covered in cashew cream halfway through making your pasta sauce is the worst.

- If you will need boiling water later, get the kettle on.

- If you haven't got time to soak cashew nuts in cold water for 4 hours or overnight (or even in boiling water for 30 minutes), you can simmer them in a pan of boiling water for 15 minutes, then drain and rinse.

- Stick any fruit or veg that needs washing in a colander and rinse it all in one go.

- Use a large bowl to collect trimmings as you cook, so you aren't pacing back and forth to the bin.

- Tuck a tea towel into your belt, for hand-drying and spill mopping.

- If you're sautéing, put a dry pan on to heat up a few minutes before you need it, then add any fat once hot. The pan will warm more quickly, and the food is less likely to stick.

- To make the clean-up quicker, have a bowl of hot soapy water on the go while you cook, and dump anything you've finished with in it for a soak.

- Batch-cook and fill the freezer for those nights where you really don't want to cook. (And even if you're not batching, save leftovers: we love finding single servings of stew, leftover roast vegetables or curry in the freezer, then magicking them into a quick solo lunch.) We've included a freezer symbol (see page 9) wherever a recipe is easy to scale up and freezes well.

HOW TO EAT OUT AS A *VEGAN*

Although it can still be tricky, more and more restaurants are happy to provide great vegan and plant-based food, so it is getting easier, especially in larger towns and cities, for vegans to eat out…and actually eat.

- Download a vegan app, or check out a vegan/vegan-friendly restaurant listing website. We love Happy Cow, which lists and reviews venues all over the world.

- Choose a chain of restaurants that is vegan-friendly, or somewhere that cooks everything from scratch. Pubs or cafés that buy in ready-made food and heat it up will struggle to tweak dishes, even vegetables and sides.

- Use Instagram. Loads of cool pop-ups and front line vegan eateries are on there, that may not have the usual media coverage.

- We try and judge when and what we need to explain. Some restaurants offer separate vegan or allergy-friendly menus, so it's always worth asking in case there is one, while in other restaurants the team might not know exactly what being vegan or plant-based means. We have had many funny conversations about how 'just a little bit of butter' still means a dish contains dairy.

- Research a new place before you visit, if you can. Phone ahead, as a really good kitchen might make up a special dish that is cooked without dairy, say, especially for you. Otherwise, check out the menu online and have a game plan before you sit down, to speed things up. (This also helps if you're with a non-vegan group and feel shy about asking lots of questions.)

- Ask for swaps, particularly if there are things like beans or grains elsewhere on the menu that could be added to your meal.

- Order two or three starters, if the mains don't work.

- While traditional French or particularly cheese-heavy Italian restaurants may be off limits, Greek, Turkish, Lebanese, Spanish, Thai, Vietnamese, Mexican, Japanese and Jamaican Ital restaurants often have lots of plant-based options.

- Watch out for: meat stocks, butter or cream used in sauces; egg or butter in brioche buns; fish sauce or shrimp paste used in South East Asian dishes; ghee (clarified butter) used in Indian recipes; eggs used in fresh pasta; dishes finished with a sprinkle of cheese or drizzle of butter.

- Some wines, beers and spirits are clarified using animal products. In the UK, vegan wine can be labelled as such, while anything that has been clarified with fish by-products or milk should say so on the label. Lots of bars and restaurants now go out of their way to offer vegan drinks.

1

BREAKFAST & BRUNCH

FLUFFY AMERICAN-STYLE PANCAKES

MAKES 10 PANCAKES

90ml **aquafaba** (tinned chickpea water, see page 12)

1 teaspoon **lemon juice**

150g **plain flour**

½ teaspoon **bicarbonate of soda**

½ teaspoon **baking powder**

1 tablespoon **caster sugar**

a pinch of **salt**

150ml **plant milk** (use non-nut or non-soya to keep NF or SoF)

1 tablespoon **neutral cooking oil**, plus extra for cooking

1 teaspoon **vanilla extract**

1 teaspoon **vegan cider vinegar**

zest of ½ **lemon**

PREP TIME: 18 MINS · REST TIME: 10 MINS
COOK TIME: 15 MINS

When you're happy with this basic recipe, start adding extras: we love a good pinch of fresh nutmeg, ground cardamom or cinnamon, or a little desiccated coconut, some ground almonds or – especially for kids – some mashed ripe banana. If you prefer, you can use melted and cooled coconut oil in place of the cooking oil in the batter. Serve the pancakes with maple syrup, non-dairy yoghurt, fresh fruit or compote.

1. Pour the aquafaba into the spotlessly clean bowl of a stand mixer fitted with the whisk attachment (or a large mixing bowl if using an electric hand whisk). Add the lemon juice, then whisk until the mixture forms stiff white peaks, about 5 minutes. Set aside.

2. In a large bowl, sift together the flour, bicarbonate of soda and baking powder. Add the sugar and salt and mix well. In a jug, mix together the milk, oil, vanilla, cider vinegar and lemon zest. Add the wet ingredients to the dry and mix briefly until just combined – it will be lumpy, thick and quite sticky.

3. Next, fold in the whisked aquafaba, keeping as much air in the mix as possible, until just combined; it doesn't need to be smooth. Allow the batter to stand for 10 minutes (but no longer) to let the gluten develop slightly (this improves the texture of the pancakes, but the raising agents are most active when cooked quickly).

4. Add a tiny splash of oil to a large frying pan, then wipe it over the base using kitchen paper. Heat over a medium-low heat, then drop generous tablespoons of the batter into the hot pan. Spread gently, if necessary, to make thick pancakes about 8cm in diameter. Cook for 3–4 minutes (they take a little longer than traditional pancakes), until the bases are golden, bubbles appear and the tops begin to set. Turn over and cook the other sides until golden. Keep warm while you cook the remaining batter, wiping a little more oil over the pan, if necessary.

TIP

Use a metal spoon to fold in the aquafaba, swiping and lifting it through the batter, rather than stirring in the usual way.

BANANA BREAKFAST LOAF

1 LOAF

oil, for greasing

1 tablespoon **ground flaxseeds**
   or **chia seeds**

2 tablespoons **water**

175g **plain flour**

75g **wholemeal flour**

1 teaspoon **ground cinnamon**

a pinch of **freshly grated nutmeg**

½ teaspoon **bicarbonate of soda**

1 teaspoon **baking powder**

110ml **unsweetened plant milk**
   (use non-soya to keep SoF)

1 teaspoon **vanilla extract**
   or **vanilla bean paste**

2 tablespoons **agave nectar**, **maple
   syrup** or **golden syrup**

45g **soft brown sugar** (or **coconut**
   or **palm sugar**)

1½ teaspoons **vegan cider vinegar**

50ml **refined** or **extra virgin
   coconut oil**, melted

175g ripe **bananas**, mashed

75g **nuts**, such as **walnuts**,
   hazelnuts or **almonds**, or a
   mixture, chopped

50g **dried fruit**, chopped into small
   pieces if necessary (optional)

a pinch of **salt**

PREP TIME: 20 MINS · COOK TIME: 50 MINS

You can use spelt flour to make this loaf, but the results will be firmer in texture with less of a rise than with ordinary flour. To make it more cake-like, you could add some dairy-free chocolate chips or chunks, or drizzle it, while still warm, with icing sugar mixed with a little water.

1. Heat the oven to 180°C/350°F/gas mark 4. Grease a small loaf tin (about 20 × 10cm) and line with 2 long strips of baking parchment. Place the strips at 90 degree angles to each other and allow to hang over the edges of the tin.

2. In a large bowl, mix together the ground flaxseeds or chia seeds and the water and allow to soak for 5 minutes.

3. Meanwhile, in a separate bowl, mix together the flours, cinnamon, nutmeg, bicarbonate of soda and baking powder.

4. Stir the milk, vanilla, agave nectar or syrup, sugar and cider vinegar into the soaked seeds. Mix well, then add the melted coconut oil and mashed bananas.

5. Working fairly quickly (to maximize the lift from the raising agents), mix together the wet and dry ingredients, adding the chopped nuts and dried fruit, if using, and the salt. Stir until just combined, then pour into the prepared loaf tin.

6. Bake in the oven for 45–50 minutes, until the loaf has risen to about twice its original height, the top is golden and firm to the touch, and a skewer inserted into the centre comes out clean. Allow to cool in the tin for 10 minutes, then transfer to a wire rack.

7. You can serve the loaf warm, but don't cut into it when it's still hot because the moisture will escape as steam and the loaf will dry out. The loaf will keep for a couple of days in a sealed container, but we reckon it is best eaten the day it is made, or frozen as soon as it is cool.

TIP
Cut the cooled loaf into slices or fingers before freezing, then tuck the frozen pieces into lunchboxes – they will be ready to eat by midday.

OVERNIGHT OATS

SERVES 1

(GF) (WF) (NF) (SoF)

50g **jumbo oats** (for a chunkier texture) or **rolled oats**

250ml **plant milk** (use non-nut or non-soya to keep NF or SoF)

maple syrup, **date syrup** or **agave nectar**, to sweeten (optional)

PREP TIME: 5 MINS · SOAK TIME: OVERNIGHT
COOK TIME: 5 MINS

When it comes to oats, some people worry about phytic acid, which occurs naturally in oats and other grains and pulses. The idea is that phytic acid binds with nutrients and makes it harder for our bodies to absorb them. There are a lot of conflicting theories, and the science isn't clear about whether phytic acid is bad for us or not – some studies suggest our gut might increase production of phytase, which breaks down the acid, when needed; others think it may have anti-cancer properties, since phytic acid is an anti-oxidant. If you are concerned, one option is to soak the oats in water, drain and rinse them, then add plant milk for cooking. Alternatively, add a little lemon juice or vegan cider vinegar to the milk when soaking. Some theories suggest that the probiotics found in fermented products like live yoghurt help to break down phytic acid, so you could add some to the soaking mixture, or serve this with a dollop on top or with a live yoghurt smoothie alongside.

1. Pour the oats and milk into a bowl or large jar with a lid. Mix well, then cover and soak in the fridge overnight.

2. In the morning, transfer the oat mixture to a pan and cook over a medium-low heat for 3–5 minutes (soaked oats cook quickly), until hot and creamy. Eat as it is, or sweeten if you like, then top with your choice of fruit, seeds or yoghurt.

> *TIP*
> Try topping the cooked oats with fresh fruit or compote (made with berries, apples or pears), toasted seeds (see page 243) or a handful of granola (see opposite). Serve with a dollop of non-dairy live yoghurt or coconut cream.

GRANOLA

3 tablespoons **neutral cooking oil**, plus extra for greasing

300ml **maple syrup**

300g **gluten-free oats**

150g **mixed seeds** (**pumpkin**, **sunflower** and/or **flaxseeds**)

150g **mixed nuts**, such as **walnuts**, **Brazil nuts**, **almonds**, **hazelnuts** and **pecans**, chopped

150g **mixed dried fruit**, such as **raisins**, **sultanas**, **cranberries**, **blueberries**, **sour cherries**, chopped **dates** or **apricots**

PREP TIME: 5 MINS · COOK TIME: 25 MINS

Serve at breakfast with non-dairy yoghurt and fresh fruit or as a topping for puddings like poached pears or baked peaches.

1. Heat the oven to 150°C/300°F/gas mark 2.

2. Whisk together the oil and maple syrup. Place the oats, seeds and nuts in a large bowl. Pour over half the maple syrup mixture, then toss together. Pour over the rest of the syrup mixture and toss again, making sure everything in the bottom of the bowl gets a coating.

3. Spread out the granola on 2 lightly greased baking trays. Bake for 10 minutes, then give each tray a good stir. Bake for another 10–15 minutes, or until the oats and nuts are golden. Allow to cool.

4. Tip the granola into a large bowl, add the dried fruit and mix together.

5. When completely cool, store in an airtight container for up to 2 weeks.

BLUEBERRY POPPY SEED MUFFINS

MAKES
9

1 tablespoon **ground flaxseeds**

2 tablespoons **water**

75ml **vegetable oil**

175ml **plant milk** (use non-soya to keep SoF)

1 teaspoon **vinegar**

zest of ½ **lemon**

250g **plain flour**

1½ teaspoons **baking powder**

½ teaspoon **bicarbonate of soda**

a pinch of **salt**

150g **caster sugar**

150g **blueberries**

2 tablespoons **ground almonds** (optional)

1 tablespoon **poppy seeds**

2 tablespoons **demerara sugar** (optional)

PREP TIME: 20 MINS · COOK TIME: 35 MINS

Light and fruity muffins – make at the weekend for a lazy brunch, freeze the leftovers, then pop frozen muffins into lunchboxes first thing and they will be ready to eat by noon.

1. Heat the oven to 190°C/375°F/gas mark 5. Line a muffin tray with 9 paper muffin cases.

2. In a small bowl, mix together the flaxseeds and water and allow to soak for 5 minutes. In a separate bowl, whisk together the oil, milk, vinegar and lemon zest.

3. Sift the flour, baking powder and bicarbonate of soda into a large bowl. Add the salt and caster sugar and mix together well. Reserve 27 blueberries (3 per muffin), then add the ground almonds, if using, the poppy seeds and remaining blueberries to the dry ingredients and mix again (coating the berries in flour makes them less likely to sink).

4. Add the oil mixture and soaked flaxseeds to the dry ingredients and stir until just combined (it doesn't need to be perfectly smooth and over-mixing will make the muffins tough). Divide the mixture between the paper cases, then push the reserved berries into the tops of the muffins. Sprinkle with the demerara sugar, if using.

5. Bake for 30–35 minutes, until light golden, firm and a skewer comes out clean. Allow to cool in the tin for 5–10 minutes, then transfer to a wire rack and allow to cool completely.

6. These are best eaten the day they are made but will keep in an airtight container for a couple of days. Alternatively, freeze once cool.

SAVOURY BREAKFAST MUFFINS

MAKES 14

225g **smoked tofu** or **extra-firm plain tofu**, cut into 5mm cubes

2 tablespoons **olive oil**, plus extra for greasing (optional)

250g **chestnut mushrooms**, sliced

I **leek**, halved and thinly sliced

1 tablespoon finely chopped **fresh sage**

salt and **freshly ground black pepper**

FOR THE BATTER:

300g **gram flour**

2 tablespoons **olive oil**

600ml **unsweetened almond milk**

I teaspoon **gluten-free baking powder**

2 teaspoons **onion powder**

2 teaspoons **garlic powder**

2 tablespoons **vegan Dijon mustard**

I teaspoon **vegan vegetable bouillon powder**

2 tablespoons **nutritional yeast**

½ teaspoon **black salt** (see page 38) or a generous pinch of **fine sea salt**

a generous pinch of **freshly ground black pepper**

2 tablespoons finely chopped **fresh chives**

PREP TIME: 20 MINS · COOK TIME: I HOUR 10 MINS

For breakfasting on the run, for filling up the freezer, for kids, for grown-ups and even for lunch. (When Chantal developed these, her son, Ethan, managed to eat a whole batch.) You can replace the tofu with mushroom or tempeh bacon (see pages 40–1), if you like.

1. Heat the oven to 180°C/350°F/gas mark 4.

2. Place the tofu on a baking tray. Pour over 1 tablespoon of the oil and toss gently to coat. Bake for 25 minutes, or until crisp and golden all over, turning once halfway through.

3. While the tofu is cooking, make the batter. Sift the gram flour into a large bowl, add the remaining ingredients and whisk until smooth. Set aside.

4. Heat the remaining oil in a frying pan. Add the mushrooms, leek and sage and sauté gently over a medium heat until the vegetables are soft, about 10 minutes.

5. When the tofu is cooked, remove it from the oven, leaving the oven on. Grease your muffin tray or line it with petal or tulip paper cases (see Tip). Divide the cooked vegetables and tofu between the cases or tray, then pour over the batter. Bake for 30–45 minutes (depending on the muffin size), until they are puffed up, golden brown and firm to the touch. Allow to cool in the tin slightly before removing and cooling on a wire rack.

6. Serve the muffins warm or at room temperature. If you like, you can reheat them or split and toast under a low grill.

TIP

If you use a deep muffin tin, this recipe will make 12, but using a shallower tin will make up to 16. Use flat muffin cases rather than pleated cupcake cases, or grease the tin and omit the lining papers.

FOUR WAYS WITH AVOCADO TOAST

4–8 slices of **bread**, depending on their size (we like sourdough)

2–3 **avocados**, depending on their size and your hunger, mashed

PREP TIME: 5 MINS · COOK TIME: 2 MINS

1. Toast the slices of bread, then spread with the mashed avocados.

2. Top with one of the following toppings.

1. WHITE BEAN, ROASTED TOMATO & OLIVE

PREP TIME: 10 MINS · COOK TIME: 20 MINS
Warm and earthy.

200g **cherry tomatoes**, quartered
2 tablespoons **olive oil**
200g **white beans**, rinsed and drained
20 **dried black olives**, pitted and chopped into 5mm pieces
1 tablespoon finely chopped **fresh thyme**, **parsley** or **oregano**
extra virgin olive oil, for drizzling
salt and **freshly ground black pepper**

1. Heat the oven to 190°C/375°F/gas mark 5.

2. Toss the tomatoes in the olive oil and season with salt and pepper. Arrange in a single layer on a baking sheet and roast for 15 minutes. Add the beans and olives and toss together, then cook for a further 3–4 minutes, until warmed through. Remove from the oven and add the herbs.

3. Top the avocado toast with the warm mixture. Season well with pepper and a little more salt, to taste. Drizzle with extra virgin olive oil and serve immediately.

2. KIMCHI

PREP TIME: 3 MINS
Hot and spicy.

6 heaped tablespoons **kimchi**, at room temperature
salt and **freshly ground black pepper**

1. Drain the kimchi if it is quite wet and roughly chop if it is in large chunks.

2. Spoon over the avocado toast and season to taste. Serve immediately.

TIPS

Fermented tofu or bean curd is also brilliant with avocado, especially the versions that include red chilli. Instead of the kimchi, try tossing 100g chopped cucumber with 2 tablespoons crumbled fermented bean curd.

You can also top your avo toast with the mushroom bacon on page 40, the roasted chickpeas on page 242, the almond feta on page 154, or the salsa verde on page 231.

3. MARINATED TOMATO & BASIL

PREP TIME: 5 MINS
MARINATING TIME: 20 MINS
Fresh and summery.

150g **cherry tomatoes**, quartered

½ teaspoon **vegan sherry vinegar** or **vegan red wine vinegar**

½ teaspoon finely chopped **garlic** or very finely **chopped shallot** (optional, but recommended)

1 tablespoon **extra virgin olive oil**, plus extra for drizzling

a large handful of **fresh basil**, leaves roughly torn

salt and **freshly ground black pepper**

1. Toss together the tomatoes, vinegar, garlic or shallot, if using, and the oil, then season with salt and pepper. Allow to marinate at room temperature for at least 20 minutes, preferably an hour or two.

2. Add the basil, then check the seasoning. Top the avocado toast with the mixture, leaving most of the liquid behind in the bowl. Drizzle over a little extra olive oil and serve immediately.

4. FENNEL, RADISH & DILL

PREP TIME: 10 MINS
Crunchy and cool.

½ small head of **fennel**, cut into very thin rounds

6cm chunk of **cucumber**, cut into very thin strips

100g **radishes**, cut into very thin strips

1 tablespoon finely chopped **fresh dill**

1 teaspoon **lemon juice**

2 teaspoons **extra virgin olive oil**

salt and **freshly ground black pepper**

1. Toss together all the ingredients and season with salt and pepper.

2. Top the avocado toast with the fennel slaw and serve immediately.

FRENCH TOAST WITH POACHED RHUBARB

SERVES
4

NF SoF

FOR THE RHUBARB:

1 tablespoon **caster sugar**

75ml **water** or **orange juice**

zest of ½ **orange** (optional)

250g **rhubarb**, cut into
    4–5cm pieces

FOR THE TOAST:

200ml **unsweetened plant milk**
    (use non-nut or non-soya to keep
    NF or SoF)

2 tablespoons **sugar**, plus extra
    for sprinkling

3 tablespoons **gram flour**

1½ teaspoons **ground cinnamon**

1½ teaspoons **vanilla extract**

a pinch of **salt** or a small pinch of
    black salt (see page 38, optional)

a large pinch of **nutritional yeast**,
    crumbled to a powder

neutral oil, for frying

8 slices of good-quality **bread**

PREP TIME: 15 MINS · COOK TIME: 20 MINS

We were pretty pleased – if we do say so – when, after lots of experimenting, we found that gram flour makes excellent French toast. You can make this with any kind of bread, but a softer bread will naturally lead to a squidgier end result, while robust breads like sourdough will be sturdier and retain some crunch after cooking.

1. First, poach the rhubarb. Put the sugar, water or orange juice and zest, if using, in a non-reactive pan over a medium heat and bring to a simmer. Add the rhubarb, cover and cook for 4–5 minutes. (Rhubarb quickly becomes mushy and releases liquid as it cooks, so don't worry if the initial amount of liquid doesn't look like much.) When the rhubarb is tender but still has some bite, remove from the heat and uncover. Leave in the pan to keep warm.

2. Pour 2 tablespoons of the milk into a bowl, then add the sugar, flour, cinnamon, vanilla, salt and yeast. Mix to form a smooth paste, then add the rest of the milk and whisk until smooth again.

3. Heat 1–2 tablespoons oil, as needed, in a large frying pan over a medium-low heat. Dip the slices of bread into the milk mixture, then slide into the hot pan in batches. Sprinkle the top of each slice with a little pinch of sugar – this will caramelize slightly when you turn them over. Don't rush the cooking, as you need to slowly cook out the bean flavour of the flour. When the bottom of the bread is a light golden brown, after about 3 minutes, flip over and cook the other side.

4. Serve the toasts with the warm poached rhubarb.

TIP

This is good served with non-dairy yoghurt or dollops of whipped sweetened cashew cream (see page 257). When rhubarb isn't in season, use any fresh or poached fruit you like, or serve with compote or maple syrup and non-dairy yoghurt.

CARROT SMOKED 'SALMON'

SERVES
4

2 large **carrots**, washed

2 tablespoons **salt**, plus extra to taste

2 teaspoons **neutral cooking oil**

a pinch of **lemon zest**

1 teaspoon **lemon juice**

1 teaspoon **liquid smoke**
(we use hickory)

a pinch of **kelp powder**

TO SERVE:

finely chopped **fresh dill**

4 toasted **bagels**

vegan cream cheese or
**homemade vegan herbed
labneh** (see page 118)

lemon wedges

*PREP TIME: 25 MINS · COOK TIME: 50 MINS
MARINATING TIME 2 HOURS*

**You just have to try this. We love it with tofu scramble (see page 38)
as well as on bagels. You can luxe it up by adding vegan caviar aka
seaweed pearls – these are widely available online, but also from Ikea.**

1. Heat the oven to 200°C/400°F/gas mark 6.

2. Place the carrots on a sheet of foil and sprinkle with the salt.
   Fold the foil around the carrots to seal, then bake for 50 minutes.
   When cool enough to handle, rinse off the salt and pat dry.
   Rub or trim off the carrot skin. Slice the remaining flesh into
   long strips, as thinly as possible and no thicker than 1mm.

3. Place the strips in a bowl and add the oil, lemon zest and juice, liquid
   smoke and kelp powder. Toss gently until the strips are coated, then
   add a little more salt to taste (salt will cause the carrot to firm up,
   so be sparing to keep its soft texture). Leave to marinate for at least
   2 hours, or overnight in the fridge.

4. Serve with sprigs of fresh dill on toasted bagels with vegan cream
   cheese or labneh and lemon wedges on the side.

5. The carrot 'salmon' will keep, covered, in the fridge for a couple
   of days, but bring up to room temperature before serving.

TIP
Liquid smoke is now easy to find in supermarkets as well as online; it is an
excellent storecupboard standby for the vegan cook.

ACKEE SCRAMBLE

SERVES
2

2 tablespoons **neutral cooking oil**

2 **spring onions**, finely chopped

75g **cherry tomatoes**,
    deseeded and diced

1 tablespoon finely chopped **red chilli**
    (less if you're serving to little ones)

1 clove of **garlic**, minced

100g **spinach**, stems removed,
    finely chopped

1 × 540g tin of **cooked ackee**,
    drained

salt and **freshly ground
    black pepper**

hot toast, to serve

PREP TIME: 15 MINS · COOK TIME: 15 MINS

Ackee is a fruit from West Africa, but when cooked it looks and tastes amazingly like scrambled egg. Keep a few tins in the cupboard for weekend brunches – you'll find it in stores that stock Caribbean ingredients, or large supermarkets. Alternatively, crumble in some soft tofu when you add the garlic.

1. Heat the oil in a large frying pan over a medium heat, add the spring onions and tomatoes and sauté for 5 minutes. Add the chilli and garlic and fry, stirring, for 2 minutes, then add the spinach and cook for another 3 minutes, or until wilted.

2. Tip in the drained ackee and cook for 3 minutes, stirring gently to warm the ackee without breaking it up too much. Season to taste with salt and pepper.

3. Serve piled on to hot toast.

TIP
A pinch of eggy black salt (see page 38) works wonders here, if you have any, or stir in some hot smoked paprika or vegan chipotle paste, in place of or as well as the chilli.

REALLY CREAMY SCRAMBLED EGGY TOFU

3 tablespoons **vegan butter**
  or **margarine**

2 tablespoons **gram flour**

a generous pinch of **ground
  turmeric**

a generous pinch of **onion powder**

½ teaspoon **garlic powder**

150ml **unsweetened almond milk**

1 teaspoon **vegan Dijon mustard**

1 tablespoon **nutritional yeast**

1 teaspoon **vegan vegetable
  bouillon powder**

½ teaspoon **black salt**

olive oil, for frying

300g **firm tofu**

freshly ground black pepper

TO SERVE:
hot toast
finely chopped **fresh chives**

PREP TIME: 15 MINS · COOK TIME: 15 MINS

You can use drained tinned cooked ackee (see page 36) in this recipe instead of tofu, if you prefer. There is no need to fry it separately as it is very delicate and crumbly – just add to the sauce to warm it through. This recipe will serve 4 if part of a big vegan fry-up breakfast.

1. Melt the butter in a pan over a medium-high heat, add the flour, turmeric, onion powder and garlic powder, then cook, stirring, for 1 minute, until it forms a smooth paste. Slowly drizzle in the almond milk, whisking constantly until smooth. Stir in the remaining ingredients, except the tofu, and cook over a medium-low heat for about 10 minutes, until thick and smooth.

2. Meanwhile, drizzle some oil into a frying pan over a high heat. Crumble the tofu into the pan so it is in small chunks and cook for 3 minutes, stirring twice.

3. Gently stir the tofu into the sauce until incorporated, taking care not to break it up too much.

4. To serve, pile up on toast, scatter with the chives and season with pepper.

TIP
Black salt is a condiment often used in Indian cooking; it is rich in sulphuric compounds and lends a delicious eggy flavour to vegan dishes. It is easy to find in Asian food stores as well as large supermarkets.

CHIA SEED YOGHURT

PREP TIME: 5 MINS · CHILL TIME: 2 HOURS

Keep it simple and serve this with muesli, toasted nuts, seeds, dried fruit or berries. Alternatively, try this with some of our favourite toppings below.

150ml **unsweetened almond milk**

100g **non-dairy plain yoghurt**

1 tablespoon **maple syrup**

4 tablespoons **chia seeds**

1 teaspoon **vanilla bean paste**

1. Place all the ingredients in a glass bowl and mix until fully combined.

2. Cover and chill in the fridge for at least 2 hours, or overnight.

TRY THESE TOPPING IDEAS:

Thinly sliced **peach & raspberries** (delicious with almond yoghurt).

Finely chopped **mango, passion fruit & lime zest** (great with coconut yoghurt)

Grated **dairy-free dark chocolate, sliced banana & hazelnut butter** (decadent and dessert-like with almond yoghurt)

Chopped **strawberries topped with sweetened cashew cream** (see page 228) **& toasted flaked almonds** (indulgent and creamy with cashew yoghurt)

VEGAN BACON

Fake bacon. Fake-on? Use these in the breakfast muffins on page 28, with tofu or ackee scramble (see pages 38 and 36), in a sandwich with avocado, lettuce and tomato, crumbled into Caesar salad or anywhere else you fancy. Coconut bacon is best in salads, while tempeh bacon works well in bakes, burgers and fry-ups.

MUSHROOM BACON

3 large **portobello mushrooms**
1 tablespoon **gluten-free tamari soy sauce** (to keep this GF and WF) or 2 teaspoons **Maggi liquid seasoning** (to keep this SoF)
1 tablespoon **toasted sesame oil**
1 tablespoon **sweet smoked paprika**
1 teaspoon **garlic powder**
½ teaspoon **fine salt**
2 teaspoons **neutral cooking oil**

PREP TIME: 10 MINS · MARINATING TIME: 15 MINS
COOK TIME: 40 MINS

1. Brush any dirt from the mushrooms, but don't wash them. Remove the stalks and trim. Remove the gills, then slice the caps and stalks into thin strips.

2. In a large bowl, stir together the rest of the ingredients except the cooking oil. Add the mushrooms and toss gently to coat. Marinate for 10–15 minutes.

3. Heat the oil in a large frying pan over a medium heat, then add the mushroom slices in a single layer to allow them to crisp up without stewing in their juices – you may need to work in batches, depending on the size of your pan. Cook for about 20 minutes, turning occasionally, until crisp and brown. Keep watch – you want the mushrooms to be smoky and brown, not burnt and bitter. Using tongs or a slotted spoon, remove the slices, allowing the excess oil to drain back into the pan. Drain on kitchen paper.

4. The 'bacon' will keep in the fridge for up to 2 days, but may need to be crisped up again before using.

TIP
Any large fresh mushrooms work well in this recipe – try it with king oyster or shiitake.

COCONUT BACON

SERVES 5

(GF) (WF) (NF) (SoF)

1 tablespoon **refined** or
   extra virgin coconut oil
1 tablespoon **liquid smoke**
½ teaspoon **sweet smoked**
   paprika
1 tablespoon **toasted sesame oil**
2 teaspoons **gluten-free tamari**
   soy sauce (to keep this GF and WF)
   or **Maggi liquid seasoning**
   (to keep this SoF)
1 tablespoon **maple syrup**
½ teaspoon **salt**, plus extra to taste
100g **dried coconut flakes**
   (choose the largest you can find)

PREP TIME: 10 MINS · COOK TIME: 15 MINS

1. Heat the oven to 180°C/350°F/gas mark 4. Spoon the coconut oil into a baking tray, then place in the oven until melted.

2. In a large bowl, mix all the remaining ingredients together except the coconut flakes until combined. Add the flakes and toss thoroughly, ensuring every flake is coated.

3. Carefully remove the tray from the oven, tip in the flakes and spread them out so they are in more or less a single layer. Bake for 7 minutes, then toss and continue to cook for another 7 minutes, until deep golden brown (keep an eye on them for the last few minutes). Allow to cool slightly, then check the seasoning and add a little more salt, if needed, and toss again.

4. When completely cool, store in a sealed container for up to a week. If necessary, crisp up in a low oven before use.

TEMPEH BACON

SERVES 10

(GF) (WF) (NF)

200g **tempeh** (in a block)
2 teaspoons **olive oil**, for greasing

FOR THE MARINADE:
1 teaspoon **liquid smoke**
1 teaspoon **sweet smoked paprika**
3 tablespoons **gluten-free tamari**
   soy sauce
1 tablespoon **maple syrup**
2 teaspoons **garlic powder**
½ teaspoon **black pepper**
1 teaspoon **vegan cider vinegar**

PREP TIME: 15 MINS · COOK TIME: 50 MINS

1. To make the marinade, mix all the ingredients together.

2. Slice the tempeh as thinly as you can (it is easiest to do this on a diagonal) to make 10–12 slices, then toss with the marinade in a heatproof dish that fits inside your steamer.

3. Place in a steamer, cover and steam for 20 minutes, until the tempeh slices have absorbed the marinade.

4. Heat the oven to 200°C/400°F/gas mark 6 and lightly grease a baking sheet.

5. Carefully transfer the tempeh slices to the baking sheet, brush over any remaining marinade, then bake for 30 minutes, or until crispy and darker in colour.

6. When completely cool, store in a sealed container for up to 3 days. If necessary, crisp up in a low oven before use.

TOFU SHAKSHUKA

SERVES
4

70ml **olive oil**

I large **onion**, finely diced

8 cloves of **garlic**, finely chopped

I stick of **celery**, finely diced

I **carrot**, finely diced

I–2 **red chillies**, to taste, deseeded
and finely chopped

I **red pepper**, cut into strips

I **green pepper**, cut into strips

I **yellow pepper**, cut into strips

I tablespoon **cumin seeds**

I tablespoon **ground coriander**

I **cardamom pod**, bruised

½ teaspoon **ground turmeric**

I teaspoon **ground cinnamon**

I teaspoon **sweet smoked paprika**

I teaspoon **freshly ground
black pepper**

2 teaspoons **salt**

270g **cherry tomatoes on
the vine**

450ml **tomato passata** or I × 400g
tin of **chopped tomatoes**

200ml **water**

I tablespoon **sugar**

350g **firm silken tofu**, at room
temperature

a large handful of **fresh coriander**,
leaves roughly chopped, to serve

PREP TIME: 20 MINS · COOK TIME: I HOUR 10 MINS

**Shakshuka is a Middle Eastern creation that has been adopted as a
brunch dish the world over.**

1. Heat the oil in a large heavy-based pan, add the onion, garlic, celery,
    carrot, chillies and peppers and cook over a medium heat for about
    20 minutes, stirring occasionally, until slightly caramelized. Add all
    the spices, the black pepper and salt and cook for 1 minute, stirring,
    then add the cherry tomatoes. Cover and cook for 10 minutes,
    stirring occasionally.

2. Pour in the passata or tinned tomatoes and the water (rinse the tin
    and use this water, if using tinned tomatoes). Bring to a simmer, re-
    cover and cook for 30 minutes. Stir in half the sugar, then taste and
    add the rest if needed.

3. Using a large spoon, divide the tofu into 4 rounded portions. Place on
    top of the tomato sauce, then remove from the heat, cover and allow
    to stand for 10 minutes, until the tofu has warmed through.

4. Serve scattered with the fresh coriander.

BREAKFAST CRUMBLE

300g **blackberries**
(or other **mixed berries**)
5 **apples** or **pears**, peeled, cored
and chopped
1 tablespoon **oat flour**
1 tablespoon chopped **pitted dates**
non-dairy, non-soya yoghurt,
to serve

FOR THE TOPPING:
60g **walnuts**, chopped
60g **almonds**, chopped
125g **oat flour**
80g **rolled oats**
30g **coconut sugar** (or **soft
brown sugar**)
100g **pitted dates**, chopped
120g **refined** or **extra virgin
coconut oil**, chopped into
small pieces
2 teaspoons **ground cinnamon**

PREP TIME: 20 MINS · COOK TIME: 40 MINS

**The night before you want to eat this, you can make the crumble
topping and filling, store them separately in the fridge, then combine
and cook in the morning while you shower. Once cooked, this keeps in
the fridge for up to 3 days, and is just as good cold as hot. Alternatively,
serve it as a pudding with vegan custard (see page 249).**

1. Heat the oven to 180°C/350°F/gas mark 4.

2. To make the topping, place all the ingredients in a bowl. Mix together
   using your fingertips until crumbly. In another bowl, mix the fruit,
   oat flour and dates together.

3. Tip the fruit filling into an ovenproof dish, then cover with the
   topping. Bake for 35–40 minutes, until golden and crisp on top.
   If it's browning too fast, cover the top with foil or baking parchment.

4. Serve hot or warm, with non-dairy yoghurt.

VARIATION

Mango & pineapple breakfast crumble

For a mango and pineapple version, omit the cinnamon from the topping
and add 80g desiccated coconut or coconut flakes. For the filling, swap the
apples or pears and berries for 500g fresh or frozen mango and 1 small
pineapple, both peeled and diced (or 500g tinned or frozen pineapple)
and add the zest and juice of 1 lime. Assemble and cook as above.

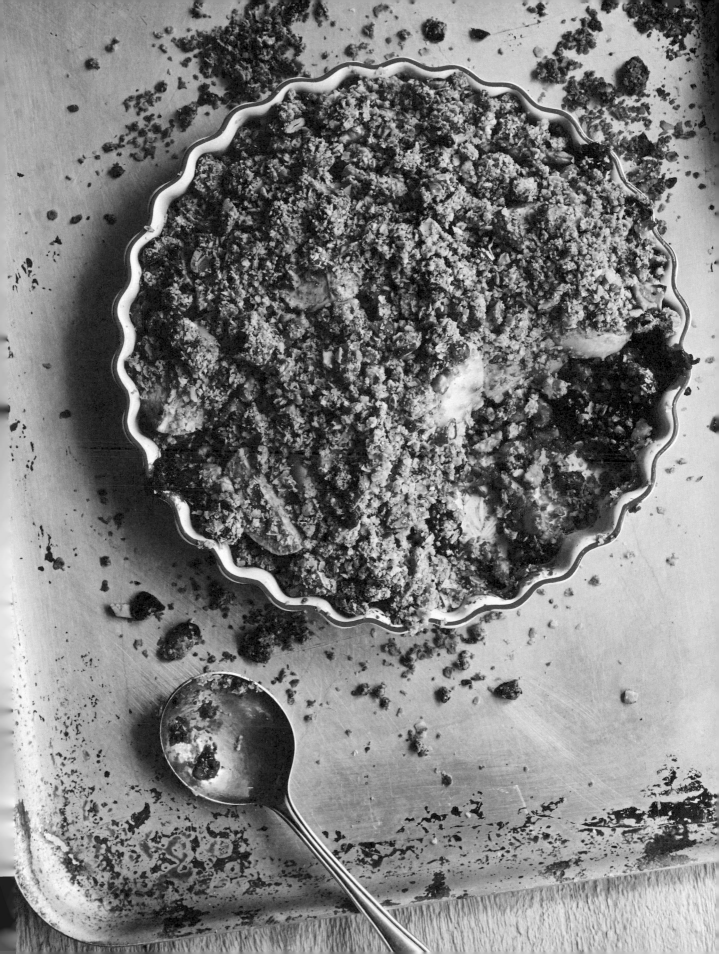

2

QUICK SUPPERS

SINGAPORE RICE NOODLES

SERVES
4

 GF WF SoF

375g **thin rice noodles**

1 tablespoon **refined** or **extra virgin coconut oil**

3cm piece of **fresh ginger**, peeled and cut into thin julienne strips

6 cloves of **garlic**, very thinly sliced

1 **red chilli**, deseeded to taste, thinly sliced into half-moons

1 **onion**, thinly sliced into half-moons

6 **spring onions**, white parts cut into 3cm pieces, green parts finely sliced

1 **red pepper**, cut into long thin strips

1 **green pepper**, cut into long thin strips

120g **shiitake mushrooms**, thinly sliced

225g **water chestnuts**, cut into 2cm pieces

200g **beansprouts**

100g **cavolo nero**, thinly sliced

FOR THE SAUCE:

60ml **gluten-free tamari soy sauce** (to keep this GF and WF) or **Maggi liquid seasoning** (to keep this SoF)

3 tablespoons **rice wine** (use gluten-free to keep this GF and WF)

3 teaspoons **curry powder**

1 teaspoon **palm sugar** (or any **soft brown sugar**)

1 teaspoon **sesame oil**

TO SERVE:

50g **cashew nuts**, roasted (see page 242)

a handful of **fresh coriander**, leaves roughly chopped

PREP TIME: 25 MINS · COOK TIME: 15 MINS

Oddly, you will probably never find Singapore noodles served in Singapore.

1. Place the noodles in a large heatproof bowl, cover with boiling water and allow to soak for 5 minutes (or cook according to the packet instructions).

2. Meanwhile, combine all the ingredients for the sauce in a small bowl, whisking with a fork until the sugar is dissolved. Set aside.

3. Drain the noodles and rinse under cold running water. Return to the bowl and add the sauce, turning to coat. While you stir-fry the veg, move the noodles about now and again so they don't clump together.

4. Heat the coconut oil in a large wok over a high heat until smoking hot, then add the ginger, garlic and chilli. Stir-fry briefly, then add the onion, white parts of the spring onions, peppers and shiitake. Stir-fry for another 3–4 minutes, until the vegetables start to colour slightly. Add the water chestnuts, beansprouts and cavolo nero and stir-fry for 2 minutes.

5. Add the noodles and any sauce remaining in the bowl and stir to combine with the vegetables. Cook for 3 minutes, stirring frequently.

6. Serve topped with the cashew nuts, coriander and finely sliced spring onions.

BATCHED JACKFRUIT

MAKES
1kg

  (GF) (WF) (NF) (SoF)

3 tablespoons **olive oil** or
neutral cooking oil

2 **onions**, finely chopped

6 × 565g or 400g tins of **young
green jackfruit in brine**
or **water**, drained

4 cloves of **garlic**, crushed

500ml hot **vegan vegetable stock**
(see page 140 for homemade)

PREP TIME: 15 MINS · COOK TIME: 25 MINS

**Having batches of prepared jackfruit for curries, stews, soups, pasta,
sandwiches and tacos in the freezer is incredibly useful – it can replace
cooked chicken in lots of recipes, and even makes delicious tuna-mayo
style sandwiches (see page 118). It comes in water or brine – don't
make the mistake of buying jackfruit in syrup. If you find tinned young
green jackfruit in unsalted water, taste and season at the end of the
cooking time. The drained weight of jackfruit from a 565g or 400g tin
is usually the same (220g).**

1. Heat the oil in a large frying pan, add the onions and fry gently over a
    medium-low heat for about 8 minutes, until translucent.

2. Meanwhile, trim away the hard woody core from each chunk of
    jackfruit and discard, leaving only the softer flesh. (You will have
    about 150g from each tin.) Roughly shred the flesh, using your hands.
    Rinse well under cold running water, then tip into a clean tea towel
    and pat dry.

3. Add the crushed garlic to the onions and cook for another 2 minutes.
    Turn up the heat to medium and add the shredded jackfruit. Cook
    for about 5 minutes, stirring frequently, until the jackfruit and
    onions begin to brown. (Fish out any jelly-like seeds or hard bits of
    core that may emerge as the flesh breaks down.) Add the stock and
    bring to a simmer, then cook until the stock has almost evaporated,
    about 10 minutes.

4. When the pan is almost dry, remove from the heat and allow the
    jackfruit to cool slightly, then roughly mash with a potato masher to
    further shred the flesh.

5. Use immediately or divide into 100g (for curries, pies, sauces) or 50g
    (for sandwiches) portions and freeze.

TIP
If you want to make this with
only 1 tin of jackfruit, use
1 tablespoon oil, ½ onion, 1 clove
of garlic and 150ml stock.

WILD MUSHROOM & TARRAGON STEW

SERVES
4

20g **dried porcini mushrooms**, chopped

400ml **boiling water**

60ml **olive oil**

1 large **onion**, thinly sliced into half-moons

1 **leek**, thinly sliced into half-moons

1 stick of **celery**, finely diced

1 **carrot**, finely diced

6 cloves of **garlic**, crushed

1 **bay leaf**

150ml **vegan white wine**

250g **chestnut mushrooms**, sliced but leave a few small ones whole or halved

240g **mixed wild mushrooms**, sliced

1 tablespoon **vegan vegetable bouillon powder**

½ teaspoon **freshly ground black pepper**

1 teaspoon **vegan Dijon mustard**

80ml **coconut cream** (from the top of an unshaken tin)

leaves from 1 small bunch of **fresh tarragon**, finely chopped

salt

PREP TIME: 20 MINS · COOK TIME: 40 MINS

This is Chantal's anglicized and veganized version of stroganoff. Although made with coconut cream, you can't taste it; instead, this is rich, savoury and comforting.

1. Soak the dried porcini mushrooms in the boiling water for 20 minutes.

2. While the porcini are soaking, heat 2 tablespoons of the oil in a large pan over a medium-high heat. When hot, add the onion, leek, celery and carrot and cook for 5 minutes, stirring occasionally. Add the garlic and cook for another 5 minutes, until slightly caramelized. Add the bay leaf and wine, turn the heat down to low and simmer for 5 minutes.

3. Meanwhile, heat the remaining oil in a frying pan, add the fresh mushrooms and fry over a high heat for 10–15 minutes, stirring every 5 minutes. Stir the mushrooms into the vegetable mixture.

4. Drain the dried mushrooms, reserving the soaking water. Pour the soaking water into the frying pan you cooked the fresh mushrooms in to deglaze it, then pour it into the veg mixture. Add the bouillon powder, pepper and mustard and stir well.

5. Turn up the heat to medium and simmer for 10 minutes, then add the coconut cream and cook for another 3–5 minutes, until thick and creamy. Take off the heat and add the tarragon, then check the seasoning and serve.

TIP
This is lovely served with crusty bread, or try it with olive oil mashed potatoes (see page 217) or creamy polenta (see page 211).

MUSTARDY MUSHROOM & BASIL GNOCCHI

3 tablespoons **olive oil**

800g **mushrooms** (any chunky,
   firm mushroom), cut into 2cm
   wedges or chunks

2 cloves of **garlic**, crushed

1 teaspoon **fennel seeds**

4 tablespoons chopped or
   crumbled **walnuts** (optional)

½ teaspoon **dried oregano**

a generous pinch of **dried thyme**

125ml shop-bought **vegan cream**
   (non-nut to keep this NF, non-soya
   to keep this SoF, we use an **oat
   cream**), plus extra if needed

2 heaped teaspoons **vegan Dijon
   mustard**, plus extra to taste

½ teaspoon **dried red chilli flakes**,
   plus extra to taste

400g **gnocchi**

leaves from 4 sprigs of **fresh basil**,
   roughly torn

salt and **freshly ground
   black pepper**

PREP TIME: 20 MINS · COOK TIME: 20 MINS

This is a family favourite in Rebecca's house, and is based on an old recipe by Nigel Slater, vegan-ified. If making for kids and adults, add the chilli flakes to the grown-ups' bowls at the end, instead of adding to the pan. The walnuts add heft and crunch, but you can leave them out and use a non-nut vegan cream if you need this to be nut free. An Italian herb mixture can be used in place of the dried oregano and thyme.

1. Heat the oil in a large frying pan over a medium-high heat, add the mushrooms and sauté, stirring regularly, for about 8 minutes, or until golden. (If you don't have a big enough pan, you may need to do this in 2 batches or use 2 frying pans.)

2. Add the garlic, fennel seeds and walnuts, if using, and cook for 2 minutes, stirring frequently, then add the dried herbs. Stir well, then remove from the heat and add the cream (it's best to do this off the heat as some vegan creams have a tendency to split if heated too quickly). Add the mustard and chilli flakes, plus plenty of pepper and a pinch of salt. Add more mustard or chilli, to taste.

3. Cook the gnocchi in a pan of boiling salted water according to the packet instructions.

4. Drain the gnocchi and toss it together with the creamy mushroom sauce. If it's too dry, add a little more cream or water and stir until heated through. Add the torn basil and serve.

ARTICHOKE, BASIL & SPINACH PASTA

PREP TIME: 10 MINS · COOK TIME: 15 MINS

Tangy artichoke is an excellent substitute for Parmesan in this pesto-like sauce – this is a great way to slip some extra vegetables past small children, too.

400g **dried pasta**

1 clove of **garlic**

50g **walnut pieces**

30g **fresh basil leaves**, washed and patted dry

150g **marinated** or **grilled artichokes** from a jar, roughly chopped

zest of ½ **unwaxed lemon**

90ml **extra virgin olive oil**

100g **frozen chopped** or **leaf spinach**, defrosted and any excess liquid squeezed out

1–2 teaspoons **lemon juice**

salt and **freshly ground black pepper**

1. Cook the pasta in boiling water for 1 minute less than the packet instructions, until al dente. If you prefer a milder flavour, blanch the garlic with the pasta for 3 minutes, then remove with a slotted spoon and drain.

2. Meanwhile, toast the walnut pieces in a hot dry pan for a couple minutes until fragrant. Tip into a food processor or blender (or use a stick blender) with the basil, artichokes, lemon zest, oil, garlic, spinach and plenty of black pepper. Pulse until the texture of pesto, then add the lemon juice and salt, to taste.

3. Drain the pasta, reserving 4 tablespoons of the cooking water. Return to the hot pan over a low heat and add the sauce. Toss well and heat for a minute or two, loosening with a little of the reserved pasta water if it is dry. Serve immediately.

PASTA ALLA PUTTANESCA

PREP TIME: 10 MINS · COOK TIME: 15 MINS

This garlicky, spicy tomato sauce is traditionally made with anchovies. Although it's not essential, adding a pinch of seaweed powder mimics their umami flavour.

400g **dried pasta**

3 tablespoons **olive oil**

2 cloves of **garlic**, bruised

1 tablespoon **tomato purée**

1 teaspoon finely chopped **red chilli**, or more to taste

200g **tomato passata** or tinned **chopped tomatoes**

2 tablespoons **capers**, rinsed, drained and roughly chopped

10 **dried black olives**, pitted and roughly chopped

a good pinch of **dried red chilli flakes** (optional, less if you're serving to little ones)

a pinch of **kelp powder** (optional)

1 tablespoon finely chopped **fresh flat-leaf parsley**

salt and **freshly ground black pepper**

1. Cook the pasta in boiling salted water for 1 minute less than the packet instructions, until al dente.

2. Meanwhile, heat the oil in a pan over a medium-low heat and add the garlic cloves and tomato purée. Cook, stirring, for 2 minutes. Add the chilli, passata or chopped tomatoes (crush any lumps with the back of a spoon or a potato masher), capers and olives. Cook for 3 minutes, stirring, or until the mixture is saucy.

3. Remove from the heat, fish out the garlic cloves, then taste the sauce and add the chilli flakes, if you like. Add the kelp powder, if using, and some pepper; you probably won't need more salt.

4. Drain the pasta, then toss in the sauce. Stir through the parsley just before serving.

MUSTARDY MUSHROOM & BASIL GNOCCHI

ARTICHOKE, BASIL & SPINACH PASTA

PASTA ALLA PUTTANESCA

PESTO PASTA

SERVES 4

PREP TIME: 15 MINS · COOK TIME: 15 MINS

A lot of vegan pesto recipes include nutritional yeast – aka 'nooch' – for its cheesy flavour, but we ran out of it one day and discovered that it really isn't essential (although it does deliver a valuable dollop of vitamin B12). If you want, add 1 tablespoon. Blanching the garlic gives a milder flavour to the pesto.

450g **dried pasta** or **gnocchi**

1 large clove of **garlic**

60g **pine nuts**

75ml good-quality **extra virgin olive oil**, plus extra if needed

a large pinch of **sea salt**

75g **fresh basil leaves**, roughly chopped

1. Cook the pasta in boiling water for 1 minute less than the packet instructions, until al dente. If you prefer a milder flavour, blanch the garlic with the pasta for 3 minutes, then remove with a slotted spoon, drain and crush.

2. Meanwhile, using a pestle and mortar (or use a stick blender), pound the blanched garlic, pine nuts, oil and salt to a rough paste. Add the basil and pummel again until the leaves begin to break down. If necessary, add more oil, tablespoon by tablespoon, to make the pesto your preferred consistency. Taste and add more salt, if necessary.

3. Drain the pasta, then return it to the pan. Stir through the pesto, tossing to coat the pasta. Serve immediately.

PEPPER & CAPER PASTA

SERVES 4

PREP TIME: 10 MINS · COOK TIME: 15 MINS

A fast fix for a quick meal and a tasty alternative to tomato pasta for kids.

400g **dried pasta**

1–2 cloves of **garlic**

200g **roasted peppers** (or **roasted pepper paste**) from a jar, deseeded

2 tablespoons roughly chopped **fresh basil**, plus a few sprigs to serve

2 tablespoons roughly chopped **fresh parsley**

1 tablespoon **capers**, rinsed and drained

1 tablespoon **pine nuts** or **ground almonds**

salt and **freshly ground black pepper**

1. Cook the pasta in boiling salted water for 1 minute less than the packet instructions, or until al dente. If you prefer a milder flavour, blanch the garlic with the pasta for 3 minutes, then remove with a slotted spoon and drain.

2. Place the blanched garlic in a food processor or blender (or use a stick blender) with the peppers, herbs, capers and pine nuts or almonds, then briefly blitz to form a pesto-like sauce. Season with salt, if needed (the peppers and capers are quite salty) and freshly ground black pepper.

3. Drain the pasta, then return to the hot pan. Add the sauce and toss together to coat well. Serve immediately, with a little more basil.

TIP FOR PESTO PASTA

For a creamier, richer sauce, mash or blitz a whole ripe avocado into the pesto with the oil. In Liguria, pesto is served with long green beans and boiled new potatoes tossed together with the pasta; we like adding roughly crushed peas. Switch some or all of the pine nuts for ground almonds, chopped walnuts or unsalted pistachios.

SALT-N-PEPPER TOFU & PINEAPPLE STIR-FRY

SERVES
2

PREP TIME: 25 MINS · COOK TIME: 40 MINS

The salt-n-pepper tofu can also be served on its own with satay (see page 80) or sweet chilli sauce, or it can be added to vegetable stir-fries or sliced up and used in sushi rolls (see pages 180–1).

FOR THE SALT-N-PEPPER TOFU:

280g **extra-firm tofu**

1 teaspoon **Sichuan peppercorns**

4 tablespoons **potato starch**

2 teaspoons **salt**

2 teaspoons **freshly ground black pepper**

2 teaspoons **garlic powder**

2 tablespoons **neutral cooking oil**, plus extra for greasing

6 **spring onions**, cut on an angle into 4cm pieces

1 **red chilli**, deseeded and thinly sliced into half-moons

1 **red pepper**, cut into 2cm chunks

FOR THE STIR-FRY:

1 × 260g tin of **pineapple cubes in pineapple juice**

1 tablespoon **cornflour**

3 tablespoons **gluten-free tamari soy sauce**

2 tablespoons **vegan rice wine** (use gluten-free to keep this GF and WF)

1 tablespoon **vegan rice vinegar**

1 teaspoon **Chinese five-spice**

2 tablespoons **refined coconut oil** or **neutral cooking oil**

200g **cashew nuts**

3cm piece of **fresh ginger**, peeled and cut into thin julienne strips

5 cloves of **garlic**, very thinly sliced

1 **green pepper**, thinly sliced

125g **baby corn**, thinly sliced on an angle

100g **bok choi, choi sum** or **Chinese leaf**, shredded

a handful of **fresh coriander**, leaves roughly chopped

steamed rice (allow 60g uncooked rice per person), to serve

1. Heat the oven to 200°C/400°F/gas mark 6. Slice the tofu in half widthways, then into 2cm cubes. In a clean tea towel or kitchen paper, squeeze the liquid from the tofu, then pat as dry as possible.

2. Grind the Sichuan pepper, then stir together with the potato starch, salt, pepper and garlic powder. Add the tofu and toss to coat well. Tip into a greased baking tray and spread out in a single layer. Bake for 20 minutes, then add the spring onions, chilli and red pepper, toss in the oil and cook for another 20 minutes, until golden and crispy.

3. While the tofu is baking, drain the pineapple, reserving the juice. Whisk the cornflour with 1 tablespoon of the soy sauce until smooth. Stir in the reserved pineapple juice, the rest of the soy sauce, the rice wine, rice vinegar and five-spice. Set aside.

4. Heat the oil in a large wok over a high heat until very hot. Add the cashew nuts and cook, tossing, for 1 minute. Add the ginger and garlic and stir-fry for a few seconds, then add the green pepper, baby corn and leafy greens. Gently stir-fry for 2 minutes, until the vegetables start to soften.

5. Add the reserved pineapple and the baked tofu and vegetables and stir to combine, then add the soy sauce mixture. Cook, stirring gently, for 1–2 minutes, until the sauce thickens.

6. Stir through the coriander and serve immediately with steamed rice.

QUICK SUPPERS

FALAFEL & HUMMUS WITH PARSLEY SALAD

PREP TIME: 30 MINS · COOK TIME: 25 MINS

We do love a good falafel at LEON. The hummus will make more than you need, so freeze it, or keep in the fridge for up to 4 days. Turn into roasted pepper hummus by adding a couple of tablespoons of roasted pepper paste. The falafel freezes well too. (Keep the chickpea water to use as aquafaba in baking.)

FOR THE FALAFEL:

1 × 400g tin of **chickpeas**, drained

1 small **onion**, roughly chopped

2 cloves of **garlic**, roughly chopped

a generous pinch of **salt**

1 teaspoon **ground cumin**

1 teaspoon **ground coriander**

a generous pinch of **baking powder**

a pinch of **cayenne pepper**

6 tablespoons **gram flour**

3 tablespoons chopped **fresh coriander**

3 tablespoons chopped **fresh parsley**

olive oil, for frying

freshly ground black pepper

FOR THE TOMATO SALAD:

150g **cucumber**, deseeded and diced

150g ripe **cherry tomatoes**, diced

1 **spring onion**, very finely chopped

2 tablespoons finely chopped
   fresh parsley

2 teaspoons **extra virgin olive oil**

a pinch of **sea salt flakes**

FOR THE TAHINI DRESSING:

2 tablespoons **tahini**

2 teaspoons **lemon juice**

1–2 tablespoons **water**

a pinch of **salt**

FOR THE HUMMUS:

1 × 400g tin of **chickpeas**, drained

a generous pinch of **salt**

2 teaspoons **lemon juice**

2 tablespoons **tahini**

2 tablespoons **water**

extra virgin olive oil, for drizzling

za'atar or **paprika**, for sprinkling

TO SERVE:

8 toasted **mini pitta breads**

hot sauce (optional)

1. First, make the falafel. Place all the ingredients except the fresh herbs in a food processor and season with pepper. Blitz to form a textured purée, then add the fresh herbs and blitz again. The mixture should be quite firm, and not at all sloppy. If it seems at all wet, add another tablespoon of gram flour. Set aside to firm up while you make the salad, dressing and hummus.

2. Toss all the ingredients for the salad together and set aside for 10–15 minutes at room temperature to allow the flavours to develop.

3. Whisk all the ingredients for the tahini dressing together, adding enough water to make a smooth and creamy dressing. Set aside.

4. Place all the hummus ingredients, except the olive oil and za'atar or paprika in a food processor or blender and blitz until smooth. Scrape out into a bowl. When ready to serve, make a groove in the surface of the hummus. Drizzle in a little oil, then sprinkle with za'atar or paprika.

5. To cook the falafel, heat about 1cm of oil in a deep heavy-based pan over a medium heat to 180°C/350°F, or until a cube of day-old bread browns in 30 seconds.

6. Using 2 dessertspoons, scoop up walnut-sized dollops of the falafel mixture. Transfer the mix from spoon to spoon, shaping as you go to make 12 balls. Carefully lower into the hot oil in batches and cook each batch for about 4–5 minutes, turning once or twice, until the balls are deep golden brown all over. The exteriors should be crisp and the inside pale, steaming hot and fluffy. (Don't overcrowd the pan as this will lower the temperature of the oil and make the falafel greasy. Allow the oil to return to 180°C/350°F between each batch.) Remove with a slotted spoon and drain on kitchen paper. Keep the falafel warm while you cook the remaining mixture.

7. Serve with the tahini dressing, salad and hummus, with pitta bread or flat breads, or as a salad with the tahini dressing and hot sauce, if using, drizzled over the falafel.

CRUNCHY FRIED AVO TACOS

neutral cooking oil (not coconut oil), for frying

3 tablespoons **plain flour**

a pinch of **spices**, such as **cayenne pepper**, **chilli powder**, **smoked paprika**, **mustard powder** or **ground cumin** (optional)

3 tablespoons **unsweetened plant milk** (use non-nut or non-soya to keep this NF or SoF)

50g **panko breadcrumbs**

2 ripe **avocados**

12 small **dairy-free corn** or **wheat tortillas**

salt and **freshly ground black pepper**

lime wedges, to serve

FOR THE TOPPINGS:

Mexican slaw (see page 162)

pico de gallo (see page 231)

cashew soured cream (see page 228), or **shop-bought vegan soured cream** (use non-nut or non-soya to keep this NF or SoF)

vegan chipotle paste or **sauce**, or **hot sauce**

almond feta (see page 154) (optional, if you don't need this to be NF)

PREP TIME: 15 MINS · COOK TIME: 10 MINS

Peel the avos as carefully as you can – the flesh closest to the peel is richest in nutrients. Fun fact – eating the kind of fats found in avocados actually helps the body absorb more nutrients from the rest of your meal. The fried avocado pieces will keep warm for a few minutes, but these are best made just before you are ready to serve and eaten quickly while hot and crisp with, maybe, some ice-cold vegan beers… So get your toppings ready before you start cooking.

1. When ready to cook, heat about 4cm of oil in a deep heavy-based pan over a medium-high heat to 180°C/350°F, or until a cube of day-old bread browns in 30 seconds.

2. Pour the flour on to a plate and season well with salt and pepper (add any of the spices now, if using). Pour the milk into a bowl. Tip the breadcrumbs on to another plate.

3. Slice each avocado into 6 or 8 long pieces, depending on their size and ripeness. Roll each piece in the seasoned flour, then dip into the milk, ensuring each piece is thoroughly wet. Finally, roll gently in the panko breadcrumbs.

4. Using a slotted spoon, carefully lower 2 or 3 slices into the hot oil. Cook for about 1 minute, or until the crumb is golden, then lift out using tongs, allowing the excess oil to drain back into the pan. Drain on kitchen paper and keep warm while you cook the remaining slices.

5. Meanwhile, warm the tortillas in a low oven or in a hot dry frying pan, or very briefly directly over a gas flame. Wrap in a clean tea towel to keep warm.

6. Serve a pile of warm tortillas with the fried avocado, your chosen toppings and lime wedges for squeezing over, then let your guests load their tacos as they like.

FOR FISH-STYLE TACOS FOR 4

Follow the recipe for 'fish' and chips (see page 98), but cut the banana blossom into smaller pieces before frying (and omit the chips). Serve with corn tortillas, Mexican slaw (see page 162) and avocado crema (see page 234).

FOR A SIMPLE TACO FILLING FOR 2

Heat a drained 400g tin of black beans or haricot beans with 1 teaspoon oil, 1 teaspoon vegan chipotle paste, 1 crushed clove of garlic, 1 teaspoon ground cumin, 4 tablespoons sweetcorn kernels and a couple of handfuls of finely shredded kale or other dark green cabbage. When the greens are cooked, add a good squeeze of lime juice, some salt, pepper and fresh coriander leaves. Serve with tortillas and one or two of the toppings as above, or some guacamole (see page 234).

'MEATY' VEGAN TACOS

Nuggets of chorizo-style seitan, smoky seitan, tempeh bacon (see page 41), cooked batched jackfruit (see page 50), extra-firm or smoked tofu, ready-made vegan mince or the chickpea and mushroom mince used in the larb salad (see page 158) can all be added to tacos – just sauté whichever you choose until browned and beginning to crisp up (but not dry). Dress with lime juice and fresh or dried chilli, then serve with tortillas and your choice of toppings as above, perhaps with some crisp shredded lettuce.

OTHER GREAT MIX-AND-MATCH FILLINGS INCLUDE:

Roasted sweet potato or **squash**

Grilled courgette

Aubergine or **peppers**

Roasted cherry tomatoes

Roasted or **buffalo cauliflower**
(see pages 72 and 106)

Roasted nuts or **toasted seeds**
(see pages 242 and 243)

CRUNCHY FRIED AVO TACOS

BUTTERNUT, ROASTED GARLIC & SAGE RISOTTO

300g **butternut squash**, **pumpkin**
or **other firm orange-skinned**
squash, peeled, deseeded and
chopped into 3cm chunks

7 cloves of **garlic**, 5 large ones still in
their skins, 2 finely chopped

5 tablespoons **olive oil**

50g **walnut pieces**

1 **onion**, finely diced

300g **risotto rice**

125ml **vegan white wine**

1 litre hot **vegan vegetable stock**
(see page 140 for homemade)

28 **fresh sage leaves**

2 teaspoons **nutritional**
yeast (optional)

2 teaspoons **lemon juice**

salt and **freshly ground**
black pepper

PREP TIME: 15 MINS · COOK TIME: 40 MINS

Sweet butternut with earthy sage and toasty walnuts for crunch.

1. Heat the oven to 200°C/400°F/gas mark 6. Tip the squash and whole cloves of garlic into a baking tray and add 1 tablespoon of the oil. Toss to coat, then roast for 30 minutes, turning once after 15 minutes, until tender and beginning to brown. Spread the walnuts out on a second baking tray, and place in the oven 5 minutes before the end of the squash cooking time, until roasted and browned.

2. Remove the squash and garlic, and the walnuts from the oven and set the walnuts aside. When the garlic is cool enough to handle, pop the cloves out of their skins, then roughly mash them with the squash.

3. While the squash is cooking, make the risotto. Heat 1 tablespoon of the oil in a large heavy-based pan over a medium heat. Add the onion and a pinch of salt and fry gently until translucent, but not brown. Add the chopped garlic and cook, stirring, for 1 minute. Add another tablespoon of the oil and the rice. Cook, stirring, until the rice is well coated in the oil and beginning to become translucent.

4. Pour in the white wine. Stir again and allow the wine to bubble away and be absorbed by the rice. Slowly add the hot stock, one ladleful at a time, stirring often and waiting until the last ladleful has been absorbed before adding the next. Cook until the rice is creamy but still retains a little bit of bite; you may not need all the stock.

5. Heat 1 tablespoon of oil in a frying pan over a low heat. When hot, add 24 of the sage leaves. Cook briefly until just crisp, then immediately remove or they will burn and become bitter. Set aside.

6. When the risotto is cooked, remove from the heat. Finely chop the remaining sage, then stir into the risotto with the mashed squash and garlic, the remaining oil, the yeast, if using, the lemon juice and some salt and pepper. Check the seasoning. Serve topped with the roasted walnuts and crisp sage leaves.

TIP

For both risottos, use an olive oil with a mild, not bitter, flavour.

LEMON, PEA & BASIL RISOTTO

SERVES 4

PREP TIME: 10 MINS · COOK TIME: 30 MINS

A light risotto that tastes of spring. In season, add thinly sliced asparagus or ribbons of courgette, podded and shelled broad beans, sugar snap peas or even edamame beans.

---

3 tablespoons **olive oil**

1 **onion**, finely diced

2 cloves of **garlic**, finely diced

350g **risotto rice**

125ml **vegan white wine**

1.15 litres hot **vegan vegetable stock**
    (see page 140 for homemade)

150g **frozen peas**

zest of ½ **lemon**

leaves from 3 sprigs of **fresh basil**, finely chopped

1 tablespoon **nutritional yeast** (optional)

a large handful of **pea shoots** or sprigs of **watercress**
    (any thick stems removed)

3 tablespoons **toasted pine nuts**

salt and **freshly ground black pepper**

1. Heat 1 tablespoon of the oil in a large heavy-based pan over a medium heat. Add the onion and a pinch of salt and fry gently until translucent, but not brown. Add the garlic and cook, stirring, for 1 minute. Add another tablespoon of the oil and continue to cook for 1 minute, then mix in the rice. Cook, stirring, until the rice is well coated in the oil and beginning to become translucent.

2. Pour in the white wine. Stir again and allow the wine to bubble away and be absorbed by the rice. Slowly add the hot stock, one ladleful at a time, stirring frequently and waiting until the last ladleful has been absorbed before adding the next. Cook until the rice is creamy but still retains a little bit of bite; you may not need all the stock.

3. While the rice is cooking, place the peas in a pan of boiling water. Bring back to the boil, then drain. Transfer to a food processor or blender and blitz to a coarse purée or crush with a potato masher.

4. When the risotto is cooked, remove from the heat and add the puréed peas, the remaining oil, the lemon zest, chopped basil and yeast, if using, and season with salt and pepper. Stir well and check the seasoning. Serve in shallow bowls, topped with the pea shoots or watercress and the toasted pine nuts.

SHIITAKE & CASHEW STIR-FRY WITH BLACK BEAN SAUCE

150g **cashew nuts**

1 tablespoon **neutral cooking oil**

2 cloves of **garlic**, thinly sliced

1 thumb-sized piece of **fresh ginger**, peeled and sliced into very thin matchsticks

1 **red chilli** (less if you're serving to little ones), thinly sliced

1 large **onion**, thickly sliced into half-moons

240g **shiitake mushrooms**, halved

100g **Tenderstem broccoli** or **green beans**, cut into thirds

6 **spring onions**, 4 each cut into 4 pieces, 2 finely sliced

1 teaspoon **sesame oil**

steamed rice (allow 60g uncooked rice per person), to serve

FOR THE BLACK BEAN SAUCE:

2 tablespoons **fermented black beans**

1 **vegan vegetable stock cube** or 1 tablespoon **vegan vegetable bouillon powder**

300ml **hot water**

1 tablespoon **neutral cooking oil**

5 cloves of **garlic**, finely chopped

1 thumb-sized piece of **fresh ginger**, peeled and finely chopped

2 tablespoons **tamari soy sauce** (use gluten-free to keep this GF and WF)

2 tablespoons **vegan mirin**, **Chinese rice wine** or **dry sherry** (use sherry to keep this GF and WF)

PREP TIME: 20 MINS · COOK TIME: 20 MINS

Fermented black beans are available in Asian supermarkets or online. You could also make this with about 200ml of a really good black bean sauce from a jar if you want a super-quick dinner, or if you can't get hold of any fermented black beans.

1 teaspoon **coconut sugar** (or **soft brown sugar**)

1 teaspoon **cornflour**

1 tablespoon **cold water**

1. To make the sauce, rinse the black beans to remove the salt, then roughly mash. Mix the stock cube or bouillon powder with the hot water and set aside.

2. Heat the oil in a small pan over a medium-high heat, then add the crushed beans and finely chopped garlic and ginger and stir-fry for 2–3 minutes. Add the stock, tamari, mirin, rice wine or sherry and sugar and bring to the boil, then reduce the heat and simmer for 10–15 minutes, or until the sauce has reduced by about half. Mix the cornflour and cold water together, then add to the pan and cook for a few minutes, stirring, until thickened.

3. Meanwhile, toast the cashew nuts in a hot wok or heavy-based frying pan over a

medium-high heat for 3–5 minutes, stirring frequently, until golden. Remove from the pan and set aside.

4. Heat the oil in the wok or frying pan over a high heat until smoking hot, then throw in the garlic, ginger and chilli. Stir-fry for 30–60 seconds, then add the onion and stir-fry for another minute. Add the mushrooms, broccoli or beans and spring onion pieces and continue to stir-fry for 2–3 minutes.

5. Add the toasted cashew nuts and the black bean sauce and stir to combine, then cook for 1 minute. Remove from the heat and stir in the sesame oil.

6. Serve with steamed rice, sprinkled with the finely sliced spring onions.

JACKFRUIT TINGA

SERVES
4

  (GF) (WF) (SoF)

4 medium **sweet potatoes**

3 large **tomatoes**

2 heaped teaspoons **vegan chipotle paste**, plus extra to taste

2 cloves of **garlic**, crushed

I teaspoon **dried oregano**

2 teaspoons **soft brown sugar**

2 teaspoons **vegan cider vinegar**

I teaspoon **ground cumin**

I tablespoon **olive oil**

I heaped teaspoon **tomato purée**

400g cooked **batched jackfruit** (see page 50)

I **bay leaf**

400ml **hot water**

salt and **freshly ground black pepper**

hot sauce or **lime wedges**, to serve

FOR THE TOPPINGS (all optional):

guacamole (see page 234)

cashew soured cream (see page 228) or shop-bought **vegan soya-free soured cream**

Mexican slaw (see page 162)

romaine lettuce leaves

fresh coriander leaves

PREP TIME: 20 MINS · COOK TIME: 45 MINS

Tinga de pollo is a Mexican chicken dish; jackfruit (see page 50) is a brilliant replacement for the meat. Chef and food writer Thomasina Miers turned us on to the power of burnt tomatoes in Mexican sauces; this is an adaptation of one her recipes.

1. Heat the oven to 180°C/350°F/gas mark 4. Put the sweet potatoes on a baking sheet and bake in the oven for 45 minutes.

2. While the potatoes are cooking, make the jackfruit tinga. Cook the tomatoes in a dry pan over a high heat, turning frequently, until blackened and beginning to soften, about 8–10 minutes. Leave the tomatoes to cool slightly, then transfer to a food processor or blender with the chipotle paste, garlic, oregano, sugar, vinegar and cumin. Blitz to form a rough purée.

3. Heat the oil in a large pan, add the tomato purée and cook for a couple of minutes over a medium-low heat, then tip in the blitzed tomatoes, the jackfruit, bay leaf and plenty of pepper. Pour in 200ml of the water, bring to a simmer and cook for about 20 minutes, stirring often and topping up with more of the water if the mixture becomes dry.

4. Taste the tinga – it should be spicy, smoky and tart. Add more chipotle paste and salt or pepper, if needed, and remove the bay leaf.

5. Remove the sweet potatoes from the oven and serve each with a generous dollop of tinga. There should be enough for you to pile it high. Add additional toppings at the table as desired.

TIP

If you don't fancy sweet potatoes, serve the tinga with steamed rice and a small salad of diced avocado, tomato, shallot and coriander, aka pico de gallo with added avocado (see page 231).

THREE WAYS WITH ROASTED CAULIFLOWER

SERVES
2

PREP TIME: 5 MINS · COOK TIME: 15 MINS

1 **cauliflower**

2 tablespoons **neutral cooking oil**, plus extra for greasing

salt and **freshly ground black pepper**

1. Heat the oven to 200°C/400°F/gas mark 6.

2. Cut the cauliflower into 4cm florets, halving any very big pieces. Place on a greased baking sheet, season and drizzle with the oil. Roast for 15 minutes (or 5 minutes for Miso ginger cauliflower).

3. Continue, following the method for your chosen flavouring (1–3) below.

1. MISO GINGER

PREP TIME: 15 MINS · COOK TIME: 25 MINS

2 teaspoons **white** or **yellow miso paste**

6cm piece of **fresh ginger**, peeled and finely grated

2 teaspoons **vegan mirin**

1 teaspoon **toasted sesame oil**

1 teaspoon **sesame seeds**

2 cloves of **garlic**

½ teaspoon **salt**

1 tablespoon **maple syrup** or **agave nectar** (or **sugar**)

2 tablespoons **water**

freshly ground black pepper

6 **spring onions**, finely sliced, to serve

1. Prepare the cauliflower as above and roast for 5 minutes.

2. Mix together all the ingredients except the spring onions.

3. Remove the cauliflower from the oven and coat with the miso mixture. Roast for another 10 minutes, or until sticky-looking and beginning to brown.

4. Sprinkle with the spring onions before serving.

2. TANDOORI

PREP TIME: 15 MINS · COOK TIME: 35 MINS

1 **shallot**, roughly chopped

2 cloves of **garlic**, roughly chopped

4cm piece of **fresh ginger**, peeled and roughly chopped

juice of ½ **lemon**

½ teaspoon **fennel seeds**

seeds from 4 **green cardamom pods**

seeds from 1 **black cardamom pod**

1 teaspoon **ground coriander**

1 teaspoon **ground cumin**

1 teaspoon **garam masala**

2 teaspoons **paprika** (hot if you want spice, or sweet if not)

a generous pinch of **ground turmeric**

100g **coconut yoghurt**

TO SERVE:

1½ small handfuls of **fresh coriander**, chopped

tzatziki (see page 230)

1. Heat the oven to 220°C/425°F/gas mark 7.

2. Before roasting, blitz all the tandoori ingredients together in a food processor or blender.

3. Coat each floret in the tandoori marinade. Place on a greased baking sheet, drizzle with the oil and roast for 35 minutes, turning twice, until the edges are beginning to char, the marinade is darkening and the flesh is tender.

4. Serve with coriander, tzatziki or minted yoghurt.

3. MIDDLE EASTERN (PICTURED)

PREP TIME: 15 MINS · COOK TIME: 25 MINS

2 tablespoons **dukkah** (see page 243)

2 tablespoons **harissa** (see page 206 for homemade)

1 teaspoon **lemon juice**

1 teaspoon **neutral cooking oil**

1 teaspoon **water**

a small handful each of **fresh mint**, **coriander** and **parsley**, leaves roughly torn

60ml **tahini dressing** (see page 206)

seeds from ½ **pomegranate**

1. Roast the cauliflower (see opposite).

2. Remove the cauliflower from the oven, scatter over the dukkah and stir to coat. Roast for another 10 minutes. (This can be batch-cooked as the undressed, roasted cauliflower will keep in a sealed container in the fridge for up to 3 days.)

3. Meanwhile, mix the harissa, lemon juice, oil and water together to make a dressing.

4. Place the roasted cauliflower on a serving plate and sprinkle over the herbs. Drizzle over the harissa and tahini dressings and sprinkle over the pomegranate seeds. Serve either warm or at room temperature.

MISO JACKFRUIT WITH NOODLES

SERVES
4

2 × 565g or 400g tins of **young green jackfruit in brine** or **water**, drained

I heaped teaspoon **mild white** or **yellow miso paste**

zest and juice of ½ **lime**

I tablespoon **vegan mirin** or ½ teaspoon **sugar** and I tablespoon **vegan white wine**

I teaspoon **toasted sesame oil**

2 teaspoons **gluten-free tamari soy sauce** (to keep this GF and WF) or **Maggi liquid seasoning** (to keep this SoF), plus extra to serve

I clove of **garlic**, grated

2cm piece of **fresh ginger**, peeled and grated

2 tablespoons **neutral cooking oil**

60ml **water**

2 **spring onions**, finely chopped

FOR THE NOODLES:

3 heads of **pak choi**

I tablespoon **neutral cooking oil**

I clove of **garlic**, bruised (optional)

600g **ready-cooked rice noodles** (to keep this GF and WF) or **wheat noodles**

PREP TIME: 15 MINS · COOK TIME: 25 MINS

Cooked with miso, lime, ginger and garlic, this jackfruit is punchy and perfect with noodles and pak choi.

---

1. Heat the oven to 200°C/400°F/gas mark 6.

2. Trim the hard woody core away from each chunk of jackfruit and discard, leaving only the softer flesh. In a medium-sized bowl, whisk together the miso, lime zest, mirin or white wine and sugar, sesame oil, soy sauce or liquid seasoning, garlic and ginger. Add the jackfruit pieces and toss together.

3. Heat 1 tablespoon of the oil in a pan over a medium heat. Add the dressed jackfruit and cook, stirring, for a minute or so, then add the water. Turn up the heat and allow the mixture to bubble away for 6–8 minutes. When almost dry, remove from the heat.

4. Shred the jackfruit with 2 forks, removing any seeds or bits of stem. Pour the remaining oil on to a non-stick baking sheet, then spread out the jackfruit on top. Bake for 8–12 minutes, until the edges begin to char very slightly.

5. Meanwhile, prepare the noodles. Chop the pak choi into bite-sized pieces. Heat the oil in a large pan or wok over a medium heat, add the pak choi and bruised garlic, if using. Stir-fry for 1 minute, then add the noodles and cook for 3 minutes, stirring. Remove and discard the garlic.

6. Divide the noodles and greens between warmed shallow bowls. Top with the miso jackfruit, scatter with the spring onions and squeeze over a little of the lime juice. Serve with extra soy sauce or Maggi on the side.

SPICED MOROCCAN TOFU

1 tablespoon **rose water**

2 tablespoons **extra virgin olive oil**

1 teaspoon **ground cumin**

½ teaspoon **ground cinnamon**

1 teaspoon **ground ginger**

a generous pinch of **ground turmeric**

seeds from 2 **cardamom pods**, ground

a pinch of **saffron**

1 teaspoon **ground coriander**

1 teaspoon **garlic powder**

280g **extra-firm tofu**

salt and **freshly ground black pepper**

FOR THE COUSCOUS:

200g **couscous**

leaves from 1 small bunch of **fresh parsley**, finely chopped

2 tablespoons very finely chopped **fresh chives** or **spring onions**

zest of ½ **lemon**

salt

PREP TIME: 20 MINS · MARINATING TIME: 2 HOURS
COOK TIME: 20 MINS

This is delicious as it is but you could serve this fragrant North African-style tofu with the date and preserved lemon chutney on page 231, or the tomato and pomegranate salad on page 156. You could swap the couscous for bulgur or freekeh, or for quinoa or rice to make this gluten and wheat free, or leave it out and eat with the Spanish chickpea stew on page 140, or the Middle Eastern stuffed pumpkin on page 142.

1. Combine all the ingredients except the tofu in a shallow dish. Slice the tofu into 4 steaks, then coat in the marinade. Marinate in the fridge for at least 2 hours, or overnight.

2. Place the couscous in a heatproof bowl. Pour over boiling water until it is covered to about 5mm above the grains. Add a good pinch of salt, then cover with clingfilm (don't let it touch the water) and allow to stand for 10 minutes, until it has absorbed all the water and puffed up. Fluff up with a fork. Allow to cool slightly.

3. Meanwhile, heat a dry griddle pan over a high heat. Remove the tofu steaks from the marinade and cook in the hot pan for 2–3 minutes until char marks appear on the bottom, then turn them 90 degrees and continue cooking to create a criss-cross pattern for another 2–3 minutes. (You shouldn't need any oil.) Turn the steaks over and repeat.

4. Toss together the couscous, parsley, chives or spring onion, lemon zest and salt to taste. Serve the tofu with the warm herbed couscous.

PERSIAN HERB FRITTATA

SERVES
8

FOR THE BATTER:

200g **gram flour**

500ml **unsweetened plant milk**
(use non-nut or non-soya to keep this
NF or SoF)

I tablespoon **extra virgin olive oil**

I tablespoon **garlic powder**

I tablespoon **mustard powder**

2 tablespoons **nutritional yeast**

2 teaspoons **onion powder**

½ teaspoon **black salt** (see page 38)
or **fine salt**

I teaspoon **ground turmeric**

I teaspoon **baking powder** (use
gluten-free to keep this GF and WF)

FOR THE FILLING:

I tablespoon **olive oil**

I large **onion**, thickly sliced
into half-moons

200g **baby spinach**

2 tablespoons **toasted pine nuts**

4 **spring onions**, finely sliced

I bunch of **fresh parsley**, leaves
finely chopped

a large handful of **fresh dill**, leaves
finely chopped

a large handful of **fresh coriander**,
leaves finely chopped

I tablespoon **dried barberries** or
chopped **dried sour cherries**

salt and **freshly ground
black pepper**

**PREP TIME: 15 MINS · REST TIME: 30 MINS
COOK TIME: I HOUR**

Chantal's grandfather was Persian – she likes to imagine her ancestors
eating a version of this egg-less frittata, spiked with tart berries. Dried
barberries are a small and sour dried berry used in Persian cuisine.
They can be found in Middle Eastern shops and large supermarkets, or
can be replaced with sour cherries or cranberries.

1. Sift the gram flour into a large mixing bowl, then whisk in the milk
   and continue whisking until you have a smooth batter. Add the rest
   of the batter ingredients except the baking powder and mix until
   smooth. Allow to rest for 30 minutes.

2. Midway through the resting time, start the filling. Heat the oven to
   180°C/350°F/gas mark 4.

3. Heat the oil in an ovenproof frying pan over a high heat, add the
   onion and cook for about 10 minutes, stirring occasionally, until
   slightly golden and caramelized. Stir in the spinach and cook until
   wilted, about 2 minutes. Take the pan off the heat, stir in the rest of
   the filling ingredients and season with salt and pepper.

4. Stir the baking powder into the batter, then pour it over the filling
   ingredients and mix to evenly distribute. Bake in the pan for
   40–50 minutes, or until a skewer comes out clean. Serve warm or
   at room temperature.

> **TIP**
> Serve with the tomato & pomegranate salad on page 156.

SATAY TOFU WITH PINEAPPLE SALSA

300g **firm tofu**

I teaspoon **ground coriander**

½ teaspoon **ground turmeric**

I tablespoon **tamari soy sauce** (use gluten-free to keep this GF and WF)

3 cloves of **garlic**, minced

2 teaspoons **neutral cooking oil** (or **refined coconut oil**, melted), plus extra for greasing

steamed rice (allow 60g uncooked rice per person), to serve

FOR THE SATAY SAUCE:

2 tablespoons **refined** or **extra virgin coconut oil**

4 **shallots**, finely diced

8 cloves of **garlic**, finely chopped

I **red chilli**, deseeded

3cm piece of **fresh ginger**, peeled and finely chopped

I tablespoon **ground coriander**

I teaspoon **ground turmeric**

400ml **coconut milk**

60ml **tamari soy sauce** (use gluten-free to keep this GF and WF)

2 tablespoons **palm sugar** (or **soft brown sugar**)

2 stalks of **lemongrass**, bashed to bruise

I **fresh kaffir lime leaf**

150g **crunchy peanut butter**

PREP TIME: 25 MINS · MARINATING TIME: 30 MINS
COOK TIME: 40 MINS

Satay is a peanut sauce from Malaysia. This is based on a satay sauce created by chef Gizzi Erskine with LEON – we have made a vegan version.

FOR THE PINEAPPLE SALSA:

½ **cucumber**, peeled and diced

I **red chilli**, deseeded and thinly sliced

I small **pineapple**, diced

I large **white onion**, diced

a large handful of **fresh coriander**, leaves roughly chopped

zest and juice of I **lime**

salt

1. Slice the tofu into 4 equal-sized steaks. In a shallow dish, mix the ground spices, soy sauce, garlic and 2 teaspoons oil together. Add the tofu steaks and allow to marinate for 30 minutes.

2. To make the satay sauce, heat the oil in a pan over a medium-high heat. When hot, add the shallots, garlic, chilli and ginger. Fry, stirring occasionally, for 5 minutes, then add the ground spices, stir and cook for 1 minute. Add the coconut milk, soy sauce, sugar, lemongrass and lime leaf and simmer for 20 minutes, until reduced by half. Stir in the peanut butter and continue to simmer for another 10 minutes.

3. Meanwhile, heat the oven to 200°C/400°F/gas mark 6. Place the tofu steaks on a greased baking sheet and bake for 20 minutes, turning once halfway through.

4. If you want a really smooth sauce, remove the lemongrass and lime leaf from the satay sauce and blend the sauce in a blender (or use a stick blender) until smooth (work in batches if your blender can't cope with hot liquids).

5. In a bowl, mix all the salsa ingredients together.

6. Serve the baked tofu on steamed rice, with the satay sauce and pineapple salsa.

VIETNAMESE CRISPY PANCAKES

refined or **extra virgin coconut oil**, for frying

280g **firm tofu**, cut into 1cm cubes

1 **onion**, thinly sliced into 2mm half-moons

2 cloves of **garlic**, very thinly sliced

400g **beansprouts**

salt

a small handful each of **fresh mint**, **Thai basil** and **coriander**, leaves roughly chopped, to serve

FOR THE PANCAKES:

130g **rice flour**

20g **cornflour** (or **ground tapioca** or **arrowroot**)

400ml **coconut milk**

a pinch of **salt**

½ teaspoon **freshly ground black pepper**

½ teaspoon **ground turmeric**

20–50ml **water**

2 **spring onions**, finely sliced

FOR THE SAUCE:

1 clove of **garlic**, finely chopped

1 small **red** or **green chilli**, finely chopped

a pinch of **freshly ground black pepper**

1 teaspoon **sweet white miso**

2 tablespoons **vegan rice vinegar**

1 teaspoon **sugar**

2 tablespoons **water**

3 tablespoons **tamari soy sauce** (use gluten-free to keep this GF and WF)

PREP TIME: 15 MINS · REST TIME: 30 MINS
COOK TIME: 40 MINS

Chantal first tasted these perched on a child's plastic chair at the side of the Hoi An river in Vietnam. It was the best thing she'd eaten on her solo trip around Vietnam, Cambodia and Thailand. Today, it takes her back every time she cooks them.

1. To make the pancake batter, whisk together the flours, coconut milk, salt, pepper and turmeric until smooth. The batter should be the consistency of double cream, so if necessary add the water, a little at a time. Stir in the spring onions, then allow to rest for at least 30 minutes.

2. Meanwhile, combine all the ingredients for the sauce, then set aside to infuse.

3. Heat the oven to 80°C/175°F/gas mark ¼.

4. Heat a little coconut oil in a 25cm cast-iron or non-stick frying pan over a medium heat. When hot, pour in about 3 tablespoons of the batter and swirl to coat the base of the pan. Cook for 7–10 minutes without flipping, until the bottom is golden and crispy. Slide the pancake on to a baking tray lined with baking parchment and keep warm in the low oven while you cook the remaining 3 pancakes. Cover each pancake with baking parchment so they don't stick together.

5. While the pancakes are cooking, squeeze and pat the tofu dry. Heat about 1 tablespoon of coconut oil in a wok over a high heat. When hot, add the tofu and allow to crisp up before turning it over. Cook until crisp on all sides, about 5–10 minutes (depending on the thickness of your wok). Add the onion and cook for 1 minute, then add the garlic and beansprouts. Stir-fry for another minute. Season with a pinch of salt, then remove from the pan and keep warm.

6. Place the pancakes on serving plates. Divide the tofu mixture, herbs and sauce between the pancakes, then fold in half. Serve immediately.

> **TIP**
> The pancakes are made with a mixture of rice flour and cornflour, but you can substitute 150g gluten-free plain flour (we use Doves Farm), which is usually a blend of both.

ACKEE FRIED RICE

SERVES
2

1 tablespoon **neutral cooking oil**

125g **long-grain rice**, cooked
and cooled

3 **spring onions**, finely chopped

1 small clove of **garlic**, crushed

1 heaped teaspoon grated **fresh
ginger**

a pinch of **black salt**
(see page 38, optional)

50g **frozen peas**

1 teaspoon **gluten-free tamari
soy sauce** (to keep this GF and
WF), **Maggi liquid seasoning**
(to keep this SoF) or **coconut
aminos** (to keep this GF, WF and
SoF), plus extra to serve

1 × 280g tin of **cooked ackee**,
drained

TO SERVE:

lime juice

1–2 teaspoons **toasted sesame oil**

2 tablespoons **roasted peanuts**,
chopped

2 teaspoons finely chopped **red chilli**
(less if you're serving to little ones)

sriracha hot sauce (optional)

PREP TIME: 10 MINS · COOK TIME: 6 MINS

**We had the idea of using cooked ackee (see page 36) in fried rice
(rather than the more commonly used silken tofu – which you could,
of course, use instead), where its creamy flavour and texture works
perfectly. If you have some black salt to hand this will add an even
more rich eggy flavour – but only add a tiny pinch. Have all the
ingredients prepped and ready to go before you start cooking.**

1. Heat the cooking oil in a large wok over a high heat. When very
   hot, add the cooked rice and most of the chopped spring onions,
   reserving a few to garnish. Quickly add the garlic, ginger, black
   salt, if using, peas and soy sauce, liquid seasoning or aminos and
   stir well.

2. Add the drained ackee and cook for 2–3 minutes, until heated
   through, stirring gently so that it doesn't completely fall apart.

3. Spoon into warmed serving bowls and squeeze over a little lime
   juice and a drizzle of sesame oil. Top with the peanuts, if using,
   the chopped chilli and a splash of sriracha. Serve immediately.

TIP

Every country in Asia (and quite a few beyond) has its own version of
fried rice: add a splash of coconut milk to make coconut fried rice, or
1 teaspoon curry powder for curry fried rice. For heft, add 100g sliced
cooked mushrooms or cubes of fried tofu. Alternatively, drain and
finely chop 3 tablespoons kimchi and add with the ackee. Experiment
with garnishes: try chopped coriander or parsley, toasted sesame
seeds, warm edamame beans, Japanese aonori seaweed flakes, pickled
vegetables like radish or cucumber (see page 237), pickled ginger or
crispy onions (see page 160). You could even serve with shop-bought
Indonesian kecap manis sauce.

MASALA DOSA

SERVES
4

FOR THE DOSA BATTER:

a pinch of **fenugreek seeds**

100g **gram flour**

60g **rice flour**

a pinch of **salt**

1 teaspoon **baking powder** (use
  gluten-free to keep this GF and WF)

300ml **water**

2 teaspoons **lemon juice**

freshly ground black pepper

1 teaspoon **neutral cooking oil**

FOR THE DOSA FILLING:

600g **white potatoes**, unpeeled and
  cut into small chunks

1 **carrot**, finely diced

2 tablespoons **neutral cooking oil**

1 **onion**, finely diced

a pinch of **salt**

2 cloves of **garlic**, grated

2cm piece of **fresh ginger**, peeled
  and grated

1 teaspoon **mustard seeds**
  (ideally **black**)

10 **curry leaves**, crumbled or torn

2 teaspoons finely chopped **green
  chilli** (less if you're serving to little
  ones) , deseeded to taste

1 teaspoon **ground turmeric**

1 teaspoon **garam masala**

75g **spinach**, stems removed,
  roughly chopped

1 tablespoon finely chopped
  fresh coriander

1 teaspoon **lemon juice**

red lentil sambar (see page 88)
  and **coconut chutney** (see page
  231), to serve (optional)

PREP TIME: 20 MINS · COOK TIME: 40 MINS

Masala dosa are fermented lentil pancakes from South India, stuffed with spiced potatoes. This quickie version is a bit of a cheat, since it is leavened with baking powder and made with gram flour and rice flour. But we still love it. The filling freezes well so make a big batch.

1. Make the dosa batter. Toast the fenugreek seeds in a hot dry pan for 1–2 minutes, then grind to a powder using a pestle and mortar. Place half the ground fenugreek in a large bowl with plenty of black pepper and the rest of the batter ingredients, except the oil. Whisk until smooth, then set aside to rest while you make the filling.

2. Place the potatoes and carrot in a large pan, cover with hot water and bring to the boil. Simmer until completely tender.

3. Meanwhile, heat 1 tablespoon of the oil in a frying pan over a medium heat, add the onion and salt and cook for about 10 minutes, until just beginning to brown. Add the garlic and ginger and cook for 1 minute, then add the remaining oil and the mustard seeds, curry leaves, chilli, remaining ground fenugreek and ground spices. Stir and cook for another minute, then add the spinach and cook until wilted.

4. Drain the potatoes and carrot, then roughly mash. Scrape the spinach mixture into the potatoes, then stir in the coriander and lemon juice. Keep warm.

5. When you are ready to cook the dosa, pour a splash of oil into a large frying pan and use kitchen paper to wipe it around the pan – you need very little to cook the dosa. Place over a low heat. Pour 1 ladleful of the batter into the hot pan, then quickly tilt the pan to spread the batter out thinly to form a circle. Cook for about 5 minutes (tiny cracks will appear all over the surface as it cooks). Check the bottom of the dosa – it needs to cook slowly otherwise the bean-y flavour of the gram flour won't cook away, so it should not brown quickly. When the dosa is completely set and very slightly browned on the bottom but isn't yet crisp, slide it out of the pan and on to a warm serving plate. Keep warm and repeat to make the remaining 3 dosa.

6. Spoon a quarter of the potato filling on to one side of each dosa, then fold over to enclose the filling. Serve with sambar and coconut chutney, if liked.

RED LENTIL SAMBAR

SERVES
4

  (GF) (WF) (NF) (SoF)

200g **red lentils**

500ml **water**

240g **basmati rice**, rinsed

2 teaspoons **tamarind paste**

100–200g **cooked vegetables**
(such as sliced **carrot**, **green
beans**, chunks of **aubergine** or
cooked **squash** or **okra**), fresh or
frozen (optional)

1 tablespoon **neutral cooking oil**

1 clove of **garlic**, grated

6 **curry leaves**, crumbled

½ teaspoon **ground turmeric**

a generous pinch of **chilli powder**

2 pinches of **salt**

dairy-free, soya-free or **nut-
free yoghurt**, to serve

PREP TIME: 10 MINS · COOK TIME: 35 MINS

**Sambar is a tamarind and lentil soup traditionally served on the
side of dosa, or with rice and yoghurt. It freezes well so is great for
batch-cooking.**

1. Place the lentils and water in a pan and bring to the boil. Skim off any
   foam or scum on the surface, then turn the heat down to a simmer, cover
   and cook until the lentils are falling apart, about 30 minutes.

2. Meanwhile, in a separate pan, add the rice and cover with water. Add a
   pinch of salt, cover and cook over a medium heat according to the packet
   instructions, until tender.

3. Remove the lentils from the heat and stir in the tamarind paste and
   cooked vegetables, if using. Heat the oil in a small frying pan over a
   medium-low heat, add the garlic and sizzle for 1 minute, then remove
   from the heat and immediately add the curry leaves, turmeric and chilli
   powder. Stir well, then tip into the lentils with the salt. Stir and taste – it
   should be mildly spicy and tangy.

4. Drain the rice and serve with the sambar in small bowls and the yoghurt
   on the side.

TOFU KATSU CURRY

SERVES
4

FOR THE KATSU CURRY SAUCE:

2 teaspoons **neutral cooking oil** or **refined coconut oil**

I large **onion**, finely diced

I **leek**, halved and finely sliced

4 cloves of **garlic**, crushed

2cm piece of **fresh ginger**, peeled and finely grated

2 tablespoons **mild curry powder**

I tablespoon **plain** or **gluten-free plain flour**

500ml **water**

I small **carrot**, quartered lengthways and diced

2 tablespoons **tamari soy sauce** (use gluten-free to keep this GF and WF)

2 tablespoons **vegan mirin**

pinch of **salt**

I teaspoon **sugar**

FOR THE BREADED TOFU CUTLETS:

300g **firm tofu**

50g **plain** or **gluten-free plain flour**

50g **cornflour**

I tablespoon **water**

100g **traditional** or **gluten-free breadcrumbs**

2 tablespoons **neutral cooking oil** or **refined coconut oil**

salt and **freshly ground black pepper**

TO SERVE:

steamed rice (allow 60g uncooked rice per person)

steamed **broccoli** (allow 75g per person)

PREP TIME: 15 MINS · COOK TIME: 30 MINS

Katsu is a Japanese technique involving breading and frying, and the results are often served with a mild curry sauce. This is our vegan version.

1. To make the curry sauce, heat the oil in a pan, add the onion, leek, garlic and ginger and fry over a medium heat for 10 minutes, stirring occasionally. Stir in the curry powder to coat all the vegetables and cook for 1 minute. Add the flour and cook for another minute, then gradually add the water, stirring constantly to make a smooth sauce. Stir in the carrot, soy sauce, mirin, salt and sugar and cook for about 15 minutes, or until the sauce has reduced by half and thickened.

2. Meanwhile, place the tofu in a clean tea towel and press firmly to squeeze out the liquid, then pat dry. Slice into 4 equal-sized steaks.

3. Prepare 3 bowls, one with flour seasoned with salt and pepper, one with the cornflour mixed with the water, and one with the breadcrumbs. Heat the oil in a large frying pan over a medium heat.

4. Dredge the tofu steaks, one at a time, in the flour, then the cornflour mixture and finally, in the breadcrumbs. Fry in the hot oil for 5–8 minutes, turning once, until golden on both sides. Drain on kitchen paper.

5. Serve with steamed rice and broccoli, with the sauce poured over.

SUPER-GREEN GREEN CURRY

SERVES
4

PREP TIME: 20 MINS · COOK TIME: 35 MINS

Thai sticky rice is easy to find in big supermarkets, as is galangal, but you could use basmati if you prefer and simply leave out the galangal. Miso paste is also widely available – along with the lime juice and salt, its intense savoury flavour replaces the fish sauce traditionally used in Thai curries. You can find soya-free versions online.

240g **Thai sticky rice**

3 tablespoons **neutral cooking oil**

2 **aubergines**, cut into 2cm pieces

600ml **coconut milk** (from 2 well-shaken tins)

a pinch of **dried red chilli flakes** (less if you're serving to little ones), plus extra to taste (optional)

125g **broccoli**, broken into florets

125g **long green beans**, trimmed and cut into short lengths

125g **spring greens** (or other soft, sweet **green cabbage**), shredded

100g **cauliflower**, broken into florets

1 tablespoon **lime juice**, plus extra to taste

salt

fresh **Thai** or **Italian basil leaves**, to serve

FOR THE CURRY PASTE:

a pinch of **ground coriander**

a pinch of **ground cumin**

½ teaspoon **fine salt**

1 teaspoon **galangal paste** or finely chopped **fresh galangal** (optional)

1 heaped teaspoon **white** or **yellow miso paste** (use soya-free to keep this SoF)

4cm piece of **fresh ginger**, peeled and roughly chopped

15 **kaffir lime leaves**

2 teaspoons **soft dark brown sugar**

1 stalk of **lemongrass**, tough outer leaves removed and finely chopped

3 small **shallots**, roughly chopped

3 cloves of **garlic**, roughly chopped

1 bunch of **fresh coriander**, leaves and stalks roughly chopped

1 **hot green chilli**, deseeded to taste, roughly chopped

1. Rinse the rice, then tip into a pan and cover with cold water to about 1cm above the grains. Add a pinch of salt and bring to the boil, then turn the heat down, cover and simmer for 10 minutes. Remove from the heat and allow to steam, covered, for about 20 minutes, or until the curry is ready.

2. Meanwhile, heat 2 tablespoons of the oil in a large frying pan, add the aubergines and fry gently over a medium heat for about 15 minutes, turning the pieces frequently, until golden brown all over. Set aside.

3. While the rice and aubergines are cooking, make the curry paste. It is quickest to throw all the ingredients into a food processor or blender and process until fairly smooth. Alternatively, you can pound the ingredients together in a pestle and mortar.

4. Heat the remaining oil in a large deep pan over a medium heat, then add the curry paste and fry for 2 minutes, stirring constantly, until fragrant. Turn the heat right down and add the coconut milk. Slowly and gently bring to a simmer (going too fast may make the coconut milk split). Add the red chilli flakes, if you feel the curry needs extra heat.

5. Add the broccoli, beans, greens and cauliflower. Stir well so that the vegetables are submerged in the sauce. Cook for 4 minutes, then add the cooked aubergines and cook for another minute. Check the vegetables – they should be tender, but still quite crisp.

6. Remove from the heat and stir in the lime juice. Check the seasoning, adding more salt, chilli flakes or lime juice, to taste.

7. Fluff up the sticky rice. Serve the soupy green curry, scattered with the basil, in bowls with the rice in small bowls alongside.

PULLED JACKFRUIT BURGERS

SERVES **2**

- 1 tablespoon **olive oil** or **neutral cooking oil**
- 1 **onion**, finely diced
- 1 × 565g or 400g tin of **young green jackfruit in brine** or **water**, drained
- 1 clove of **garlic**, crushed
- 150ml hot **vegan vegetable stock** (see page 140 for homemade)
- 1 teaspoon **vegan Dijon mustard**
- ½ teaspoon **sweet smoked paprika**
- 1 teaspoon **gluten-free tamari soy sauce** (to keep this GF and WF) or **Maggi liquid seasoning** (to keep this SoF)
- 4 tablespoons **vegan barbecue sauce** (see page 223 for homemade)

TO SERVE:
- 4 **vegan burger buns**, **vegan brioche** (see page 241) or **gluten-free burger buns** (to keep this GF and WF) split and lightly toasted
- **coleslaw** (see page 162)
- **sweet pickled cucumbers**, sliced
- **pickled jalapeños** (optional)
- **French fries**

PREP TIME: 15 MINS · COOK TIME: 30 MINS

We were amazed when we first tried pulled jackfruit – the unripe green fruit works so well in place of traditional pulled pork, is super-healthy and completely guilt-free. (You can also use the cooked batched jackfruit from page 50 here and start the recipe at Step 4.)

1. Heat the oil in a large frying pan, add the onion and fry gently over a medium-low heat for about 8 minutes, until translucent.

2. Meanwhile, trim away the hard woody core from each chunk of jackfruit and discard, leaving only the softer flesh. (You will have about 150g.) Roughly shred the flesh, using your hands. Rinse well under cold running water, then tip into a clean tea towel and pat dry.

3. Add the crushed garlic to the onion in the pan and cook for another 2 minutes. Turn up the heat to medium and add the shredded jackfruit. Cook for about 5 minutes, stirring frequently, until the jackfruit and onion begin to brown. (Fish out any jelly-like seeds or hard bits of core that emerge as the fruit breaks down.) Add the stock and bring to a simmer, then cook until the stock has almost completely evaporated, about 10–15 minutes.

4. (Or, if you are using batched jackfruit, re-heat it with a little oil in a large frying pan, until heated through.)

5. When the pan is almost dry, add the mustard, sweet smoked paprika and soy sauce or Maggi. Stir to coat well, then remove from the heat. Mash roughly using a potato masher to further shred the flesh. Return to a low heat and add the barbecue sauce. Toss well to coat and cook for 3–4 minutes.

6. Serve in split toasted buns, topped with the coleslaw and pickles, and fries on the side.

TIP
If you don't want burgers, serve the pulled jackfruit with mac-n-no-cheese (see page 114), or even add it as a layer in the middle before baking, or over nachos with guacamole (see page 234).

JEMIMA'S CHICKPEA & CAULIFLOWER STEW

2 tablespoons **refined** or **extra virgin coconut oil**

3 **shallots** or small **onions**, finely diced

5 cloves of **garlic**, very finely chopped

3cm piece of **fresh ginger**, peeled and very finely chopped

1 teaspoon **ground turmeric**

1 teaspoon **paprika**

1 × 400g tin of **chopped tomatoes**

2 tablespoons **white** or **yellow miso paste**

1 teaspoon **tamari soy sauce** (use gluten-free to keep this GF and WF)

400ml **coconut milk**

1 × 400g tin of **chickpeas**, drained (or 240g cooked **chickpeas**)

1 **red pepper**, cut into long 5mm-wide strips

½ **cauliflower** (or 1 whole small one), broken into small florets

lemon juice, to taste

salt and **freshly ground black pepper**

TO SERVE:

fresh coriander leaves

steamed rice (allow about 60g uncooked rice per person), to serve

PREP TIME: 15 MINS · COOK TIME: 35 MINS

We asked LEON's Instagram and Twitter followers to submit their favourite original vegan recipes. Jemima Grant was a 19-year-old self-taught cook when she submitted this dish. It's halfway between a stew and a curry and came out as a a a clear winner.

1. Heat the oil in a large pan, add the shallots or onions and fry over a medium-high heat, stirring frequently, for about 5 minutes, or until beginning to soften. Add the garlic and ginger and continue to cook for a few minutes until the onions are soft and starting to caramelize. Add the spices and stir to coat the onions. Cook for 30–60 seconds, until fragrant.

2. Stir in the chopped tomatoes, miso paste and soy sauce and cook for 5 minutes, stirring occasionally, until the sauce has thickened slightly.

3. Mix in the coconut milk, chickpeas and red pepper, then bring to a gentle simmer and cook for 10 minutes, stirring occasionally to prevent sticking. Add the cauliflower, mix again and cook for another 10 minutes, or until the stew has reduced and thickened and the cauliflower is tender.

4. Take off the heat, add lemon juice and a little salt and pepper, to taste. Scatter with the coriander leaves and serve with steamed rice.

VIDA'S MUSHROOM & KALE FILO PIE

SERVES
4

2 tablespoons **olive oil**, plus 50ml
    for brushing
2 small **red onions**, thickly sliced into
    half-moons
2 cloves of **garlic**, finely chopped
leaves from 1 bunch of **fresh thyme**
300g **portobello mushrooms**,
    roughly chopped
120g **shiitake mushrooms** or other
    wild mushrooms, roughly
    chopped (leave any small ones whole)
200g **kale** or **cavolo nero**, or a
    mixture, thick stems removed
100g roughly chopped **pitted olives**
    or **vegan feta** (non-nut and non-
    soya shop-bought to keep this NF and
    SoF or see page 154), or a mixture
    of both
12 sheets of **filo pastry**
salt and **freshly ground
    black pepper**
green vegetables, to serve

PREP TIME: 25 MINS · COOK TIME: 1 HOUR 5 MINS

**Vida Scannell is in charge of well-being and engagement at LEON.
'This is my homage to Greek spanakopita. There is something
indulgent about cooking with filo pastry and rich wild mushrooms
yet at the same time this is such a simple and quick recipe. It also uses
kale to give weight and earthiness, while the vegan feta adds a punch
of saltiness and sharpness. It's our Sunday favourite, there are never
any leftovers, and it tastes good with simple steamed green vegetables
alongside.'**

1.   Heat the oven to 180°C/350°F/gas mark 4.

2.   Heat 1 tablespoon of the oil in a deep frying pan over a medium-low
     heat, add the onions and garlic with a pinch of salt and pepper and
     cook for 8–10 minutes, until soft and translucent.

3.   Add the thyme leaves, mushrooms and another tablespoon of the oil
     and cook for another 10 minutes, stirring frequently. Add the kale or
     cavolo nero and cook, stirring continuously, until wilted. Take off the
     heat and if using olives, mix them in. Set aside.

4.   Pour the 50ml oil into a small cup or bowl. Grease a small pie dish,
     about 25 × 25cm. Place a sheet of the filo pastry in the dish so that it
     hangs over the sides, then lightly brush with oil. Repeat with another
     5 sheets, brushing each with oil.

5.   Spoon in the mushroom mixture and spread out gently. Top with
     small spoonfuls of the feta, if using. Fold the corners and sides of
     pastry over the filling, then place a sheet of pastry on top, tucking
     the sides in. Lightly brush with oil and repeat with another 6 sheets,
     brushing each with oil.

6.   Bake for about 40 minutes, or until golden brown. If the pie browns
     too early, place a sheet of foil or baking parchment over the top to
     allow it to cook through. Serve with green vegetables.

3

FAST FOOD

MAISIE'S 'FISH' & CHIPS

1 or 2 × 500g tins of
banana blossom
300ml **warm water**
2 tablespoons **lemon juice**
2 teaspoons **kelp powder**

FOR THE BATTER:
125g **plain flour**, plus extra for coating
1 tablespoon **baking powder**
1 teaspoon **salt**
250ml **cold water**
neutral cooking oil, for frying

TO SERVE:
oven-baked chips or **fries**
vegan tartare sauce (see page 222)
lemon wedges
450g cooked and crushed or puréed
garden peas

PREP TIME: 20 MINS · MARINATING TIME: OVERNIGHT
COOK TIME: 15 MINS

Maisie Manterfield is one of the founders of Burgerlolz (now The Burger Garden), a brilliant vegan fast food restaurant in Sheffield. She introduced Rebecca to the joys of battered banana blossom, which when seasoned with seaweed is a perfect sub for white fish. You will need to prepare the blossom the day before you cook it. Some tins contain lots of small pieces, so it is worth buying two to ensure you have enough large chunks.

1. Drain the blossom and place in a large bowl. Gently squeeze the firm stems to soften. Add the water, lemon juice and kelp powder, gently stir and allow to marinate overnight.

2. When ready to cook, mix the dry batter ingredients together, then add the cold water and stir thoroughly. Allow to rest for 5–10 minutes, then stir again.

3. Heat about 6cm of oil in a deep heavy-based pan over a medium heat to 170°C/340°F, or until a cube of day-old bread browns in 30 seconds.

4. Drain the marinated blossom in a sieve, then gently pat dry. Pour some flour on to a plate, then, working with a few pieces of blossom at a time, coat them in the flour then dip in the batter, turning to ensure they are well coated.

5. Using tongs, carefully place the blossom in the hot oil, a couple of pieces at a time. Cook for about 2 minutes on each side, or until the batter is crisp, bubbly and golden. Remove and drain on kitchen paper. Keep warm while you repeat with the rest of the blossom.

6. Serve with chips, tartare sauce, lemon wedges and crushed peas.

> **TIP**
> You will find banana blossom in tins in Asian supermarkets (it is used as a vegetable in South East Asian and Indian cooking) or online. It can be cut into smaller pieces before cooking and used in 'fish' tacos (see page 63) or hot wraps (see page 103).

JACKFRUIT FRIED 'CHICKEN'

6 tablespoons **rice flour**

6 tablespoons **ground flaxseeds**

250ml **water**

500g cooked **batched jackfruit** (see page 50)

neutral cooking oil, for frying

FOR THE CRUMB COATING:

250ml **unsweetened plant milk** (use non-nut or non-soya to keep this NF or SoF)

2 teaspoons **vegan cider vinegar**

125g **plain flour**

100g **cornflour**

1 teaspoon **cayenne pepper** (optional)

2 teaspoons **sweet smoked paprika**

2 teaspoons **mustard powder**

2 teaspoon **garlic powder**

1½ teaspoons **sea salt**, crumbled until fine

freshly ground black pepper

TO SERVE:

fries

vegan hot sauce

garlicky vegan aioli or **vegan chipotle mayo** (see page 222)

Mexican slaw or **miso-sesame slaw** (see page 162 or 163)

PREP TIME: 25 MINS · COOK TIME: 25 MINS

We use a plant-based buttermilk and classic spiced crumb for these incredibly moreish crunchy patties. Rebecca first tried fried jackfruit 'wings' at Biff's Jack Shack in London, where they serve jackfruit deep-fried around a sugar-cane 'bone'. These are inspired by Biff's incredible creations, simplified for home-cooking. Choose an oil with a very high smoke point, like sunflower oil, for this recipe.

1. In a small bowl, mix together the rice flour, flaxseeds and water and allow to soak for 5 minutes. Strain the thickened liquid through a sieve, pressing the solids with the back of a spoon and reserving the liquid. Discard the solids. Mix the liquid with the shredded jackfruit and set aside.

2. Pour the milk and vinegar into a large shallow bowl. In a separate large shallow bowl, stir together the flours, cayenne, if using, paprika, mustard powder, garlic powder and sea salt. Season with plenty of pepper.

3. Heat about 1cm of oil in a large deep pan over a medium-high heat. Meanwhile, divide the jackfruit mixture into 12, then shape into patties by squeezing the flesh firmly until even and neat.

4. When the oil is shimmering hot (190°C/375°F), begin triple dipping the jackfruit: hold 1 patty in your hand and spoon over the milk mixture, then gently roll in the spiced flour. Repeat the wetting and rolling process twice more, ensuring each patty is well covered in batter with no fruit visible.

5. Carefully lower 3 or 4 patties at a time into the hot oil. (Don't overcrowd the pan, as this will lower the temperature of the oil and make the patties greasy and soggy.) Cook for about 3 minutes on each side, until golden and very crisp. Remove with a slotted spoon, allowing the excess oil to drain back into the pan. Drain on kitchen paper and keep warm while you cook the rest of the patties.

6. Serve with fries, hot sauce, mayo and slaw.

> **TIP**
> If you love buffalo wings, when cooked, drench each patty in vegan buffalo hot sauce before serving.

VARIATIONS - JACKFRUIT NUGGETS & BURGERS

To make these into nuggets suitable for kids, halve the size of each patty. When making the crumb, omit the cayenne and paprika and halve the amount of mustard and salt in the flour mix. Cook until golden, as above. To make this into fried jackfruit 'chicken' burgers, shape into 4–6 larger patties about 1.5cm thick. Gently shallow-fry in about 5mm oil for 5 minutes on each side – as they are bigger, they will be much more fragile, so use 2 large spatulas to flip them gently when the bottom is golden.

SMOKY BEAN BURGERS

3 tablespoons **neutral cooking oil**
or **olive oil**

1 **onion**, very finely diced

2 cloves of **garlic**, finely chopped

1 teaspoon **ground cumin**

½ teaspoon **ground coriander**

½ teaspoon **mustard seeds**

1 teaspoon **sweet smoked paprika**

½ teaspoon **vegan chipotle paste**
(less if you're serving to little ones)

1 × 400g tin of **kidney beans**, drained

1 × 400g tin of **black beans**, drained

1 **ready-cooked beetroot** (not
in vinegar), about 80–90g, peeled and
roughly chopped

4 tablespoons **breadcrumbs**

2 tablespoons chopped **fresh
coriander** (leaves and stalks)

2 tablespoons chopped **fresh parsley**
(leaves and stalks)

2 tablespoons **vegan mayonnaise**
(see page 224 for homemade)

2 tablespoons **refined coconut oil**

salt and **freshly ground
black pepper**

TO SERVE:

vegan burger buns or **vegan
brioche** (see page 241), warmed
or toasted

crisp lettuce and **sliced tomato**

dill pickles, sliced

burger relish

garlicky vegan aioli or **vegan
chipotle mayo** (see page 222)

fries

PREP TIME: 20 MINS · COOK TIME: 30 MINS

Here, we use refined coconut oil along with vegan mayo and breadcrumbs to help bind our burgers – being fat-free may sound healthy, but it makes for very squishy, crumbly burgers.

1. Heat 1 tablespoon of the neutral or olive oil in a large frying pan over a low heat, add the onion, garlic and a pinch of salt and cook gently, stirring often, for 8–10 minutes, until beginning to turn translucent.

2. Next, add the spices and plenty of pepper. Cook, stirring, for a minute or two, until the spices are fragrant, then add the chipotle paste. Stir again and add the kidney beans and black beans.

3. Scoop half the bean mixture into a food processor or blender, leaving the rest in the pan. Add the beetroot, breadcrumbs, coriander, parsley and vegan mayo. Blitz to form a rough purée that is not totally smooth.

4. Scrape the puréed bean mixture back into the pan and return to a medium heat. Add the coconut oil and cook, stirring frequently, for about 10 minutes, until the oil has been absorbed and the mixture has thickened, allowing any excess liquid to cook away. Set aside until cool enough to shape into patties.

5. Divide the mixture equally into 4–6 patties, depending on the size of your buns. Using your hands, shape into neat burgers, pressing firmly to help them hold their shape when cooking.

6. Wipe out the frying pan and add the remaining neutral or olive oil. Reduce the heat to medium-low and fry the patties for about 3 minutes on each side, until browned. Use a thin spatula to carefully turn them, but otherwise leave them alone in the pan as they can be slightly fragile.

7. Serve in warmed burger buns with lettuce, sliced tomato, dill pickles, relish, chipotle mayo or aioli, with fries on the side.

> **TIP**
> If not using immediately, stack the patties, separated by squares of baking parchment and when cool, freeze. Defrost completely before cooking.

HOT WRAPS

LOTS OF OUR RECIPES WORK WELL ROLLED UP IN FLAT BREADS. HERE ARE A FEW OF OUR FAVOURITE IDEAS.

There are lots of gluten-free wraps available now, as well as wraps made with rice, charcoal or blue corn. Check your wrap ingredients – some pittas and other flat breads contain milk.

Stir-fried seitan or tempeh strips dressed with soy sauce, lime juice and grated ginger, with spring onions and cucumber strips, and/or leftover miso-sesame slaw (see page 163).

Warm roasted vegetables with spicy vegan mayo (see page 224), harissa or tzatziki (see page 230), toasted nuts or seeds (see pages 242–3), sliced tomatoes and crisp lettuce.

Fried banana blossom 'fish' (see page 98), vegan tartare sauce (see page 222), cucumber and lettuce.

Reheated leftovers: chilli (see pages 126 or 139), tinga (see page 70), Spanish omelette (see page 150), frittata (see page 78), breaded tofu (see page 89), jackfruit fried 'chicken' (see page 100), 'meatballs' (see page 134), curry (see pages 90 or 133) with salad and/or rice.

Salt-n-pepper tofu (see page 58), thinly sliced spring onions, thinly sliced cucumber, Chinese leaves, beansprouts and hoisin sauce.

Warmed refried beans from a tin, salsa, lettuce, cucumber, coriander, lime juice, and/or leftover Mexican slaw (see page 162).

Refried beans, guacamole (see page 234), lettuce, corn salsa, cashew soured cream (see page 228) and chilli/hot sauce.

Onion bhaji, mango chutney (see page 235), salad and tzatziki (see page 230).

Chickpeas warmed and dressed with sweet smoked paprika, ground cumin, salt, lemon juice and a pinch of cayenne, wrapped up with vegan tzatziki (see page 230), roasted vegetables or salad.

Jackfruit tikka masala (see page 144) with rice and raw vegetables.

Garlic mushrooms, fried onions, watercress, vegan Dijon mustard and vegan mayo (see page 224).

TOFU BURGERS

250g **shiitake mushrooms**

olive oil, for frying

1 **onion**, finely diced

2 cloves of **garlic**, minced

½ teaspoon finely chopped **fresh thyme**

½ teaspoon finely chopped **fresh rosemary**

280g **extra-firm tofu**

2 tablespoons **plain** or **gluten-free plain flour**

2 tablespoons **ground flaxseeds**

1 tablespoon **ground chia seeds**

3 tablespoons **gluten-free tamari soy sauce**, plus extra if needed

2 tablespoons **vegan mayonnaise** (see page 224)

3 tablespoons **sunflower seeds**, toasted

salt and **freshly ground black pepper**

TO SERVE:

vegan burger buns, **vegan brioche** (see page 241) or **gluten-free vegan burger buns**, split and toasted

crisp lettuce, **sliced tomato** and **dill pickles**

sliced avocado or **guacamole** (see page 234)

chipotle mayo or **garlicky aioli** (see page 222)

burger relish

fries

**PREP TIME: 20 MINS · COOK TIME: 40 MINS
CHILL TIME: 20 MINS**

These make a great swap for meat burgers and work brilliantly with our vegan brioche (see page 241). We love adding creamy avocado or guacamole as well as classic burger garnishes.

1. Place a large frying pan over a medium heat. Chop the mushrooms into very small pieces, then add to the pan with just enough oil to coat the bottom of the pan. Fry for 10 minutes, stirring frequently to prevent sticking, until the mushrooms have reduced in size by about three-quarters. Add a drop more oil and the onion, garlic, thyme and rosemary and fry for another 10–15 minutes, until the onions are translucent. Remove from the heat and allow to cool.

2. In a clean tea towel or kitchen paper, squeeze the liquid from the tofu, then pat as dry as possible. Crumble the tofu into small pieces, leaving some chunky bits for texture.

3. When the mushroom mix is cool enough to handle, add the tofu, flour, ground seeds, soy sauce, mayo and sunflower seeds. Season well and gently mix. Take a small nugget of the burger mix and fry briefly in a splash of olive oil to check the seasoning. Add more salt, pepper or soy sauce to the mix if needed, then form into 6–8 patties. Chill for 20 minutes in the fridge, to help firm up. Heat the oven to 180°C/350°F/ gas mark 4.

4. In the same pan, heat a splash more oil over a medium heat and fry the patties until browned on both sides. Transfer to a baking sheet and bake for 10 minutes.

5. Serve in split toasted buns, piled with the lettuce, tomato and pickles, then topped with the burgers and avocado and any sauces or relish you want to add.

> **TIP**
> These burgers don't freeze well, so if you don't need this many, halve the recipe.

BAKED BUFFALO CAULIFLOWER WINGS

PREP TIME: 15 MINS · COOK TIME: 35 MINS

Fiery and unbelievably moreish. Serve with vegan mayo (see page 224), garlicky aioli (see page 222) or ranch dressing (see page 223).

1 **cauliflower**

90ml **unsweetened plant milk** (use non-nut or non-soya to keep this NF or SoF)

1 teaspoon **vegan cider vinegar**

120ml **neutral cooking oil**, plus extra for greasing

4 tablespoons **plain flour**

1 tablespoon **cornflour**

2 teaspoons **sweet smoked paprika**

1 teaspoon **mustard powder**

2 teaspoons **garlic powder**

½ teaspoon **salt**

150g **panko breadcrumbs**

8 tablespoons **vegan buffalo wing sauce** or **vegan American-style hot sauce** (we love Frank's Red Hot)

freshly ground black pepper

1. Heat the oven to 180°C/350°F/gas mark 4. Remove the leaves from the cauliflower and break it into fairly large 4–5cm florets.

2. Whisk the milk, vinegar and 75ml of the oil together. In a large bowl, mix together the flours, sweet smoked paprika, mustard powder, garlic powder, salt and plenty of pepper. Stir the wet ingredients into the dry and mix to form a smooth, thick batter.

3. Place the panko breadcrumbs in a separate bowl.

4. Dip each floret into the thick batter and use your fingers to work it into the crevices. Scrape off any excess batter – each piece should be thoroughly coated, but not thickly. Next, dip the floret into the breadcrumbs, rolling to coat it all over, then place on a baking sheet lined with baking parchment and lightly greased with oil. Repeat with the rest of the florets.

5. Whisk the remaining oil and the hot sauce together in another bowl and set aside.

6. Bake for 15 minutes, turning once halfway through. Using tongs, dip each floret in the hot sauce, turning to ensure all the breadcrumbs are well coated in the sauce, then return to the sheet and cook for another 20 minutes, turning twice, until the cauliflower is just tender and the coating is deep red and very crunchy.

7. Drain on kitchen paper for 3–4 minutes to drain the excess oil and allow to cool slightly before serving.

ARANCINI

 ARANCINI BALLS

PREP TIME: 15 MINS · COOK TIME: 20 MINS

Deep-fried balls of risotto joy.

neutral cooking oil, for frying

100g **plain** or **gluten-free plain flour**

75–90ml **unsweetened plant milk** (use non-nut or non-soya to keep this NF or SoF)

150g **traditional** or **gluten-free breadcrumbs**

1 × quantity chilled **butternut squash** or **pea & lemon risotto** (omit the toppings; see pages 66–7) or 500–600g any **vegan risotto**, chilled

salt and **freshly ground black pepper**

lemon wedges, to serve

1. Heat about 6cm of oil in a large, deep heavy-based pan over a medium heat to about 180°C/350°F, or until a cube of day-old bread browns in 30 seconds. When the oil is hot, turn down the heat slightly to keep it at a steady temperature.

2. Meanwhile, pour the flour into a bowl and season with salt and pepper. Pour the milk into another bowl, then the breadcrumbs into a third bowl.

3. Using a dessertspoon, scoop up ping-pong-ball-sized nuggets of risotto, then use your hands to shape into neat balls. Roll each one first in the seasoned flour, then dip in the milk, then roll in the breadcrumbs, ensuring each ball is well coated.

4. Using tongs, carefully lower 3 or 4 balls at a time into the hot oil. (Don't overcrowd the pan as this will lower the temperature of the oil and make the arancini soggy and greasy.) Cook for about 4 minutes, until the shells are golden and crisp, turning once or twice if necessary. Remove with tongs or a slotted spoon, allowing the excess oil to drain back into the pan. Drain on kitchen paper and keep warm while you cook the rest of the arancini. Serve warm with lemon wedges to squeeze over.

TIP

Chilling the risotto helps to firm it up. If you have found a vegan mozzarella or blue cheese that you love, tuck a little nugget inside each ball, or if using a plain risotto, you could include fillings like finely chopped grilled artichoke or cooked garlicky mushrooms. Just make sure they are well covered by a good layer of rice, and don't overfill the balls.

FAST FOOD

PIZZA

× 20–25CM PIZZAS

PREP TIME: 35 MINS · RISE TIME: 4–6 HOURS
COOK TIME: 10 MINS PER PIZZA

If you know and love a vegan mozzarella, Parmesan, blue cheese, feta or goat's cheese, you should definitely experiment with using it here. Mix and match the toppings to your taste. The proved uncooked dough freezes well too.

FOR THE DOUGH:

250ml **lukewarm water**

2 teaspoons **dried active yeast**

1 teaspoon **sugar**

2 tablespoons **olive oil**, plus extra

375g **strong white bread flour**

100g **'00' flour** (or use **all-bread flour**)

1 teaspoon **fine salt**

polenta or **flour**, for dusting

FOR THE MARINARA PIZZA SAUCE:

200ml **tomato passata**

½ teaspoon **dried oregano**

1 clove of **garlic**

1 tablespoon **extra virgin olive oil**

freshly ground black pepper

TOPPINGS:

artichoke hearts in oil

mushroom bacon (see page 40)

capers

olives

cooked and squeezed out **spinach**

shredded **uncooked kale** or **Brussels sprouts**

walnuts, crumbled

cubes of **roasted squash**

sun-dried or **halved cherry tomatoes**

roasted peppers

roasted onions

roasted mushrooms or **mushrooms in oil**

asparagus spears, halved lengthways

shaved **courgette ribbons**

pine nuts

fresh or **dried chillies**

quartered figs

rocket or **basil**, added after cooking

1. To make the bases, mix together the water, yeast and sugar. Allow to stand for 10 minutes, or until a frothy head has formed. Add the olive oil, then mix with the flours and salt in a large bowl. Using your hands, work the mixture until it forms a rough dough, then continue to work until smooth. Turn out on to a clean work surface dusted with flour and knead for 5 minutes, until it feels soft and elastic. (Alternatively, use a stand mixer fitted with a dough hook.)

2. Place the dough in a clean, lightly oiled bowl and cover with clingfilm. Allow to rise in a warm place for at least 4 hours, preferably 6, until doubled in size. Knock back the dough, using your knuckles to press it back, then divide into 4 equal-sized balls. Allow to prove for another 20 minutes, or until ready to cook.

3. Meanwhile, make the marinara sauce. Mix all the ingredients together and set aside until ready to use.

4. Heat the oven to its highest setting. Place a pizza stone or two in it to heat up, or use a couple of up-turned baking sheets.

5. When the oven is hot, roll or stretch out a dough ball to form a circle about 20–25cm in diameter. (Stretching it is trickier, but it will allow you to create a crust.) Repeat with a second dough ball if you have 2 stones or sheets. Remove the hot sheets or stones from the oven and dust them with flour or polenta. Slide the prepared bases on to the sheets and working quickly, use a large spoon to smear a thin layer of the sauce over the dough, leaving at least 2cm for the crust all the way around.

6. Quickly add your chosen toppings, then bake for 5–10 minutes, checking every minute or two after 5 minutes have elapsed (how long they need will depend on how hot your oven is).

7. Add any toppings that don't need to be cooked (like rocket or pesto). Repeat with the remaining bases. Serve immediately.

CEM & ROJ'S LAHMACUN

 LAHMACUN

FOR THE DOUGH:

1 tablespoon **dried active yeast**

300ml **warm water**

1½ teaspoons **sugar**

500g **plain flour**

25ml **olive oil**, plus extra for greasing

1¼ teaspoons **salt**

polenta or **flour**, for dusting

FOR THE SAUCE:

100g **soya mince**

1 × 400g tin of **plum tomatoes**, excess juice drained off

½ small **onion**, finely chopped

½ **red pepper**, chopped

2 teaspoons **red pepper purée** or **paste** (ideally Turkish **biber salçasi**)

2 tablespoons **sunflower oil**

1 teaspoon **garlic powder**

½ teaspoon **black pepper**

1 teaspoon **paprika**

a generous pinch of **salt**

a small handful of **fresh parsley**, leaves finely chopped

> **TIP**
> Serve with tzatziki (see page 230) and tomato and parsley salad (see page 60).

PREP TIME: 30 MINS · RISE TIME: 1½–2 HOURS
COOK TIME: 12 MINS PER LAHMACUN

Cem and Roj run What the Pitta (www.whatthepitta.com), a vegan kebab shop in London – if you find yourself near one of their branches (in Shoreditch, Camden or Croydon), you have to taste their vegan doner. They also serve lahmacun, a traditionally cheese-free Turkish pizza. They are made with a yeasted dough base, plus a tomato, herb and red pepper sauce. You can use any mince replacement here, or substitute cooked Puy lentils for the mince. If you like a bit of spice, try adding some chopped fresh chilli or dried chillies.

1. To make the dough, whisk the yeast with the water and half the sugar until the yeast is dissolved. Allow to stand for 5–10 minutes, or until a frothy head has formed. Add the rest of the sugar to the flour in a large bowl. Make a well in the flour and add the yeast mixture, olive oil and salt. Mix to form a dough, then knead for 10–12 minutes, until smooth and pliable. (Alternatively, use a stand mixer fitted with a dough hook.) Place the dough in a clean, oiled bowl. Cover with a clean tea towel or clingfilm and allow to rise in a warm place for 1½–2 hours, until doubled in size.

2. Meanwhile, make the sauce. Soak the soya mince for 10–15 minutes in hot water until soft, then drain and squeeze out as much water as you can. Put the plum tomatoes, onion, red pepper, red pepper purée or paste and sunflower oil in a food processor or blender and blend until smooth. Pour into a large bowl and add the rest of the ingredients with the squeezed-out soya mince. Taste for seasoning and spice.

3. Heat the oven to its highest setting. If you have a pizza stone, place it in the oven to heat up. If not, use 2 or 3 of your largest baking sheets, turned upside down if they have a rim or lip.

4. Divide the risen dough into 6 × 120g portions. Shape into neat balls and set aside for a further 10 minutes.

5. When ready to cook, roll out 2 or 3 dough balls on a clean work surface dusted with flour to form circles about 25cm in diameter. Remove the stone or hot sheets from the oven, dust with polenta or flour to prevent sticking, then carefully slide the dough discs on to them. Use a ladle to portion out the sauce and smear it thinly over the dough, leaving a gap around the crust.

6. Bake for 6–12 minutes (how long depends on how hot your oven is), or until the dough is lightly browned and bubbled. Repeat until all the dough has been used up, ideally eating each one as soon as it comes out of the oven.

CRISPY TOPPED MAC-N-NO-CHEESE

5 tablespoons **ground almonds**

75ml **water**

150g **white potatoes**, peeled and
roughly chopped

350g **squash**, peeled, deseeded and
roughly chopped

1 **carrot**, peeled and roughly chopped

350g small **pasta tubes**, such as
macaroni or **spirali** (not quick-
cook macaroni)

2 tablespoons **olive oil**

2 tablespoons **plain flour**

500ml **unsweetened plant milk**
(use non-soya to keep this SoF), plus
extra to taste

2 teaspoons **nutritional yeast**, plus
extra to taste

2 teaspoons **English mustard
powder**, plus extra to taste

1 teaspoon **garlic powder**

a really large pinch of **sea salt**

a large pinch of **freshly
grated nutmeg**

50g **sauerkraut** or
pickled cabbage

lots of **white pepper**

neutral cooking oil, for greasing

FOR THE TOPPING:

50g slightly stale **bread**

1 clove of **garlic**

a pinch of **sea salt**

1 tablespoon **olive oil**

PREP TIME: 25 MINS · COOK TIME: 40 MINS

**Pickled cabbage may seem like a mad ingredient to add, but it lends
this a subtle lactic tang – we got the idea from Isa Chandra Moskovitz,
a blogger whose recipe for mac and 'shews (cashews) is widely loved.**

1. Heat the oven to 200°C/400°F/gas mark 6. Mix the almonds and water
    together and allow to soak.

2. Cook the potatoes, squash and carrot in a pan of boiling water for 10
    minutes, until just tender. Drain.

3. Meanwhile, cook the pasta in a separate pan of boiling salted water for
    3 minutes less than the packet instructions. Drain.

4. While the vegetables and pasta are cooking, blitz the bread and garlic
    clove in a food processor to create breadcrumbs for the topping.
    Toss the crumbs in the oil, then tip into a bowl and wipe out the food
    processor bowl.

5. To make the béchamel sauce, heat the oil in a large pan over a
    medium heat. When hot, add the flour. Turn the heat to low and cook,
    stirring, for a couple of minutes to form a paste (don't let it brown).
    Gradually add the milk, a couple of tablespoons at a time, until about
    half has been incorporated, then stir in the rest of the milk. Cook,
    stirring, for 5 minutes. At this point, the sauce will be very loose.

6. Working in batches if necessary, place the vegetables in a food
    processor (or use a high-powered blender) and add the béchamel,
    yeast, mustard powder, garlic powder, salt, nutmeg, sauerkraut,
    pepper and soaked ground almonds. Blitz until completely smooth,
    scraping the sides down twice. (A high-powered processor or blender
    should make the sauce smooth, so keep going until this happens.)

7. Taste the sauce and add more mustard, pepper, yeast or salt, if
    needed. It should be tangy, cheesy and creamy. Stir into the drained
    pasta. If dry, add more milk to loosen, remembering it will thicken
    when it cooks. Tip into a large greased gratin dish and sprinkle
    over a thick layer of the breadcrumbs. Bake for 20 minutes, or until
    the sauce is bubbling and the top is golden brown. (To reheat from
    frozen, place the leftover mac in an ovenproof dish. Add a splash of
    unsweetened plant milk. Cover with foil and place in an oven heated
    to 200°C/400°F/gas mark 6. Cook for 10 minutes, then remove the
    foil and cook for a further 5–10 minutes, until the top has crisped up
    again.)

TIP

Some food processors and blenders have a maximum fill point for blending hot food – ignoring this can make them explode, so whizz the sauce in batches if necessary. If you taste the sauce and it doesn't have quite enough savoury tang for you, try adding ½ teaspoon – to start with – vegan Worcestershire sauce, miso paste or Maggi liquid seasoning. Add any extras a little at a time, tasting as you go. Pimp your mac by adding sliced jalapeños, sweet smoked paprika, vegan chipotle paste, cooked and squeezed out spinach, or one of our fake bacons, chopped (see pages 40–1).

MERIEL'S BEER-MARINATED SEITAN BURRITOS

PREP TIME: 20 MINS · MARINATING TIME: 10 MINS
COOK TIME: 15 MINS

Meriel Armitage created Club Mexicana, a 100% vegan Mexican street food stall, in 2014 and has never looked back – she currently serves tacos, burgers, burritos and cocktails at London's first entirely vegan pub, the Spread Eagle in Hackney, as well as at Kerb in Camden and Dinerama in Shoreditch. This is her recipe. 'There are no hard and fast rules on what you include. I've listed what I like to put in, but if you don't have time to pickle onions, don't worry.'

FOR THE MARINATED SEITAN:

250g **dark seitan** (see page 132 for homemade), shredded into thin doner-kebab-style strips

3 cloves of **garlic**, finely chopped

1 **red onion**, finely chopped

1 bunch of **fresh coriander**, leaves and stalks chopped

2 teaspoons **dried red chilli flakes** or 1 **fresh red chilli**, finely chopped

500ml **vegan beer** (a red ale or hoppy IPA would work well but avoid lager)

juice of 2–3 **limes**, to taste

a pinch of **salt**

2 tablespoons **vegetable oil**

FOR THE BURRITOS:

4 **dairy-free flour tortillas**

150g **brown** or **white long-grain rice**, cooked

200g **guacamole** (see page 234)

1 head of **romaine lettuce**, finely chopped

pink pickled onions (see opposite, optional)

200ml **unsweetened, plain vegan yoghurt** (soya-free or nut-free to keep this SoF and NF) mixed with **lemon juice**

your favourite **salsa** (or **pico de gallo**, see page 231)

hot sauce

coriander cress or **fresh coriander leaves**

2 **limes**, for squeezing over

1. Place the seitan in a large bowl or dish. Add all the marinade ingredients, except the oil, and mix well with your hands until the seitan is very well coated and all the pieces are separated so they can absorb the flavour. Cover with clingfilm and marinate in the fridge for at least 10 minutes or up to 24 hours. The longer you can leave it the better.

2. Heat the oil in a large frying pan. Remove the seitan from the marinade, reserving the marinade in the bowl. Working in batches, if necessary, add the seitan to the pan and mix gently until coated in the hot oil. Cook over a medium heat for about 5–10 minutes (depending on the pan), until brown on one side. Carefully turn over and brown on the other side until crisped all over. Add the reserved marinade, turn up the heat to medium-high and cook for 2–5 minutes, or until the liquid has almost evaporated, but being careful not to let it burn.

3. Meanwhile, heat a large dry frying pan over a high heat. Place each flour tortilla in the pan for about 10 seconds, then flip over. You want each side to puff up and be slightly charred but not burnt.

4. On a chopping board, lay out a warmed flour tortilla and fill with the following (or as many fillings as you are using): 2 tablespoons cooked rice, 2 tablespoons guacamole, a handful of lettuce, a quarter of the seitan, some pink onions, yoghurt, salsa/pico de gallo, hot sauce and coriander cress or leaves. Squeeze lime juice over, for extra zing. Fold each side of the tortilla in towards the middle, then hold the edges in place and roll the burrito away from you, pinching to create a tightly rolled wrap. Repeat to make 4 burritos.

5. Wrap in foil or baking parchment if you find this easier. Eat with your hands while hot – no cutlery allowed!

TIP

Just before you're ready to serve your burritos, start getting all your fillings ready and cook the rice so it's ready when the seitan is cooked.

PINK PICKLED ONIONS

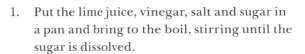

**PREP TIME: 10 MINS · COOK TIME: 5 MINS
REST TIME: 1 HOUR**

200ml **lime juice**

200ml **white vinegar**

1 tablespoon **salt**

3 tablespoons **sugar**

250g **red onions**, thinly sliced

1. Put the lime juice, vinegar, salt and sugar in a pan and bring to the boil, stirring until the sugar is dissolved.

2. Place the red onions in a non-reactive dish and pour over the pickling liquid. Allow to stand for at least 1 hour. Transfer to a clean sterilized jar and keep in the fridge for several weeks.

LEON.
VEGAN SANDWICHES

Much as we love love love hummus, sometimes it's nice to have something else for lunch.

'EGG' MAYO WITH CRESS: (NF) Allow about 75g ackee (see page 36 for more about this incredible, scrambled-egg-like fruit) or soft silken tofu per round of sandwiches. Mix with 1 heaped tablespoon vegan mayonnaise (see page 224), mashing any large pieces gently, and a pinch of black salt (see page 38). Taste and add more salt. Use as a sandwich filling with cress or watercress.

'TUNA' SANDWICHES: (NF) (SoF) For 2 people. Mix together 100g cooked batched jackfruit (see page 50) or 100g roughly crushed tinned chickpeas per person, with 1 teaspoon rinsed and chopped capers, 1 chopped spring onion, 2 tablespoons vegan mayonnaise (see page 224) and a pinch of kelp powder (optional). Taste and add a squeeze of lemon and 1 teaspoon ketchup, if needed. Use in sandwiches with lettuce, cucumber and some black pepper.

HERBED LABNEH WITH BLACK OLIVES, CARROT & MINT: Place 4 heaped tablespoons good-quality high-fat, non-dairy live plain yoghurt (we love Coyo coconut yoghurt for this, as it's very creamy) into a colander lined with muslin (or a clean tea towel) set over a bowl. Allow to drain until thick and spreadable, about 30–60 minutes. Add a pinch of garlic powder and 2 tablespoons chopped mixed fresh herbs – parsley, dill and basil all work. Spread on to crusty bread or into dairy-free pitta, with chopped pitted black olives, grated or sliced carrot and fresh mint leaves.

CHILLI CHEESE DOG: Heat a vegan hot dog, then place in a warmed hot dog bun, top with 1–2 tablespoons chilli con jackfruit (see page 126) or chilli con three beans (see page 139), some fried onions, vegan cheese of choice, such as queso (see page 230) or stringy 'cheese' sauce (see page 226) and sliced jalapeños.

MUMBAI SANDWICH: (NF) (SoF) Ottie Ise works at LEON head office and loves this India-inspired sandwich. She says: 'Make emerald chutney first by chopping and pounding together a handful each of fresh coriander and mint, 1 small clove of garlic, 1 green chilli and some lime juice and salt. Mix together a big pinch each of ground cumin, ground coriander and ground cinnamon. Spread sandwich bread with coconut oil, then fill with sliced tomato, red onions, cucumber and cooked potato, then top with the chutney and spice mix.'

AVOCADO, SUN-DRIED TOMATO AND BASIL

COCONUT BACON (see page 41), rocket, avocado and tomato

VEGAN CREAM CHEESE or **LABNEH** (see left), with beetroot and sprouted seeds

ALMOND FETA (see page 154) with tomato, cucumber, olives, red onion and fresh oregano

CARROT SMOKED 'SALMON' (see page 34) or **'GRAVLAX'** (see page 192) with vegan cream cheese, mayo or thick cashew cream, fresh dill and chopped spring onions

BABAGANOUSH (see page 232) with pomegranate seeds and walnuts

AVOCADO, TOMATO & VEGAN PESTO (see page 56) or roasted red pepper paste from a jar

CRISPY CHICKPEAS, HUMMUS (see page 60), tomato, red onion and tahini

REMOULADE (see page 172) **WITH BATTERED BANANA BLOSSOM 'FISH'** (see page 98), lettuce and watercress

HUMMUS (see page 60), **MOROCCAN TOFU** (see page 76), grated carrot, thinly sliced red cabbage and pickled red onions

BREADED TOFU (see page 89), **TAPENADE** (see page 198), cucumber, lettuce and **VEGAN TARTARE SAUCE** (see pag 222)

TAPENADE (see page 198), sliced tomatoes, spinach and rocket

FRIDGE RAIDERS

Living a plant-based life can take a bit of planning. Here is a list of our favourite 'fridge raiders' – things we like to keep in the fridge (or freezer) so that there's always something quick and satisfying to nibble. When you make the recipes below, cook more than you need on the day, and stash the leftovers.

CHIA SEED YOGHURT
(see page 39)

SPANISH OMELETTE
(see page 150)

SALT-N-PEPPER TOFU
(see page 58)

ROASTED CAULIFLOWER
(see page 72)

BUFFALO CAULIFLOWER WINGS
(see page 106)

PIZZA
(see page 110)

LAHMACUN
(see page 112)

PERSIAN HERB FRITTATA
(see page 78)

SPICED MOROCCAN TOFU
(see page 76)

JACKFRUIT FRIED 'CHICKEN'
(see page 100)

ARANCINI
(see page 108)

JACKFRUIT NUGGETS
(see page 101)

CROQUETAS
(see page 178)

SAMOSAS
(see page 182)

AUBERGINE WEDGES
(see page 206)

STUFFED AUBERGINE ROLLS
(see page 203)

COURGETTE FRITTERS
(see page 202)

SPANISH CHICKPEA FRITTERS
(see page 204)

MALAYSIAN SWEETCORN FRITTERS
(see page 200)

PARSNIP ROSTIS
(see page 199)

CELERIAC ROSTIS
(see page 194)

STUFFED FIGS
(see page 190)

FALAFEL
(see page 60)

HUMMUS
(see page 60)

BABAGANOUSH
(see page 232)

BREAKFAST MUFFINS
(see page 28)

BLUEBERRY POPPY SEED MUFFINS
(see page 26)

VERY BERRY ICE CREAM MILKSHAKE

PREP TIME: 10 MINS
FREEZE TIME: OVERNIGHT

Outrageous-looking, but still contains three of your five-a-day. If you can eat nuts, this can be made with our cashew vanilla cream ice cream (see page 284).

100g **frozen strawberries**

50g **frozen raspberries**

1 **banana**, sliced and frozen overnight

160ml **plant milk** (use non-nut or non-soya to keep this NF or SoF)

3 large scoops of **non-dairy vanilla ice cream** (use non-nut or non-soya to keep this NF or SoF, see page 284 for homemade)

1. Place the frozen fruit and milk into a blender and blend until smooth. Add the ice cream and blend again.

2. Pour into a milkshake glass or large tall glass.

BANANA PECAN ICE CREAM MILKSHAKE

PREP TIME: 10 MINS
FREEZE TIME: OVERNIGHT

Just. So. Good.

2 **bananas**, sliced and frozen overnight

80g **non-dairy vanilla yoghurt** (use non-soya to keep this SoF)

60ml **plant milk** (use non-soya to keep this SoF)

4 scoops of **non-dairy vanilla ice cream** (use non-soya to keep this SoF, see page 284 for homemade)

2 tablespoons chopped **candied maple pecans** (see page 286)

1. Place the frozen fruit and milk into a blender and blend until smooth. Add the ice cream and blend again.

2. Pour into a milkshake glass or large tall glass and top with candied maple pecans to serve.

TIP

Both the milkshakes can be topped with whipped soya cream (from a tin) or whipped chilled sweetened cashew cream (see page 257). Alternatively, try whipped coconut cream (see page 257) and a drizzle of shop-bought vegan chocolate sauce, if you like.

4

SLOW FOOD

PHO

SERVES **6**

  (GF) (WF) (SoF)

FOR THE BROTH:

3 **onions**, halved

18cm piece of **fresh ginger**, cut into big chunks

2 **carrots**, halved lengthways and cut into chunks

2 heads of **garlic**, halved through the middle

3 litres **water**

500g **shiitake mushrooms**

30g **dried mushrooms**

2 sticks of **cinnamon**

5 **star anise**

3 **black cardamom pods**

1 tablespoon **coriander seeds**

1 tablespoon **salt**

1 tablespoon **palm sugar**

½ teaspoon **freshly ground black pepper**

1 teaspoon **white** or **yellow non-soya miso paste**

1 tablespoon **gluten-free tamari soy sauce** (to keep this GF and WF), **Maggi liquid seasoning** (to keep this SoF) or **coconut aminos** (to keep this GF, WF and SoF)

PREP TIME: 20 MINS · COOK TIME: 4 HOURS 15 MINS

Pho is a noodle soup from Vietnam. There are loads of variations, but it is often served as a vegan dish, to suit vegetarians and Buddhists. Top with plain, fried or spiced firm tofu, for extra oomph (see pages 58, 80, 89 and 145). Although it takes a while to prepare the broth, this actually requires very little attention. If you have a big enough pan, prepare double the broth and freeze half.

TO SERVE:

600g **wide flat rice noodles**

100g **beansprouts**

4 **spring onions**, finely chopped

150g **pak choi**, sliced lengthways into thin wedges

leaves from 1 large bunch each of **fresh Thai basil**, **mint** and **coriander**

1 **red chilli** (less if you're serving to little ones), thinly sliced

1 **lime**, cut into 6 wedges

sriracha hot sauce or **hoisin sauce** (optional, omit if you need to keep this GF, WF or SoF)

1. First, make the broth. Put the onions, ginger and carrots, cut side down, in a hot dry frying pan and cook until blackened, then toss the garlic around in the pan until slightly charred all over. Transfer the charred veg to a large stock pot and stir in the rest of the broth ingredients.

2. Bring to the boil, then turn the heat down, cover and simmer for at least 4 hours. Top up with water now and then if it starts to get low.

3. Strain out the vegetables and spices, keeping the broth and 8 of the shiitake mushrooms. Thinly slice the mushrooms lengthways. Keep the broth hot and check the seasoning.

4. Cook the noodles according to the packet instructions, until al dente.

5. Using tongs, divide the noodles between serving bowls, then add a few slices of the shiitake mushrooms, the beansprouts, spring onions and pak choi. Pour over the hot broth. Divide the herbs between the bowls, then top each bowl with a sprinkling of red chilli and a wedge of lime to squeeze over, plus any sauce you would like.

CHILLI CON JACKFRUIT

PREP TIME: 20 MINS · COOK TIME: 1 HOUR 50 MINS

For more about the miraculously meaty jackfruit, see page 50.

2 tablespoons **olive oil**

1 **large onion**, diced

8 cloves of **garlic**, finely chopped

a handful of **fresh coriander**, stalks finely chopped and leaves picked

1 **carrot**, diced

1 stick of **celery**, diced

2 teaspoons **dried oregano**

2 tablespoons **sweet smoked paprika**

1 tablespoon **ground cumin**

1 teaspoon **ground coriander**

1 tablespoon **tomato purée**

200ml **vegan red wine**

2 × 565g or 400g tins of **young green jackfruit in water** or **brine**, drained

1 × 400g tin of **chopped tomatoes**

1 tablespoon **gluten-free tamari soy sauce** (to keep this GF and WF) or **Maggi liquid seasoning** (to keep this SoF)

2 teaspoons **vegan chipotle paste** or **powder** (less if you're serving to little ones)

400ml **water**

2 teaspoons **unsweetened cocoa powder**

1 × 400g tin of **kidney beans**

1 teaspoon **freshly ground black pepper**

1 tablespoon **vegan vegetable bouillon** powder

1 teaspoon **vegan cider vinegar**, plus extra to taste

1 tablespoon **maple syrup**, plus extra to taste

salt

TO SERVE:

steamed rice (allow 60g uncooked rice per person)

guacamole (see page 234)

1. Heat the oil in a large pan, add the onion and sweat over a medium heat for 5 minutes, then add the garlic, coriander stalks, carrot and celery. Cover and sweat for another 10 minutes, stirring occasionally.

2. Place the oregano and spices in a small bowl and stir together (this will help prevent them catching when you add them to the pan).

3. Add the tomato purée to the pan and cook for 1 minute, stirring continuously. Stir in the spice mixture, then add the wine to deglaze the pan. Allow to bubble for a couple of minutes, then add the drained jackfruit pieces and chopped tomatoes.

4. Stir in the soy sauce or Maggi liquid seasoning, chipotle, water, cocoa powder, kidney beans, black pepper and bouillon powder and a large pinch of salt. Bring to a simmer, re-cover and cook for 1 hour 30 minutes, stirring and mashing the chunks of jackfruit occasionally with a spoon to break it up slightly (fish out any jackfruit seeds, if you like).

5. Just before serving, stir through the cider vinegar, maple syrup and coriander leaves. Check the seasoning and add more salt, vinegar or syrup to taste. Serve with steamed rice and guacamole.

'CHORIZO', BUTTERNUT & CHICKPEA STEW

SERVES
4

PREP TIME: 15 MINS · COOK TIME: 50 MINS

If you can't find seitan chorizo, just leave it out, or use smoked extra-firm tofu or soya chunks in its place.

---

2 tablespoons **olive oil**

1 **onion**, finely diced

1 tablespoon **tomato purée**

2 cloves of **garlic**, crushed

60ml **vegan red wine**

350g **butternut squash**, peeled and
   cut into 2cm cubes

400ml hot **vegan vegetable stock**
   (see page 140 for homemade)

2 teaspoons **sweet smoked
   paprika**, plus extra to taste

1 × 400g tin of **chickpeas**, drained

1 × 400g tin of **chopped tomatoes**

1 tablespoon **fresh thyme leaves**

a pinch of **dried red chilli flakes**,
   plus extra to taste

300g **vegan seitan chorizo
   sausage**, crumbled

salt and **freshly ground
   black pepper**

TO SERVE:
fresh coriander or
   parsley leaves
crusty bread

1. Heat half the oil in a heavy-based pan over a medium heat, add a pinch of salt and the onion and cook, stirring frequently, for about 10 minutes, until beginning to brown. Add the tomato purée and garlic, and cook, stirring, for 2 minutes. Add the wine and allow to bubble briefly, then add the squash and hot stock.

2. Bring to a simmer and add the smoked paprika, chickpeas, tomatoes, thyme and chilli. Simmer gently, uncovered, for 30 minutes, or until the squash is tender and the sauce has reduced and thickened slightly.

3. Meanwhile, pour the remaining oil into a frying pan over a medium heat. Add the crumbled seitan sausage and fry briefly, turning the pieces so they brown all over. Remove from the heat and keep warm.

4. When the squash is cooked, season with pepper, adding a little more salt, chilli flakes or paprika to taste. Add the sausage pieces and stir them into the stew.

5. Scatter over the herbs and serve. Eat with crusty bread to mop up the sauce.

TIP
Whenever a recipe uses tinned chickpeas, save the drained water to use as 'aquafaba' in baking or meringues (see page 252), in dressings and mayo (see page 224), or even in cocktails (see page 296).

MOUSSAKA

3 tablespoons **olive oil**, plus extra
for brushing

2 **onions**, finely chopped

I **small carrot**, finely diced

2 sticks of **celery**, finely diced

I **red pepper**, finely diced

8 cloves of **garlic**, crushed

I teaspoon **ground cinnamon**

I tablespoon finely chopped
fresh thyme

I tablespoon finely chopped
fresh oregano

2 **bay leaves**

75g **pitted black olives**,
finely chopped

75g **red lentils**

I × 400g tin of **pinto beans**, drained

75ml **vegan red wine**

500ml **tomato passata**

300ml **water**

3 **aubergines**, thinly sliced lengthways

salt and **freshly ground
black pepper**

FOR THE BÉCHAMEL:

I litre **unsweetened almond milk**

60ml **olive oil**

60g **plain** or **gluten-free
plain flour**

2 tablespoons **gram flour**

2 teaspoons **garlic powder**

a generous pinch of **freshly grated
nutmeg**

I tablespoon **nutritional yeast**

salt and **freshly ground
black pepper**

PREP TIME: 25 MINS · COOK TIME: 1½ HOURS

We love this with a shepherd's salad on the side: dice 200g tomatoes, 200g cucumber and 1 small red onion, then toss with extra virgin olive oil, lemon juice, salt and pepper.

1. Heat the oil in a large heavy-based pan, add the onions, carrot, celery, red pepper and garlic and cook over a medium heat, stirring frequently, for about 10 minutes, until lightly caramelized. Add the cinnamon, herbs and olives, stir well and cook for another 2–3 minutes. Add the lentils, beans, red wine, passata and water. Bring to a simmer and cook for 30–45 minutes, stirring every now and then, until the lentils are cooked and the sauce has reduced by about half and is thick and rich. (If it is reducing very quickly, cover with a lid.)

2. Meanwhile, heat a griddle pan or grill until hot. Season the aubergine slices with salt and pepper and brush with a little olive oil. Working in batches, griddle in the hot pan or under the grill for about 5 minutes, until lightly charred on both sides (they don't need to cook through at this stage). Set aside.

3. Heat the milk in a small pan over a high heat until bubbles start to appear on the surface, then set aside. Heat the oil in a large pan over a medium heat. When hot, add the flours. Turn the heat down to low and cook, stirring constantly, to form a paste (don't let the flour brown). Add the garlic powder, then gradually add the milk, whisking constantly to form a thick white sauce. Stir in the nutmeg, yeast, ½ teaspoon salt and some pepper until smooth, then check the seasoning.

4. Heat the oven to 200°C/400°F/gas mark 6.

5. To assemble, choose an ovenproof dish that is about 25 × 30cm and 9cm deep. Place a layer of aubergine on the bottom of the dish, then a layer of the vegetable sauce, then another layer of aubergine. Repeat with a thin layer of vegetable sauce and another of aubergine, then pour the béchamel over the top. Bake for 30 minutes, or until the sauce is set and golden.

LIGHT OR CHICKEN-STYLE SEITAN

125g **vital wheat gluten flour**

3 tablespoons **gram flour**, plus extra
for dusting

1 teaspoon **tamari soy sauce** or
Maggi liquid seasoning
(to keep this SoF)

100ml **water**

½ teaspoon **nutritional yeast**,
crumbled until fine

VARIATION:
GLUTEN-FREE SEITAN

Chantal can't eat gluten,
so invented this: blend 1 ×
400g tin of butter beans and
its water until smooth. Add
2 tablespoons gluten-free
tamari soy sauce, 1 tablespoon
each of olive oil and gluten-
free bouillon powder, 2
teaspoons garlic powder,
1 teaspoon each onion
powder and miso paste and
½ teaspoon each of salt and
pepper and stir well. Add 150g
gluten-free brown bread flour
and mix to form a dough, then
knead for 5 minutes. Cook
as above, dividing the dough
into 2 sausages and greasing
the baking parchment.
When ready, the dough will
spring back when pressed.
Cool before slicing. This will
keep, covered in water in the
fridge, for up to 2 days.

PREP TIME: 15 MINS · REST TIME: 30 MINS
COOK TIME: 50 MINS

Seitan or 'wheat meat' is made from vital wheat gluten flour, which is
ordinary flour that has had its starch washed away. It has been used
for centuries in Chinese and Japanese cooking – if you've ever eaten
mock duck in a Chinese restaurant then you've already tasted a kind of
seitan. It is very high in protein and its texture means it works well as a
meat substitute. You can buy ready-made seitan, but making it at home
means you can customize it to suit your recipes, adding flavourings like
ground cumin, tomato purée, miso, chilli or sweet smoked paprika to
the mix, or slathering the cooked dough in jerk, barbecue or teriyaki
sauce. We have experimented A LOT with seitan dough, and although
many recipes suggest simmering it in stock, we find that makes the
seitan spongy and mushy; steaming works best for us.

---

1. Mix together the vital wheat gluten and gram flours. Add the soy sauce
   or Maggi and the water and mix to form a dough. Seitan needs to be
   kneaded until it is very firm, so tip the dough out on to a clean work
   surface dusted with flour and knead for 5–10 minutes, until the dough
   is smooth and tight. Cover with clingfilm or a clean damp tea towel
   and allow to rest for 30 minutes.

2. Roll the dough into a sausage shape. Wrap tightly in baking
   parchment and then in foil. Place the wrapped dough in a steamer,
   cover and steam for 50 minutes, or until the dough is waxy in
   appearance, very firm and no longer sticky to touch. Unwrap and
   allow to cool completely before using.

3. For extra flavour, slice or shred then briefly fry the seitan in a splash of
   cooking oil over a medium heat, until slightly browned, and then use.

4. Cooked seitan dough freezes well, or keep in the fridge, covered, for
   up to 2 days.

> **TIP**
> You can turn this into a beefier, dark seitan by adding an extra
> 1 tablespoon soy sauce to the dough.

CARIBBEAN PLANTAIN CURRY

2 tablespoons **refined** or **extra virgin coconut oil**

2 **onions**, diced

1 head of **garlic**, cloves peeled and finely chopped

1½ tablespoons finely chopped **fresh thyme**

2 tablespoons **mild curry powder**

½ teaspoon **ground allspice**

1 teaspoon **salt**

400ml **coconut milk**

800ml **water**

1 large **carrot**, quartered lengthways and diced

1 **red pepper**, deseeded and diced into 3cm pieces

3 **ripe plantains**, sliced on an angle into 1cm pieces

1 **Scotch bonnet**, whole (omit if serving to little ones)

1 **bay leaf**

1 tablespoon **vegan vegetable bouillon** powder

250g **spring greens**, halved and cut into 1cm ribbons

zest and juice of 1 **lime**

2 tablespoons chopped **fresh coriander**

freshly ground black pepper

roti, **dairy-free flat breads** or **coconut rice & peas** (to keep this GF and WF, see page 220), to serve

PREP TIME: 20 MINS · COOK TIME: 1 HOUR 45 MINS

This rich and creamy curry contains Scotch bonnet peppers, which give it a wonderful, almost sour, chilli heat. Choose ripe plantains with a good covering of dark brown spots.

1. Heat the oil in a large pan over a medium heat. When hot, add the onions and sweat for 5 minutes, then add the garlic and thyme and cook for another 10 minutes. Add the spices, season with black pepper and toss together.

2. Stir in the salt, coconut milk, water, carrot, red pepper, plantains, Scotch bonnet, bay leaf and bouillon powder. Simmer for 45–60 minutes, or until the plantain is tender and the sauce has reduced and thickened. Add the spring greens, cover and cook for another 30 minutes.

3. Just before serving, fish out the Scotch bonnet (if you can't find it, it will have disintegrated – which is fine, you just wouldn't want to accidentally eat it whole). Add the lime zest and juice and stir through the coriander.

4. Serve with roti, flat breads or coconut rice and peas.

AUBERGINE 'MEATBALLS'

FOR THE BALLS:

2 tablespoons **refined coconut oil**

3 tablespoons **olive oil**, plus extra
as needed

2 **aubergines**, diced

1 **onion**, diced

2 cloves of **garlic**, crushed

15 **black olives**, pitted and
roughly chopped

2 teaspoons **red pepper paste**

2 teaspoons **tomato purée**

1 teaspoon **paprika**

2 teaspoons **fennel seeds**
(optional)

2 tablespoons **sunflower seeds**

2 tablespoons **pine nuts**

1 tablespoon **ground flaxseeds**

1 tablespoon **water**

leaves from 1 sprig of **fresh
rosemary**, finely chopped

2 tablespoons **fresh parsley**,
roughly chopped

zest of ¼ **lemon**

150g **cooked Puy lentils**

5–7 tablespoons **dried
breadcrumbs**

4 tablespoons **gram flour**

1 teaspoon **baking powder**

salt and **freshly ground
black pepper**

FOR THE PASTA & SAUCE:

400g **dried spaghetti**

1 tablespoon **olive oil**

2 cloves of **garlic**, whole but bruised

300ml **tomato passata**

a large handful of **fresh basil**, leaves
roughly torn

salt and **freshly ground
black pepper**

*PREP TIME: 25 MINS · CHILL TIME: 1 HOUR
COOK TIME: 45 MINS*

These balls are even better – and much firmer in texture – if you shape
and brown them the day before serving them with pasta. Just reheat in
a hot oven, for about 10 minutes. If you don't have refined coconut oil,
don't worry, simply use more olive oil instead – coconut oil is good at
binding, so we use it to help firm up the mixture.

1. Heat the coconut oil and
1 tablespoon of the olive
oil in a large heavy-based
frying pan over a medium
heat. When hot, add the
aubergines and cook, stirring,
for about 5 minutes, then
add the onion and a pinch of
salt and sauté for 15 minutes,
stirring regularly, until the
aubergines are soft, tender
and browning and the
onion is translucent and also
beginning to brown. If the pan
seems dry at any point, add
another splash of olive oil.

2. Add the garlic, olives,
red pepper paste, tomato
purée, paprika, fennel
seeds, sunflower seeds
and pine nuts and cook,
stirring, for 3 minutes.

3. Meanwhile, in a small bowl,
mix together the ground
flaxseeds and water in a bowl
and allow to soak for 5 minutes.

4. Tip the aubergine mixture
into a food processor with the
rosemary, parsley, lemon zest
and 50g of the cooked Puy
lentils. Blitz briefly, to form a
rough purée, but don't go too
far – the balls need texture,
and too much whizzing
will make them mushy.

5. Transfer the purée to a
bowl and add the rest of the
lentils, 5 tablespoons of the
breadcrumbs, the soaked

> **TIP**
> Try this with 2 teaspoons rinsed and chopped capers added to the food
> processor (you may not need any more salt). Or, to give this dish a more
> Middle Eastern, rather than Italian, feel, add a large pinch of sumac, ½
> teaspoon ground cumin and ½ teaspoon dried red chilli flakes. Instead
> of pasta serve with couscous or dairy-free pitta bread, tzatziki (see page
> 230) and salad.

flaxseeds, the gram flour, baking powder, a generous pinch of salt and some black pepper. Mix well with a spoon, then place in the fridge to firm up for an hour.

6. When ready to cook, heat a splash of oil in a clean non-stick frying pan over a medium heat. First, cook a nugget of the mixture to check its texture and seasoning. If it seems too wet, add more of the breadcrumbs, and add more salt and pepper, if necessary.

7. Using a tablespoon, scoop out pieces of mixture and form into 16 firm, golf-ball-sized 'meatballs' using 2 spoons or floured hands. Add the remaining 2 tablespoons oil to the pan and fry the balls gently, in batches, turning often, until they are deep brown and quite crisp on the outside. Remove with a slotted spoon and keep warm while you cook the rest.

8. Meanwhile, cook the pasta in boiling salted water until al dente. To make the sauce, heat the oil in a pan over a low heat. Add the bruised garlic and allow the flavour to infuse into the oil (don't let it brown) for about 10 minutes. Remove the garlic and add the passata. Bring to a simmer, adding a pinch of salt and pepper.

9. Drain the pasta. Add the basil to the tomato sauce, then add the pasta and toss well to coat it in the sauce. Serve the pasta topped with the warm aubergine balls.

MR BAO'S SESAME & AUBERGINE BAO

8 BAO BUNS

FOR THE BAO BUNS:

1 teaspoon **dried active yeast**

1½ teaspoons **caster sugar**

100ml **warm water**

250g **plain flour**, plus extra if needed
and for dusting

a pinch of **salt**

2 tablespoons **unsweetened
plant milk** (use non-soya to keep
this SoF)

1 teaspoon **vegetable oil**, plus extra
for greasing and brushing

1 teaspoon **vegan rice vinegar**

1 teaspoon **baking powder**

FOR THE CRISPY SHALLOTS:

neutral cooking oil, for frying

6 **shallots**, cut into thin strips

FOR THE SESAME AUBERGINES:

150g **sesame sauce** (see Tip,
overleaf)

20ml **vegan mirin**

2 teaspoons **low-salt tamari soy
sauce** or **Maggi liquid
seasoning** (to keep this SoF)

2 **aubergines**, halved and cut into
1cm slices

**PREP TIME: 45 MINS · RISE TIME: 4 HOURS
COOK TIME: 35 MINS**

Mr Bao is a Taiwanese restaurant in Peckham, south London. In 2017,
the kitchen developed what they reckon is the first vegan bao bun to be
served in a London restaurant by removing the usual dairy from the
dough – and they were kind enough to give us the recipe. Try these with
some miso-sesame slaw (see page 163) on the side.

1. To make the dough, mix the yeast, sugar and warm water together
   until the yeast has dissolved. Allow to stand for 5–10 minutes, until
   a frothy head has formed. Mix the flour and salt together in a large
   bowl, then add the yeast mixture, milk, oil and vinegar. Mix to form
   a soft dough. If it is too dry, add a dash more water; if it is really sticky,
   add 1–2 tablespoons more flour. Knead the dough on a clean work
   surface dusted with flour for 10 minutes, or until smooth and elastic.
   (Alternatively, use a stand mixer fitted with a dough hook.) Place in a
   clean, oiled bowl. Cover with clingfilm or a clean damp tea towel and
   allow to rise in a warm place for 3 hours, or until doubled in size.

2. Knock back the dough on a clean work surface, using your
   knuckles to press it back to more or less its original size.
   Sprinkle over the baking powder, then knead for 5 minutes.
   Divide into 8 equal-sized pieces, then roll into neat balls.

3. Roll out each ball into an oval about 3mm thick. Brush a
   chopstick with a little vegetable oil, then brush each piece of
   dough with vegetable oil. Fold each dough oval over the oiled
   chopstick, then slowly draw the chopstick out (you may need
   to oil it again between buns). Place on a baking tray lined with
   baking parchment and loosely cover with the tea towel. Allow
   to prove in a warm place for 1 hour, until doubled in size.

4. Meanwhile, prepare the fillings. Heat about 2cm of oil in a
   large deep pan over a medium heat until shimmering hot
   (about 150°C/300°F), add the shallots and cook until golden
   and crisp (but not dark brown or they will taste bitter).
   Remove with a slotted spoon and drain on kitchen paper.

5. Mix together the sesame sauce, mirin and soy sauce or Maggi liquid
   seasoning, adding a little water if it is very dry and sticky. Add the
   aubergines slices and coat well, then marinate for 30 minutes. Heat
   the oven to 180°C/350°F/gas mark 4. Lay the aubergine slices on a
   greased baking sheet in a single layer. Bake for 10 minutes. Set aside. »

MR BAO'S SESAME & AUBERGINE BAO

FOR THE CORIANDER PESTO:

½ bunch of **fresh coriander**

1 clove of **garlic**

50ml **olive oil**, plus extra if needed

25ml **sesame oil**

1 tablespoon **vegan cider vinegar**

25g **sweet peanut powder**
(see Tip, below)

25g **roasted unsalted peanuts**

a pinch of **salt**

TO SERVE:

2 **spring onions**, cut into thin
3cm strips

seeds from 1 **pomegranate**

6. Using a stick blender, whizz all the pesto ingredients together, adding a little more olive oil if it seems too thick. Set aside.

7. When the dough has proved, cut out small squares of baking parchment, then place the buns on the paper in a steamer to prevent the buns sticking. When the water is simmering merrily, steam the buns, covered, for 8–10 minutes. (You may need to do this in batches depending on the size of your steamer.)

8. Meanwhile, heat a splash of oil in a frying pan or griddle pan over a medium-high heat and cook the baked aubergine slices until lightly browned on both sides. Keep warm.

9. Split the warm bao buns and fill with the warm aubergines, a spoonful of the pesto, some crispy shallots, the sliced spring onion and a handful of pomegranate seeds.

> ### TIP
> To make peanut powder simply roast peanuts in the oven and then roughly blend them with a tiny amount of sugar. (Or leave it out completely and use 25g extra peanuts.) Sesame sauce is a Chinese and Japanese condiment – make sure you choose one that is vegan, or use tahini, plus 1 teaspoon vegan rice vinegar and 1 teaspoon soft brown sugar, a pinch of salt and enough hot water to loosen, instead.

CHILLI CON THREE BEANS

SERVES
4

 (GF) (WF) (SoF)

PREP TIME: 20 MINS · COOK TIME: 2 HOURS

Perfect for a cold winter's evening. If you have any leftovers, use in tacos or burritos.

2 tablespoons **olive oil**

1 **red onion**, finely chopped

1 **white onion**, finely chopped

1 **carrot**, finely chopped

1 stick of **celery**, finely chopped

100g **mushrooms**, finely chopped

2 cloves of **garlic**, crushed

1 tablespoon deseeded and finely diced **red chilli**

1 × 400g tin of **chopped tomatoes**

1 teaspoon **ground cumin**

½ teaspoon **dried oregano**

1 heaped teaspoon **unsweetened cocoa powder** or **cacao powder**

½ stick of **cinnamon**

1 teaspoon **vegan hot chipotle paste**, plus extra to taste

1 small **sweet potato**, peeled and finely diced

500ml **vegan vegetable stock** (see page 140 for homemade)

1 teaspoon **vegan cider vinegar**, plus 2–3 teaspoons, to taste

1 heaped teaspoon **soft brown sugar**

1 teaspoon **sweet smoked paprika**

1 × 400g tin of **pinto beans**, drained

1 × 400g tin of **borlotti beans**, drained

1 × 400g tin of **kidney beans**, drained

salt and **freshly ground pepper**

TO SERVE:

fresh coriander leaves

steamed rice (allow 60g uncooked rice per person)

4–6 tablespoons **soured cashew cream** (see page 228, optional)

1 **avocado**, cut into chunks and roughly mashed

vegan hot sauce (optional)

lime wedges

1. Heat the oil in a large deep pan, add the onions, carrot, celery and a good pinch of salt and sauté gently over a medium-low heat for 15–20 minutes, or until the onions are translucent and just beginning to take on a little colour.

2. Add the garlic, chilli and tomatoes and cook for a couple of minutes, stirring. Add the cumin, oregano, cocoa powder, cinnamon stick and chipotle paste and cook, stirring, for 1 minute. Add the sweet potato and half the vegan stock, the 1 teaspoon vinegar, the sugar and smoked paprika and bring to a simmer. Cover and cook gently for 30 minutes. Remove the cinnamon stick, then add the remaining stock and the beans. Bring back to a simmer and cook for 1 hour, until the sweet potato is completely soft.

3. Remove a couple of ladlefuls of the chilli and blitz in a food processor or blender (or carefully use a stick blender directly in the pan for a few seconds) until smooth – this will thicken the sauce.

4. The chilli will almost certainly need more salt and vinegar, to balance the sweetness of the beans and vegetables. Add salt to taste and a teaspoon of vinegar at a time – the finished dish should be tangy and spicy, but not vinegary. If not spicy enough, add another teaspoon of chipotle paste.

5. Serve scattered with coriander leaves, with steamed rice, soured cashew cream, if liked, and mashed avocado, with a little hot sauce, if using, on the side, and lime wedges for squeezing over. Season everything with a little more salt.

SPANISH CHICKPEA STEW

PREP TIME: 15 MINS · COOK TIME: 1 HOUR 10 MINS

This recipe was a favourite on the menu at Chantal's restaurant, the Secret Pantry. Serve with steamed rice.

60ml **olive oil**

3 **red onions**, diced

4 cloves of **garlic**, finely chopped

1 stick of **celery**, diced

1 head of **fennel**, diced

1 large **carrot**, diced

1 teaspoon each of **ground cumin**, **sweet smoked paprika** and **fennel seeds**

a pinch of **saffron**

½ teaspoon **freshly ground black pepper**

1 tablespoon **vegan sherry vinegar**

zest and juice of 1 **orange**

2 × 400g tins of **chickpeas**, drained

300ml **vegan vegetable stock** (see below) or **1 tablespoon vegan vegetable bouillon powder** + 300ml **water**

3 tablespoons chopped **fresh parsley**

salt

orange wedges, to serve

1. Heat the oil in a large pan over a medium heat. When hot, add the onions, garlic, and vegetables and sweat, stirring frequently, for 15 minutes, until they begin to caramelize.

2. Add the dried spices, fennel seeds, saffron and pepper and cook for 3 minutes. Stir well, then add the vinegar and orange juice. Cook for 1 minute, then add the chickpeas, orange zest, stock or bouillon powder and water and bring to a simmer.

3. Turn the heat to low, cover and cook for 45 minutes, stirring occasionally to prevent sticking. Season with a little salt, to taste, you may not need it if using bouillon powder as it's quite salty. Stir through 2 tablespoons of the parsley, then serve scattered with the remaining parsley and with orange wedges to squeeze over.

HOMEMADE VEGAN VEGETABLE STOCK (MAKES 1.5 LITRES)

To make a rich brown stock (great for rich pies or hearty soups), heat a splash of oil in a large deep pan, add 2 onions, 2 carrots, 1 leek and 2 celery sticks (all roughly chopped) and sauté over a medium heat, stirring frequently, until they begin to caramelize, about 10 minutes. Add 8 button mushrooms and 4 garlic clove halves and cook for a further 5 minutes, continuing to stir so that nothing sticks or burns. Cover with 1–2 litres of boiling water (depending on your pan size), add 2 bay leaves, 4 sprigs of thyme, 4 parsley stalks and 10 black peppercorns. Bring to a gentle simmer and cook for 45–60 minutes. Strain out the vegetables and discard them, retaining the stock. Store, covered, in the fridge for a couple of days, or freeze in ice cube trays or ice cube bags.

To make a lighter, more summery, white stock, follow the same method but omit the oil and sautéing stage and go straight to cooking all the other ingredients with 1–2 litres of boiling water. Bring to a gentle simmer and cook for 15–20 minutes before straining and storing.

MIDDLE EASTERN STUFFED PUMPKIN

SERVES 4 AS A MAIN OR 6 AS A SIDE

(GF) (WF) (SoF)

50g **unsalted pistachio nuts**

1 **pumpkin** (approx. 1kg)

2 tablespoons **olive oil**

2 **red onions**, thinly sliced

6 cloves of **garlic**, thinly sliced

1 tablespoon **coriander seeds**

4 **green cardamom pods**, bruised

1 teaspoon **ground cinnamon**

a pinch of **freshly grated nutmeg**

a pinch of **saffron**

1 **red chilli** (less if serving to little ones), deseeded to taste, finely diced

20g **dried barberries**

20g **raisins**

50g **basmati rice**

200ml **vegan vegetable stock** (see page 140 for homemade)

1 teaspoon shredded **dried orange peel**

1 teaspoon of **rosewater**

1 tablespoon **dried edible rose petals**

pomegranate molasses, for drizzling (optional)

salad, to serve

PREP TIME: 20 MINS · COOK TIME: 1 HOUR 25 MINS

Sweet roasted pumpkin, filled with nutty, fragrant rice and sharp barberries. Serve this as a main course with a green salad or the tomato salad on page 60, or as part of a selection of mezze dishes (see pages 60, 188, 230 and 232).

1. Toast the pistachios in a hot dry pan for 2–3 minutes, turning frequently, until toasty and fragrant. Set aside.

2. Slice the top off the pumpkin, reserving the lid, and scoop out the seeds using a large spoon. If the cavity inside is quite shallow, you will need to scoop out a bit of the flesh (chop it up and keep for later).

3. Heat the oven to 220°C/425°F/gas mark 7.

4. Heat the oil in a heavy-based pan over a medium heat. Add the onions and fry for 10 minutes, until slightly caramelized. If you have scooped out some pumpkin flesh, add to the pan and cook for 2 minutes. Then add the garlic, coriander seeds, cardamom, cinnamon, nutmeg, saffron and chilli and cook for another 3 minutes, stirring regularly. Add the barberries and raisins, then the rice and toasted pistachios. Stir to coat and toast the rice for 2–3 minutes. Add the stock, orange peel and rosewater and bring to the boil. Cook for 6 minutes, then immediately remove from the heat.

5. Spoon the rice mixture into the pumpkin, add the pumpkin lid, then wrap the stuffed pumpkin in a strip of wet baking parchment and then foil, to make a parcel. Place on a baking sheet and bake for 45 minutes to 1 hour, or until the pumpkin is cooked and a sharp knife inserted into the flesh meets no resistance.

6. Serve cut into wedges, with a drizzle of pomegranate molasses, if you like, and some salad.

JACKFRUIT TIKKA MASALA

 SERVES 4

(GF) (WF) (NF) (SoF)

2 × 400g tins of **young green jackfruit in water** or **brine**, drained

2 teaspoons **garam masala**

1 tablespoon **vegan vegetable bouillon powder**

FOR THE TIKKA MASALA SAUCE:

2 tablespoons **refined** or **extra virgin coconut oil**

4 **onions**, thinly sliced into half-moons

6cm piece of **fresh ginger**, peeled and finely grated

8 cloves of **garlic**, finely grated

6 **green cardamom pods**, bruised

2 **black cardamom pods**, bruised

1 teaspoon **ground turmeric**

1 teaspoon **ground cinnamon**

1½ teaspoons **ground cumin**

2 teaspoons **ground coriander**

2 teaspoons **sweet smoked paprika**

2 teaspoons **garam masala**

400g **fresh tomatoes**, diced

400ml **coconut milk**

800ml **water**

1 tablespoon **sugar**

FOR THE TIKKA PASTE:

100g **non-dairy plain yoghurt** (use non-nut or non-soya to keep this NF or SoF)

4cm piece of **fresh ginger**, peeled and finely grated

2 cloves of **garlic**

1 **shallot**, roughly chopped

juice of ½ **lemon**

1 teaspoon **paprika**

1 teaspoon **ground coriander**

1 teaspoon **ground cumin**

seeds from 2 **green cardamom pods**

seeds from 1 **black cardamom pod**

½ teaspoon **fennel seeds**

a generous pinch of **ground turmeric**

TO SERVE:

fresh coriander leaves

steamed rice (allow 60g uncooked rice per person) or **flatbreads**

PREP TIME: 30 MINS · COOK TIME: 1 HOUR 20 MINS

For more on the magically meaty jackfruit, see page 50. The paste and sauce can also be used with tofu, seitan, chunky vegetables or cooked pulses. This is also great with the aloo kabli on page 174 or the tomato and pomegranate salad on page 156, both of which cut through the rich creamy masala sauce.

1. Place the drained jackfruit in a pan. Cover with water and add the garam masala and bouillon powder. Bring to a simmer and cook gently for 1 hour, topping up the water if necessary. Drain and allow to cool.

2. Meanwhile, make the sauce. Heat the oil in a heavy-based pan over a high heat, add the onions, then reduce the heat to low and cook until beginning to caramelize (don't allow to darken), about 20 minutes. Add the ginger and garlic and cook for 5 minutes, stirring regularly, then add all the spices and the tomatoes. Cook for 20 minutes, stirring frequently so that it doesn't stick. Turn the heat to medium, add the coconut milk and water and bring to a simmer. Cook for about 40 minutes, or until the mixture has thickened and reduced by half.

3. Add the sugar, then blend the sauce in a blender (or use a stick blender) until smooth. (Cool first or work in batches, if your blender can't cope with hot liquids.)

4. Blitz all the ingredients for the tikka paste in a food processor or blender (or use a stick blender). Pour the paste into a bowl and add the cooled jackfruit. Toss well to coat.

5. Heat the grill to its highest setting. Arrange the jackfruit on a grill rack set over a tray, then cook under the grill for about 3 minutes on each side, turning occasionally, until it begins to char slightly in places and turn golden in others.

6. Warm the tikka masala sauce, if necessary, then add the grilled jackfruit. Sprinkle over the coriander and serve with rice or flat breads.

LEMONGRASS & CHILLI TOFU

1 stalk of **lemongrass**, tough outer
leaves removed and roughly chopped

1 **red chilli**, deseeded to taste,
roughly chopped

6 cloves of **garlic**, roughly chopped

½ teaspoon **salt**

280g **extra-firm tofu**

neutral cooking oil, for greasing
and drizzling

TO SERVE:

steamed rice (allow 60g uncooked
rice per person)

2 heads of **pak choi** or other **Asian
greens**, sliced and steamed

tamari soy sauce (use gluten-free to
keep this GF and WF)

*PREP TIME: 20 MINS · MARINATING TIME: 2 HOURS
COOK TIME: 45 MINS*

This tofu is great served as a steak with rice or alongside a stir-fry, but
we also use it in our Thai rice paper rolls on page 186. Or, once cooked
and cooled, slice into thin strips and use in sushi (see pages 180–1).

1. Pummel the lemongrass, chilli, garlic and salt to a paste using a pestle
   and mortar (or use a stick blender).

2. Slice the tofu into 4 steaks. In a clean tea towel or kitchen paper,
   squeeze the liquid from the tofu, then pat as dry as possible. Rub the
   marinade into each one. Place in the fridge for at least 2 hours, or
   overnight.

3. Heat the oven to 200°C/400°F/gas mark 6. Place the tofu steaks in a
   greased ovenproof dish and drizzle over a little more oil. Cook for
   45 minutes, turning once halfway through, until golden and crispy.

4. Serve with steamed rice and steamed greens, dressed with a little
   soy sauce.

SEA-SPICED AUBERGINE

This traditional Sichuan vegetable dish gets its name from the fact that this kind of spicing is more often used with fish.

3 tablespoons **refined coconut oil** or **neutral cooking oil**

2 **aubergines**, cut into large dice

6 cloves of **garlic**, thinly sliced

3cm piece of **fresh ginger**, peeled and thinly sliced into matchsticks

1 **red chilli**, deseeded and thinly sliced

1 large **onion**, thickly sliced into half-moons

6 **spring onions**, white parts cut into 3cm pieces, green parts finely sliced

1 **red pepper**, cut into large dice

60ml **tamari soy sauce** (use gluten-free to keep this GF and WF)

60ml **rice wine** (use gluten-free to keep this GF and WF)

200ml **water**, plus 1 tablespoon

1 tablespoon **vegan vegetable bouillon powder**

1 teaspoon **coconut sugar** (or **soft brown sugar**)

1 teaspoon **white miso paste**

1 teaspoon **cornflour**

1 teaspoon **toasted sesame oil**

1 tablespoon chopped **fresh coriander**

steamed rice (allow 60g uncooked rice per person), to serve

1. Heat the oil in a large frying pan over a high heat. When hot and smoky, add the aubergines and cook for 12–15 minutes, tossing occasionally, until golden all over.

2. Add the garlic, ginger and chilli and stir-fry for 1 minute, then add the onion, white parts of the spring onions and red pepper and cook for another 5 minutes. Add the soy sauce, rice wine, 200ml water, bouillon powder, sugar and miso and simmer for 5 minutes.

3. Mix the cornflour with the remaining tablespoon of water until smooth. Add to the pan and cook until thickened, just a minute or two. Remove from the heat, drizzle over the sesame oil and top with the finely sliced spring onions and coriander.

4. Serve with steamed rice.

PUFF POT PIE

320g sheet of **ready-rolled vegan puff pastry**

3 tablespoons **neutral cooking** or **olive oil**, plus extra for greasing

I **onion**, thinly sliced

I **leek**, thinly sliced

150g **mushrooms**, thinly sliced

I clove of **garlic**, crushed

3 tablespoons **plain flour**

350–400ml hot **vegan vegetable stock** (see page 140 for homemade)

2 teaspoons **vegan wholegrain mustard** (optional)

300g **chicken-style seitan** (see page 132), shredded into small pieces

I tablespoon finely chopped **fresh parsley** or **tarragon**, or a mixture

salt and **freshly ground black pepper**

FOR THE GLAZE:

I tablespoon **unsweetened plant milk** (use non-nut to keep this NF)

I teaspoon **neutral cooking oil**

½ teaspoon **agave nectar** or **golden syrup**

TO SERVE:

mashed (see page 217) or **new potatoes**

seasonal greens

PREP TIME: 20 MINS · COOK TIME: I HOUR

It is easy to find vegan puff pastry to use as a lid for this pot pie. Feel free to play around with the filling and leave out the seitan if you like – whatever you use should add up to about 500g in total. Try using a mixture of mushrooms and cooked root vegetables in winter, or in summer, add uncooked peas, asparagus or broccoli to the sauce before the lid is added.

1. Heat the oven to 200°C/400°F/gas mark 6. Remove the pastry from the fridge and allow to come to room temperature.

2. Heat 1 tablespoon of the oil in a large frying pan, add the onion, leek and a pinch of salt and cook over a medium heat, stirring frequently, for about 10 minutes, or until beginning to brown. Add another tablespoon of the oil, the mushrooms and garlic. Cook for another 5–10 minutes, until the mushrooms are tender and beginning to caramelize.

3. Turn the heat to low, then add the remaining oil and the flour. Cook, stirring, for 2 minutes, then slowly begin to add 350ml of the stock, a little at a time, stirring well and adding more only when each amount has been incorporated. The sauce will be quite thin at this point. Bring to a simmer and cook for about 5 minutes, until thickened. Add the mustard, if using, then season with salt and pepper, if necessary. Stir in the shredded seitan, then remove from the heat. If the sauce is dry, add the remaining stock.

4. Whisk together the glaze ingredients.

5. Unroll the pastry sheet and place a pie dish upside down on it. Using a sharp knife, score out a lid, including a 2cm overhang. Grease the edge of the dish, then pour in the seitan mixture. Carefully lift the pastry lid on top, arranging the overhang neatly. Cut two 3cm vents in the centre of the pastry, to allow steam to escape and prevent a soggy underside, then brush with the glaze.

6. Bake for 25–30 minutes, or until the pastry has puffed up and is golden brown and crisp all over. Serve with potatoes and seasonal greens.

> **TIP**
> You can use mock duck (a Chinese gluten- and soya-based protein that is excellent in pies, curries and stir-fries) in place of the seitan.

SPANISH OMELETTE

SERVES 6

   (GF) (WF) (NF)

150g **gram flour**

500ml **water**

1 teaspoon **black salt** (see page 38)
or ½ teaspoon **salt**

½ teaspoon **freshly ground
black pepper**

1 teaspoon **mustard powder**

1 tablespoon **nutritional yeast**

1½ teaspoons **gluten-free
baking powder** (to keep this GF
and WF)

60g **vegan cream cheese**

3 tablespoons **olive oil**, plus extra
for greasing

2 **onions**, thinly sliced into half-moons

2 large **white potatoes**, unpeeled
and thinly sliced

2 cloves of **garlic**, thinly sliced

TO SERVE:

romesco sauce (see page 204) or a
pinch of **sweet smoked paprika**
(optional)

green salad

*PREP TIME: 15 MINS · COOL TIME: 30 MINS
COOK TIME: 1½ HOURS*

**Gram flour (chickpea flour) is a protein-rich substitute for the
traditional eggs in a Spanish omelette, especially when paired with
eggy black salt. Gram flour is commonly used in Indian cooking
to make things like poppadums and bhaji; it is easy to find in large
supermarkets and Asian food shops. Serve the omelette for supper or
cut into wedges for lunchboxes or picnics.**

1. Sift the flour into a bowl, then add the water, salt, pepper, mustard,
   yeast, baking powder and cream cheese. Mix until smooth and set
   aside while you cook the potatoes.

2. Heat the oil in a large frying pan over a low-medium heat. Add
   the onions and potatoes and sauté, turning occasionally, for
   15 minutes. Add the garlic and cook for another 15 minutes.
   Turn the heat down if the veg are browning too quickly; you want
   everything to be lightly caramelized and for the potatoes to be
   almost cooked through.

3. Heat the oven to 200°C/400°F/gas mark 6.

4. Add the batter to the frying pan and stir to mix, then pour into
   a greased springform or loose-bottomed cake tin, spreading out
   the onions, potatoes and garlic evenly around the tin. Bake for
   45–60 minutes, until firm to the touch. Allow to completely cool
   in the oven.

5. Serve at room temperature, cut into wedges, with romesco sauce or
   a dusting of sweet smoked paprika, if liked, and a green salad.

5

SALADS & SLAWS

FREEKEH SALAD WITH ALMOND FETA

SERVES 2 AS A MAIN

FOR THE SALAD:

250g **ready-cooked freekeh**

1 × 400g tin of **chickpeas**, drained

12 **pink**, **red** or **purple summer radishes**, cut into wedges

2 **spring onions**, finely chopped

½ **cucumber**, deseeded and diced

a large handful of **fresh parsley**, leaves chopped

1 × quantity **almond feta** (see below)

a large pinch of **sumac** or **za'atar**

FOR THE DRESSING:

2 tablespoons **tahini**

2 teaspoons **extra virgin olive oil**

a pinch of **salt**

FOR THE ALMOND FETA:

75g **ground almonds**

2 tablespoons **unsweetened coconut yoghurt**

1 tablespoon **olive oil**

1 teaspoon **lemon juice**

a pinch of **garlic powder**

1 teaspoon **sea salt**

¼ teaspoon **vegan cider vinegar**

3 tablespoons **water**

2 teaspoons finely chopped **fresh chives**, **parsley** or **dill**, or a mixture (optional)

PREP TIME: 20 MINS

Freekeh is a delicious toasted green wheat, with a slightly smoky and nutty flavour, which you can buy ready-cooked or dried. Find it in the supermarket as well as specialist food stores. If you can't find freekeh, use bulgur wheat, farro, wheat berries, wild rice, quinoa or giant couscous instead. Choose parsley that has soft rather than tough leaves.

1. Whisk all the dressing ingredients together, then add water in teaspoonfuls to thin it to a creamy consistency.

2. Place all the salad ingredients except the feta and sumac or za'atar in a large bowl. Drizzle over 1 tablespoon of the dressing and toss together.

3. Divide the salad between serving plates, or arrange on a large platter. Drizzle over the rest of the dressing, then crumble the feta into chunks over the salad. Scatter over the sumac or za'atar.

ALMOND FETA   *PREP TIME: 10 MINS*

Choose a coconut yoghurt that has live cultures and a mild-flavoured olive oil for this recipe. If you cut down on the salt, the feta can also be used in place of cream cheese in other dishes.

1. Place all the ingredients except the herbs in a bowl, then mix and mash together to form a crumbly mixture. Add the herbs, if using, and mash them into the 'cheese'.

2. If the 'cheese' seems at all wet, place it in a piece of muslin (or even a clean tea towel) and squeeze out the excess liquid. Taste to check the salt levels – it should be pretty salty.

3. Use immediately or store in the fridge for up to 3 days, but bring up to room temperature before serving.

> **TIP**
> We keep a few pouches of ready-cooked freekeh in the cupboard for quick lunches, but to cook it from scratch for this recipe, allow about 100g cracked or broken freekeh and cook in a 1:3 ratio of freekeh to salted water or stock, for about 15 minutes, or according to the packet instructions (wholegrain freekeh will take longer to cook). For a nut-free salad, omit the almond feta and sumac or za'atar, and serve with salsa verde (see page 231) instead.

TOMATO & POMEGRANATE SALAD

SERVES
4

  (GF) (WF) (NF) (SoF)

2 **red onions**, thinly sliced into
   half-moons

juice of 1 **lemon**

2 teaspoons **agave nectar** (or sugar
   or maple syrup)

6 **tomatoes on the vine**, sliced
   into wedges

1 bunch of **fresh parsley**, leaves
   roughly chopped

seeds from 1 **pomegranate**

2 tablespoons **extra virgin olive oil**

1 tablespoon **pomegranate
   molasses**

salt and **freshly ground
   black pepper**

PREP TIME: 15 MINS

A tart tangy salad, for mezzes or to serve with Middle Eastern dishes.
Use tomatoes that are at room temperature for this salad.

1. Place the onions in a bowl and pour over the lemon juice, then add the
   agave and a pinch of salt. Stir together.

2. Next, add the tomatoes, parsley and pomegranate seeds and stir again.

3. Add the oil and pomegranate molasses, plus a little more salt to taste
   and some pepper. Toss gently, then serve.

THAI LARB SALAD

SERVES
2 **AS A MAIN OR 4 AS A STARTER**

(GF) (WF) (SoF)

100g **Thai sticky rice**,
  plus 1 tablespoon

8 **gem lettuce leaves**

100g **cucumber**, cut into thin strips

100g **long green beans**, trimmed
  and cut on an angle into thin strips

2 **spring onions**, finely chopped

FOR THE MINCE:

2 tablespoons **neutral cooking oil**

1 **onion**, very finely chopped

125g **mushrooms**, very finely chopped

1 × 400g tin of **chickpeas**, drained

2 cloves of **garlic**, crushed

4 tablespoons **walnuts**, crumbled into
  2mm pieces using a pestle and mortar

1 teaspoon **dried red chilli flakes**
  or 2 teaspoons finely chopped **fresh
  red chilli**, plus extra to taste

1 bunch of **fresh coriander**, leaves
  roughly chopped

a small handful of **fresh Thai** or
  Italian basil, leaves roughly
  chopped, plus 2 sprigs to serve

10 **fresh mint leaves**,
  roughly chopped

FOR THE DRESSING:

1 tablespoon **soft brown sugar**

2 teaspoons **gluten-free tamari
  soy sauce** (to keep this GF and WF)
  or 1 teaspoon **Maggi liquid
  seasoning** (to keep this SoF)

1½ teaspoons **kelp powder**

1 tablespoon **toasted sesame oil**

juice of 2 **limes**, plus extra to taste

PREP TIME: 30 MINS · COOK TIME: 35 MINS

This northern Thai salad packs a real punch, with chilli, lime and raw shallots balanced by the cooling crunch of cucumber, lettuce and sliced green beans. Traditionally made with mince, we developed a vegan mince made from chickpeas and mushrooms (you could use any vegan mince or tofu, or mushrooms on their own). We use seaweed powder and miso paste rather than the usual fish sauce; sometimes larb is made with *nam prik*, a chilli paste, but as this usually contains fish, use sriracha over the salad if you need it to be even hotter.

1 tablespoon **white** or **yellow miso
  paste** (use non-soya to keep this SoF)

a pinch of **salt**

2 tablespoons **neutral cooking oil**

1 small **shallot**, very finely chopped

1. Soak the sticky rice for 15 minutes, then drain, rinse and cook according to the packet instructions. Set aside, covered, and keep warm until ready to serve.

2. Meanwhile, toast the 1 tablespoon rice in a hot dry pan over a medium heat, tossing regularly, for 10 minutes, or until each grain is a light golden brown. Grind to a fine powder using a pestle and mortar.

3. While the rice is cooking, make the mince. Heat 1 tablespoon of the oil in a large frying pan, add the onion and mushrooms and cook over a medium heat, stirring often, for about 8 minutes, or until beginning to brown.

4. Meanwhile, tip the chickpeas into a food processor or blender and blitz briefly until broken down into rough 2mm pieces, but do not blitz to a purée.

5. Add the remaining oil to the pan, then tip in the chickpeas and cook gently, stirring frequently, for 8–10 minutes, until beginning to brown. Add the garlic and crumbled walnuts. Cook for another 5 minutes, tasting as you go – the mince should not be mushy or dry. Remove from the heat and add the chilli and herbs.

6. While the mince is cooking, whisk together all the dressing ingredients except the shallot, mashing in the miso paste as it is quite hard to dissolve, until smooth. Add the diced shallot.

7. Pour the dressing over the mince and toss. The mix should be spicy, hot and sour. Add more chilli, lime juice or salt, if needed.

8. Arrange the lettuce leaves in serving bowls, with the cucumber and beans. Tip the mince over the top, then sprinkle over the spring onions and reserved ground rice. Add the sprigs of basil and serve immediately with the sticky rice.

VEGAN POKE

200g **sushi rice**

425ml **cold water**

1 tablespoon **vegan rice vinegar**
with 1 teaspoon each of **salt** and
sugar or 1½ tablespoons **vegan
ready-made sushi seasoning**

250g **ready-cooked beetroot** (not
in vinegar), cut into 1cm cubes

2 tablespoons **dried hijiki** or
wakame seaweed, or a mixture

a pinch of **sea salt**

1 small **avocado**, diced

3cm chunk of **cucumber**,
thinly sliced

2 **radishes**, thinly sliced

FOR THE CRISPY ONIONS:

1 **white onion**

neutral cooking oil, for frying

FOR THE MAYO & DRESSING:

1 tablespoon **vegan mayonnaise**
(see page 224 for homemade)

2 teaspoons **sriracha hot sauce**

2 tablespoons **toasted sesame oil**

2 tablespoons **gluten-free tamari
soy sauce**

1 teaspoon **maple syrup** or **vegan
mirin** (optional)

TO SERVE:

2 **spring onions**, cut into long
thin strips

1 **shallot**, very finely chopped
(optional)

1 tablespoon **pickled ginger**

1 teaspoon **black** or **white sesame
seeds**, or a mixture, toasted

*PREP TIME: 45 MINS · COOL & STAND TIME: 30 MINS
COOK TIME: 10 MINS*

Poke (pok-ay) is a deconstructed sushi dish from Hawaii, with a base of sushi rice and – often – raw tuna, with avocado, seaweed, sesame and onions. We've replaced the fish with beetroot marinated in seaweed, then dressed in sesame oil and soy sauce. You can make this with dried wakame or hijiki seaweed – wakame is a bit easier to find in large supermarkets, but both can be found in Chinese or Asian food stores. There are hundreds of ways to make poke: try adding crispy fried tofu, chunks of fresh pineapple or mango, toasted flakes of coconut, edamame beans, dried chilli flakes or kimchi. Swap cooked and cooled brown rice, quinoa, or even cauliflower rice, for the sushi rice.

1. To make the crispy onions, very thinly slice the white onion, using a mandolin, if you have one. Heat about 3cm of oil in a deep heavy-based pan over a medium heat until shimmering hot (or about 150°C/300°F). Drop a couple of onion strands into the pan. If they brown in less than 1 minute, the oil is too hot, so you will need to turn down the heat and test again until the onions turn light gold and crisp in about 2 minutes (but not dark brown or they will be bitter and unpleasant). Fry the onions in 3 batches until golden, then remove immediately with a slotted spoon and drain on kitchen paper. Set aside.

2. Rinse the rice under cold running water, then place in a pan with 275ml of the water. Bring to the boil, then turn down to a simmer, cover and cook for 12 minutes. Remove from the heat and allow to steam, covered, for 30 minutes. Stir in the rice vinegar, salt and sugar or sushi seasoning and fluff up with a fork, then leave to cool in the fridge until ready to serve.

3. Meanwhile, place the diced beetroot in a bowl with the dried seaweed, sea salt and the remaining water. Allow to stand for 30 minutes, until the beetroot has absorbed the seaweed flavour and the seaweed has plumped up and softened.

4. To make the sriracha mayonnaise, mix together the mayo and sriracha.

5. In a separate bowl, whisk together the sesame oil, soy sauce and maple syrup. Drain the beetroot and seaweed, then toss with half the soy sauce dressing. In another bowl, mix together the avocado, cucumber and radishes. Pour over the rest of the soy dressing and gently toss.

6. To assemble the poke, divide the cooled rice between bowls. Add the beetroot mixture on one side and the dressed vegetables on the other. Scatter over the spring onions and shallot, if using. Add the pickled ginger and a dollop of the sriracha mayo. Top with a tangle of the crispy onions, sprinkle over the sesame seeds and serve.

MEXICAN SLAW

SERVES 4

 GF   WF   NF SoF

PREP TIME: 15 MINS · COOK TIME: 2–3 MINS

This is vegan version of a recipe taught to Rebecca by chef Thomasina Miers and goes beautifully with many Mexican or South American-style main courses. Serve in or alongside tacos and burritos, or as a fresh, crisp counterpoint to nachos or burgers.

FOR THE SLAW:

50g **pumpkin seeds**

1 small **carrot**, cut into thin julienne strips, or coarsely grated

125g **red cabbage**, cored and finely shredded

2 **spring onions**, halved lengthways and finely sliced

50g **romaine lettuce** or 1 **baby gem lettuce**, shredded

3 tablespoons roughly chopped **fresh coriander**

50g **radishes**, finely chopped

2 teaspoons finely chopped **red chilli** (or ½ teaspoon **dried red chilli flakes**) (optional)

FOR THE DRESSING:

2 tablespoons **vegan mayonnaise** (see page 224 for homemade, choose soya-free to keep this SoF)

juice of ½ **lime**

a generous pinch of **salt**

1 teaspoon **vegan Dijon mustard**

½ teaspoon **vegan red wine vinegar**

½ teaspoon **ground cumin**

freshly ground black pepper

1. Toast the pumpkin seeds in a small, hot, dry pan over a medium heat until they pop. Immediately tip out of the pan to prevent them burning and becoming bitter.

2. Place the rest of the slaw vegetables in a large bowl and when cool add the popped seeds.

3. Whisk all the ingredients for the dressing together, mixing until smooth. Pour over the slaw, tossing well to ensure it is well coated. Taste – it should be crunchy, tangy, sharp and hot.

COLESLAW

SERVES 4

★ GF   WF   NF   SoF

PREP TIME: 10 MINS

Serve this creamy slaw with the pulled jackfruit burgers from page 92.

150g **red** or **white cabbage**, cored and very finely shredded

1 **carrot**, cut into thin julienne strips or coarsely grated

2 **spring onions**, finely chopped

2 tablespoons **vegan mayonnaise** (see page 224 for homemade, choose soya-free to keep this SoF)

1 teaspoon **vegan Dijon mustard**

freshly ground black pepper

1. Mix all the ingredients together and serve.

MISO-SESAME SLAW

SERVES **4**

PREP TIME: 20 MINS

This slaw is delicious topped with a couple of tablespoons of chopped roasted peanuts (if you can eat nuts, of course).

FOR THE SLAW:

65g **beansprouts**

50g **long green beans**, trimmed and sliced on an angle into 1cm strips

125g **white cabbage**, cored and finely shredded

1 small **carrot**, cut into very thin julienne strips or coarsely grated

75g **radishes**, such as **red radishes** or **daikon**, thinly sliced

75g **cucumber**, deseeded and cut into thin julienne strips

2 teaspoons **white** or **black sesame seeds**, or a mixture, toasted

FOR THE DRESSING:

1 teaspoon **gluten-free tamari soy sauce** (to keep this GF and WF) or **Maggi liquid seasoning** (to keep this SoF)

2 teaspoons toasted **sesame oil**

1 teaspoon **vegan rice vinegar** or **vegan cider vinegar**

1 teaspoon **white** or **yellow miso paste** (use soya-free to keep this SoF)

1 teaspoon **grated fresh ginger**

zest and juice of ½ **lime**

1 teaspoon **maple syrup**

a pinch of **salt**

1. Place the slaw ingredients in a large bowl. Whisk all the dressing ingredients together, mashing in the miso paste well (it is quite hard to dissolve) until smooth.

2. Pour the dressing over the slaw and toss well. Serve immediately or keep in the fridge for up to 24 hours.

TIP

Make this Asian-inspired slaw spicy by adding 2 teaspoons finely chopped fresh chilli or ½ teaspoon dried red chilli flakes. Or stir through 1–2 teaspoons vegan Asian hot sauce or chilli paste. For a tangier slaw, add 2 tablespoons drained and finely chopped kimchi.

PARSNIP, KALE & BEETROOT SALAD

PREP TIME: 20 MINS · COOK TIME: 40 MINS

Serve this warm, or at room temperature.

1 tablespoon **olive oil**

2 **parsnips**, cut into 2cm wedges

2 **apples**, cored and cut into 8 wedges

4 small **red onions**, peeled
 and quartered

a large handful of **fresh sage leaves**

4 **ready-roasted beetroot** (not in
 vinegar), quartered

200g **kale**, stems removed, roughly
 chopped

FOR THE DRESSING:

100g **walnuts**

1 **shallot**, very finely diced

2 cloves of **garlic**, minced

1 tablespoon finely chopped
 fresh parsley

1 tablespoon finely chopped
 fresh thyme

60ml **vegan cider vinegar**

100ml **extra virgin olive oil**

a generous pinch of **freshly ground
 black pepper**

1 teaspoon **salt**

1. Heat the oven to 190°C/375°F/gas mark 5. Pour the olive oil into a baking tray and add the parsnip, apples and onions. Toss to coat in the oil. Roast for 20 minutes.

2. Remove from the oven, toss again and add the sage, then roast for another 20 minutes, or until the veg and apples are soft and caramelized. If serving warm, add the beetroot 5 minutes before the end of the cooking time, to warm up.

3. Meanwhile, make the dressing. Toast the walnuts in a large dry frying pan over a medium-low heat for 3–4 minutes, turning once or twice, until golden and fragrant. Allow to cool, then chop the walnuts roughly. Put in a jar with the rest of the ingredients, seal and give it a good shake.

4. Steam the kale for a few minutes, just before the other vegetables are done.

5. To serve, arrange the kale on a serving plate, then top with the roasted vegetables (cooled or warm) and beetroot. Drizzle over the walnut dressing.

> **TIP**
>
> To serve this as a slaw, use raw beetroot and don't roast the other vegetables and apple. Grate them all, shred the kale, then toss together with the dressing.

SQUASH, KALE & LENTIL SALAD

SERVES **4**

  (GF) (WF) (SoF)

PREP TIME: 25 MINS · COOK TIME: I HOUR

Chantal first cooked this for John, at home, and he loved it so much he asked her to develop a recipe so he could use it on the LEON menu.

I **butternut squash**, peeled, deseeded and sliced into 2cm half-moons

2 tablespoons **olive oil**

60g **toasted pine nuts**

salt and **freshly ground black pepper**

FOR THE LENTILS:

I tablespoon **olive oil**

I **onion**, very finely diced

I **carrot**, very finely diced

I stick of **celery**, very finely diced

2 cloves of **garlic**, finely chopped

I teaspoon **vegan Dijon mustard**

I **bay leaf**

750ml **water**

200g **dried Puy lentils**

½–I tablespoon **vegan vegetable bouillon powder**

juice of ½ **lemon**

200g **kale**, thick stems removed, finely sliced

salt and **freshly ground black pepper**

FOR THE SAGE MAYO:

60ml **aquafaba** (tinned chickpea water, see page 12)

juice of ½ **lemon**

½ tablespoon **vegan cider vinegar**

I teaspoon **vegan Dijon mustard**

a generous pinch of **salt**

200ml **neutral cooking oil** (not coconut oil)

I clove of **garlic**, crushed to a smooth paste

2 tablespoons **dried sage** or I tablespoon very finely chopped **fresh sage**

1. Heat the oven to 200°C/400°F/gas mark 6.

2. To cook the lentils, heat the olive oil in a medium heavy-based pan, add the onion, carrot, celery and garlic and cook for 10–15 minutes, until caramelized and soft. Stir in the mustard, then add the bay leaf, water and lentils. Bring to the boil, then reduce the heat to a gentle simmer. Cook for 30–45 minutes, stirring occasionally, until the lentils are tender, and most of the water has evaporated. (Top up with water if it seems to be drying up too quickly.)

3. While the lentils are cooking, place the squash in an oven tray in a single layer and drizzle over the olive oil. Season with salt and pepper and roast for 30–40 minutes, until golden and soft, turning once halfway through.

4. To make the sage mayo, pour the aquafaba into a tall, thin container big enough for a stick blender (or use the jug of the stick blender) and whizz until fluffy and white. Add the lemon juice, cider vinegar, mustard and salt and whizz again. Very slowly, drizzle in the oil, whizzing constantly on the highest setting possible. After a few minutes, the mixture should form a rich, creamy mayonnaise. Add the garlic and sage and stir to combine.

5. Add ½ tablespoon of the bouillon powder and the lemon juice to the lentils. Stir, then add the kale and check the seasoning, adding the rest of the bouillon as needed. Divide between plates, top with the sliced roasted squash, drizzle with the sage mayonnaise and serve sprinkled with pine nuts.

CELERIAC, KALE & HAZELNUT SALAD

PREP TIME: 20 MINS · COOK TIME: 30 MINS

This earthy autumnal salad is filling and nourishing. Serve hot or cold.

1 **celeriac**

½ tablespoon **olive oil**

200g **kale**, stems removed,
   leaves chopped

salt

FOR THE DRESSING:

1 **shallot**, very finely diced

1 clove of **garlic**, minced

4 tablespoons **hazelnuts**, toasted
   and chopped

1 tablespoon **maple syrup**

3 tablespoons **vegan
   sherry vinegar**

½ teaspoon **salt**

½ teaspoon **freshly ground
   black pepper**

60ml **extra virgin olive oil**

1 tablespoon finely chopped
   fresh parsley

1. Heat the oven to 200°C/400°F/gas mark 6.

2. Wash the celeriac thoroughly (if it's very muddy, peel it instead). Slice it crossways into 1.5cm round 'steaks' – you will get 5 or 6 slices. Rub the oil over the celeriac, then place on a baking sheet and sprinkle with a pinch of salt. Roast for 30 minutes, turning once halfway through, until tender and a sharp knife inserted into the slices meets no resistance.

3. Meanwhile, whisk all the ingredients for the dressing together. Taste and add more salt, if needed.

4. Place the chopped kale in a large bowl. Pour over three-quarters of the dressing and massage into the leaves. Set aside to allow the flavours to develop while the celeriac is cooking.

5. Remove the celeriac from the oven and allow to cool slightly. To serve, divide the dressed kale between individual plates. Top each pile with a celeriac steak and drizzle over the remaining dressing.

PUY LENTIL & ROASTED RED PEPPER SALAD

**AS A MAIN OR
4 AS A STARTER**

 (GF) (WF) (SoF)

Chantal created this salad for one of the LEON twice-yearly Well-Being team events (think delicious food and spa treatments!), where it was wolfed down by the team.

2 large **red peppers**, cut into long 1cm-wide strips

2 large **red onions**, each cut into 8 wedges

325g **cherry** or small **heritage tomatoes** (choose a mix of colours, if possible)

½ teaspoon **sea salt**

1 teaspoon **freshly ground black pepper**

75–90ml **olive oil**

1 clove of **garlic**, thinly sliced

1 tablespoon finely chopped **fresh thyme**

250g **ready-cooked Puy lentils**

50g **fresh flat-leaf parsley**, roughly chopped

80g **rocket leaves**

4 tablespoons **toasted pine nuts**

FOR THE DRESSING:

1 **shallot**, thinly sliced

50g **fresh basil**, leaves very finely chopped

25g **fresh oregano**, finely chopped

20ml **vegan red wine vinegar**

75ml **olive oil**

2 teaspoons **agave nectar**

1 clove of **garlic**, minced

a generous pinch of **freshly ground black pepper**

salt

1. Heat the oven to 200°C/400°F/gas mark 6.

2. Place the red peppers, onions, tomatoes, salt, pepper and oil in a large roasting tin, then toss until well coated. Roast for 20 minutes, turning once halfway through the cooking time. Add the garlic and thyme and toss again. Roast for another 15 minutes, or until everything is sticky and just slightly charred.

3. Meanwhile, make the dressing. Whisk all the ingredients together, then add salt to taste.

4. When the vegetables are still hot, add the lentils and the dressing to the roasting tin. Toss together, mixing in all the roasting juices. Stir through the parsley.

5. Place the rocket in a serving bowl or on individual plates. Top with the roasted vegetables and pine nuts, pouring over any dressing left in the roasting dish.

CELERIAC REMOULADE

SERVES
4

1 small **celeriac**, about 1kg

2 **spring onions**, finely chopped

4 tablespoons finely chopped
   fresh parsley

leaves from 1 small bunch of **fresh
   tarragon**, finely chopped

zest and juice of ½ **lemon**

5 tablespoons **vegan mayonnaise**
   (see page 224 for homemade)

1–2 teaspoons **vegan
   Dijon mustard**

1 clove of **garlic**, minced

salt and **freshly ground
   black pepper**

PREP TIME: 15 MINS

Turn knobbly celeriac into a classy French salad.

1. Peel the celeriac, then julienne into fine 2mm strips, using a julienne peeler or a sturdy mandolin (use the hand guard!).

2. Place the strips in a large bowl with the spring onions, parsley and tarragon. Pour over the lemon juice and toss to coat (this will prevent the celeriac going brown).

3. Whisk together the lemon zest, mayo, 1 teaspoon of the mustard and the garlic, then season with salt and pepper. Taste and add more salt, pepper or mustard, if needed. Pour over the celeriac and toss well.

4. The salad will keep in the fridge for up to 2 days if you're not serving it immediately.

CAESAR SALAD

(NF) (SoF)

1 large **romaine lettuce** or 250g **baby** (or very tender) **kale**, shredded or sliced

1 quantity of **croutons** (see page 242)

FOR THE DRESSING:

60ml **aquafaba** (tinned chickpea water, see page 12)

½ tablespoon **vegan cider vinegar**

1 teaspoon **vegan Dijon mustard**

200ml **neutral cooking oil**

1 teaspoon **coconut aminos**, **Maggi liquid seasoning** or **vegan Worcestershire sauce**

½ teaspoon **kelp powder**

½ teaspoon **white** or **yellow miso paste** (use non-soya to keep this SoF)

½ teaspoon **freshly ground black pepper**

1 tablespoon **nutritional yeast**

2 cloves of **garlic**, crushed to a paste

juice of ½ **lemon**

a generous pinch of **salt**

OPTIONAL EXTRAS:

mushroom anchovies (see page 236) or **coconut bacon** (see page 41)

crunchy **roasted chickpeas** (see page 242) or drained **chickpeas from a tin**

toasted seeds (see page 243)

vegan Parmesan shavings

PREP TIME: 15 MINS

Make an old-school Caesar by using romaine lettuce, or freshen it up with baby kale instead.

1. To make the dressing, pour the aquafaba into a tall, thin container big enough for a stick blender (or use the jug of the stick blender) and whizz until fluffy and white. Add the cider vinegar and mustard and whizz again. Very slowly, drizzle in the oil, whizzing constantly on the highest setting possible. After a few minutes, the mixture should form a rich, creamy mayonnaise.

2. Add the rest of the dressing ingredients and whizz again until smooth and combined. Taste and add more salt, if needed. If you feel the dressing is too thick, very gradually add a little water until you get the desired consistency.

3. Place the lettuce or kale and croutons in a salad bowl with your choice of extra salad ingredients and pour over the dressing to serve.

TIP
The dressing can be kept in the fridge, covered, for up to 4 days.

RINKU'S ALOO KABLI

(GF) (WF) (NF) (SoF)

4 **waxy potatoes**, peeled

2 × 400g tins of **chickpeas**, drained

I **red onion**, roughly chopped

2 **green chillies**, deseeded to taste,
   finely chopped

2 tablespoons finely diced **cucumber**

3 tablespoons **lemon juice**

I teaspoon **pink salt**, plus extra
   to taste

8 tablespoons **shop-bought
   tamarind chutney**

a handful of finely chopped **fresh
   coriander**

salt

FOR THE BHAJA MASALA:

4 tablespoons **cumin seeds**

I **bay leaf**

I **dried red chilli**

PREP TIME: 15 MINS · COOK TIME: 35 MINS

Rinku Dutt is one of Rebecca's friends – she runs the Indian street food pop-up Raastawala, and regularly appears at Rebecca's door with incredible curries; somehow she always manages to appear when a miracle meal is most needed. She says: 'Aloo kabli is one of the most popular street food dishes of Kolkata and is very easy to make. A light, healthy, tangy and fresh dish that can be enjoyed as a snack, starter or as an accompaniment to a main.'

1. To make the bhaja masala, toast all the ingredients in a hot dry pan until fragrant. Tip out of the pan and allow to cool, then grind to a fine powder using a pestle and mortar or an electric spice grinder. Set aside.

2. Cook the potatoes in a pan of salted boiling water until tender. Drain and allow to cool.

3. Rinse the chickpeas well and place in a large bowl. Mix with the chopped onion, chillies and cucumber.

4. Cut the potatoes into medium-sized cubes and add to the bowl with the lemon juice, pink salt, 6 tablespoons of the tamarind chutney, the bhaja masala and the chopped coriander. Mix well, ensuring all the ingredients have a chance to meld their flavours together, but be gentle so that the potatoes don't lose their shape.

5. Finally, spoon the rest of the tamarind chutney over the salad. Taste and add more salt, if needed. Serve immediately.

TIP
Pink salt has a much milder flavour than most salts. If you don't have any, then replace it with sea salt, to taste, when the salad is made.

JARRED SALADS

DITCH THE TUPPERWARE & TAKE YOUR LUNCH TO WORK IN A LARGE, LIDDED JAR INSTEAD.

Why? Because you can stack the ingredients, starting with the dressing, and keep everything crisp until you tip everything out into a bowl and eat.

TOP YOUR JAR WITH ANYTHING YOU WANT TO STAY CRUNCHY LIKE CROUTONS OR TOASTED SEEDS.

LETTUCE OR RAW GREENS SIT HERE.

VERY SOFT INGREDIENTS (AVOCADO, ALMOND FETA ON PAGE 154, COCONUT LABNEH ON PAGE 118) SIT ON TOP.

FOLLOWED BY PASTA AND ANY OTHER SEMI-FIRM INGREDIENT (TOFU, MUSHROOMS, RAW TOMATOES).

THIS LAYER IS FOR COOKED GRAINS OR PULSES (QUINOA, LENTILS, RICE, CHICKPEAS)

HERE LIES ANY ROASTED VEGETABLES.

THEN COOKED GREENS (SPINACH, KALE).

THEN ADD THE FIRM INGREDIENTS (RAW CARROTS, COOKED BEETROOT OR POTATOES).

START WITH THE DRESSING AT THE BOTTOM OF THE JAR.

TRY IT WITH THESE SALADS:

Freekeh salad
(see page 154)

Parsnip, kale & beetroot salad
(see page 164)

Caesar salad
(see page 173)

Puy lentil & roasted red pepper salad
(see page 170)

Poke
(see page 160)

Rinku's aloo kabli
(see opposite)

6

PARTY FOOD & SMALL PLATES

LEEK & MUSHROOM CROQUETAS

SERVES 4 AS A STARTER

NF **SoF**

1 tablespoon **olive oil**, plus extra for frying the croquetas (see Tips)

100g **mushrooms**, very finely diced

½ **leek**, very finely diced

½ teaspoon **sweet smoked paprika** (optional, but strongly recommended!)

salt

4 tablespoons **vegan mayonnaise** (see page 224 for homemade, choose soya-free to keep this SoF) mixed with 1 teaspoon **sweet smoked paprika**, or **garlicky aioli** (see page 222), to serve

FOR THE BÉCHAMEL:

475ml **unsweetened plant milk** (use non-nut or non-soya to keep this NF or SoF)

½ **onion**

10 **black peppercorns**

60ml **olive oil**

60g **plain flour**

a pinch of **freshly grated nutmeg**

a generous pinch of **salt**

FOR THE COATING:

3 tablespoons **unsweetened plant milk**

3 tablespoons **plain flour**, plus extra for dusting

50–75g **panko breadcrumbs**

**PREP TIME: 20 MINS · CHILL TIME: 4 HOURS
COOK TIME: 45 MINS**

With their crisp shells and silky béchamel inside, these are impossible to stop eating once you've started. As long as the béchamel has set firmly, you can breadcrumb the croquetas up to an hour before cooking.

1. First, heat the milk for the béchamel with the onion and peppercorns in a pan over a low heat until warm, but don't allow to boil. Remove from the heat and allow to infuse for a few minutes.

2. To make the béchamel, heat the oil in a heavy-based pan over a medium-low heat. Add the flour and cook, stirring, to form a paste, for 2 minutes. Gradually begin to add the warm, infused milk, using a ladle and stirring constantly. Don't rush this step as adding the milk too fast results in a lumpy béchamel (although if this does happen, don't worry, just keep stirring until the lumps break down into the sauce). When all the milk has been added, the sauce should be silky smooth, thick and almost stretchy.

3. Add the nutmeg and salt, then cook for another 8 minutes, stirring regularly to prevent it sticking to the bottom of the pan. Don't rush this phase, as the béchamel needs to be very thick in order for it to firm up enough to roll into balls and fry.

4. Meanwhile, heat the 1 tablespoon oil in a frying pan over a medium heat, add the vegetables and sauté until the mushrooms are just beginning to brown and the leek is softened, about 8 minutes.

5. When the béchamel is cooked, stir in the vegetables and sweet smoked paprika, if using. Taste and add more salt, if needed. Pour into a bowl, cover and allow to cool, then firm up in the fridge for at least 4 hours, but ideally overnight.

6. When ready to cook the croquetas, heat about 4cm of olive oil in a deep heavy-based pan over a medium heat to 180°C/350°F, or until a cube of day-old bread browns in 30 seconds. Remove the béchamel from the fridge. For the coating, pour the flour on to a plate, the milk into a bowl and the panko breadcrumbs on to another plate.

7. Flour your hands, then scoop enough of the cold béchamel to form a cylinder about 6cm long and 2cm wide. Pat it firmly into shape, then roll gently in the flour. Briefly dip it in the milk until covered but not soggy, then roll it in the breadcrumbs, ensuring the croqueta is well coated.

8. Fry the croqueta to check the oil is the right temperature. Using a slotted spoon, carefully lower it into the hot oil. Deep-fry for 3 minutes, or until the breadcrumbs are a rich, deep gold – you may need to nudge it over to ensure it browns evenly (if the breadcrumbs burn, the oil is too hot). Remove with tongs, allowing any excess oil to drain back into the pan. Drain on kitchen paper and keep warm while you prepare and cook the rest of the criquetas, cooking no more than 3 at a time.

9. Allow to cool for a couple of minutes before serving, as the insides will remain extremely hot. Serve with the sweet smoked paprika vegan mayo or aioli.

TIPS

Don't overcrowd the pan when you fry the croquetas as this will lower the temperature of the oil and make them soggy and greasy. Allow the oil to come back to 180°C/350°F for a minute or two between batches. The croquetas can also be fried in a mixture of olive oil and neutral cooking oil (but not coconut oil). Try frying 100g very finely diced smoked tofu (if you don't need these to be soya free) or smoky seitan, until crisp, then add it to the béchamel.

TOMATO 'TUNA' FUTOMAKI SUSHI ROLLS

MAKES
24
ROLLS

1 under-ripe **tomato**

1 tablespoon **dried
wakame seaweed**

2 teaspoons **gluten-free tamari
soy sauce** (to keep this GF and WF)
or **coconut aminos** (to keep this
GF, WF and SoF), or 1 teaspoon
Maggi liquid seasoning (to keep
this SoF), plus extra to serve

560ml **water**, plus extra if needed

400g **sushi rice**

60ml **vegan rice vinegar** with
1¼ teaspoons **fine salt** and
1 tablespoon **caster sugar** or
75ml **ready-made vegan
sushi seasoning**

½ ripe **avocado**

10cm chunk of **cucumber**,
deseeded and cut into thin
julienne strips

3 sheets of **nori**

3–4 teaspoons **sesame
seeds**, toasted

TO SERVE:
pickled ginger for sushi
wasabi paste

**PREP TIME: 45 MINS · CHILL TIME: 2 HOURS
COOK TIME: 45 MINS**

Futomaki are chubby, large sushi rolls. Instead of tuna, we fill ours with tomato that has been marinated with seaweed. (We were inspired by a company called Ocean Hugger Foods in the US, who have developed a range of tomato-based raw-fish-style products; find them in WholeFoods.) Nori is a dried seaweed sheet used for wrapping sushi.

---

1. First, prepare the tomato. Fill a heatproof bowl with boiling water. Cut a shallow cross on the top of the tomato, just enough to break the skin, then plunge it into the hot water. Leave for 30–60 seconds – you should see the skin beginning to split. Using tongs or a slotted spoon, remove and when cool enough to handle, peel back the skin and discard. Halve the tomato, remove the seeds and discard. Cut the remaining flesh into 5mm strips, discarding any hard pieces of core or stem.

2. Place the tomato in a bowl with the wakame seaweed, soy sauce, aminos or Maggi liquid seasoning and 60ml of the water. Toss together, cover and marinate in the fridge for 2 hours.

3. About an hour before you want to make the sushi, rinse the rice well, then place in a small pan with the remaining water. Bring to the boil, then turn the heat down and simmer, covered, for 12 minutes. Remove from the heat and allow to steam, covered, for 30 minutes, adding extra water if needed. Once steamed, break up the rice with a fork. Mix together the vinegar, salt and sugar or sushi seasoning, then stir into the rice. Leave to cool in the fridge until ready to serve.

4. Have ready all your fillings: drain the marinated tomatoes, discarding the seaweed; slice the avocado into thin strips; have the cucumber strips nearby. Place a small bowl of water next to the ingredients.

5. Arrange a large sheet of clingfilm on a board in front of you (or use a sushi rolling mat, if you have one). Place a sheet of nori, shiny side down, on the clingfilm. Wet your hands slightly. Divide the rice into 3 portions. Use your hands to gently but firmly arrange an even layer of cooked sushi rice, about 5mm thick, all over the nori, leaving a gap of about 2cm at the top. Arrange a third of the fillings horizontally across the centre of the rice.

6. To roll the sushi up, wet the nori still exposed at the top of the sheet. Use the clingfilm to help you roll the bottom half of the rice-

PARTY FOOD & SMALL PLATES

covered nori over the fillings, using your fingers to hold the fillings in place while your thumbs do the rolling. Make sure the roll is quite tight and firm. Then continue to roll, using the clingfilm to help but without rolling it inside the sushi.

7. When you get to the top, the wet nori will stick to the dry nori. Set the roll aside, seam side down, while you repeat to make another 2 rolls. Use the clingfilm to help you gently nudge them back into cylinder shapes if they have become a bit square-looking during the filling process.

8. Wet the blade of a very sharp knife and gently slice each roll into 8 (or 6, if you prefer chunkier rolls). Serve with pickled ginger, soy sauce and wasabi.

TIP
Swap the marinated tomato with carrot 'gravlax' (see page 192) to make a salmon-style sushi roll.

PEA & POTATO SAMOSAS

MAKES 16 SAMOSAS

FOR THE PASTRY:

175g **plain flour**, plus extra for dusting

a generous pinch of **salt**

1½ tablespoons **oil**

60–100ml **water**

FOR THE FILLING:

450g **white potatoes**, peeled
and diced

1 large **carrot**, peeled and diced

1 tablespoon **neutral cooking oil**,
plus extra for frying the samosas

1 **onion**, finely diced

2 cloves of **garlic**, grated

4cm piece of **fresh ginger**, peeled
and grated

½ teaspoon **ground turmeric**

½ teaspoon **dried red chilli flakes**
(optional)

1 teaspoon **garam masala**

1 teaspoon **mustard seeds**

75g **frozen peas**

2 tablespoons finely chopped
fresh coriander

1 teaspoon **lemon juice**

salt and **freshly ground
black pepper**

TO SERVE:

tamarind yoghurt (see page 235)

coconut chutney (see page 231)

Indian pickles

PREP TIME: 45 MINS · COOK TIME: 1 HOUR

Crisp, hot samosas, stuffed with a traditional pea and potato filling.

___

1. First, make the pastry. Mix the flour and salt in a bowl, then rub in the oil using your fingers. When sandy, add just enough water to form a dough. The dough should not be at all sticky. Knead for up to 5 minutes, until smooth and elastic. Place in a clean bowl, cover with a clean tea towel and allow to rest while you make the filling.

2. Cook the potatoes and carrot in a large pan of salted boiling water until tender, about 15 minutes.

3. Heat the cooking oil in a frying pan over a medium heat, add the onion and a pinch of salt and fry for about 8 minutes, until translucent and beginning to brown. Add the garlic and ginger and cook, stirring, for 1 minute. Add the turmeric, chilli flakes, if using, garam masala and mustard seeds, plus a splash of oil if dry. Cook for 1 minute, then remove from the heat. Stir in the peas and coriander. Set aside.

4. Drain the potatos and carrot, then roughly mash. Tip in the onions and lemon juice and season with pepper. Taste for salt. Set aside.

5. Heat about 4cm of oil in a deep heavy-based pan to about 180°C/350°F, or until a cube of day-old bread browns in 30 seconds.

6. Divide the dough into 8 equal pieces, then shape into neat balls. Using a floured rolling pin and a clean work surface dusted with flour, roll out a ball to make a very thin circle of pastry, about 20cm wide. Using a sharp knife, cut in half, then shape each semicircle into a cone by folding it over itself, a third at a time. Wet the outer edge of the pastry and seal the loose pastry like a seam, pinching it firmly shut at the bottom of the cone so the filling doesn't leak when frying.

7. To fill, make a ring with your thumb and forefinger and use it to support the open-topped cone. Fill the cone about three-quarters full with the filling, then wet the remaining open edges and pinch firmly shut. Repeat until all the dough and filling are used up.

8. Carefully lower 2 or 3 samosas at a time into the hot oil. (Don't overcrowd the pan.) Cook for 2–3 minutes on each side, until golden brown and bubbly all over. Remove with a slotted spoon. Drain on kitchen paper and keep warm while you fry the rest.

9. Serve hot, with coconut chutney and tamarind yoghurt, plus Indian pickles.

BEETROOT CARPACCIO

 SERVES
4
AS A STARTER

(GF) (WF) (SoF)

2 tablespoons **walnuts**

1 teaspoon **caraway seeds**

4 **beetroot** (ideally, heritage or multi-coloured)

2 tablespoons chopped **fresh thyme**

about 1 teaspoon grated **fresh horseradish**

FOR THE DRESSING:

zest of 1 and juice of 1½ **oranges**

60ml **extra virgin olive oil**

4 cloves of **garlic**

juice of 1 **lemon**

PREP TIME: 15 MINS · COOK TIME (OPTIONAL): 1 HOUR

Slightly controversially, this carpaccio works just as well cooked as it does raw. If you prefer a cooked version, heat the oven to 180°C/350°F/ gas mark 4, wrap the beetroots in foil with a teaspoon of water and roast for 50–60 minutes. Allow to cool completely before rubbing off the skins and slicing thinly.

1. Toast the walnuts in a hot dry pan for a couple of minutes. Tip on to a plate and allow to cool, then roughly chop. Toast the caraway seeds in the same pan for 30 seconds–1 minute.

2. To make the dressing, place all the ingredients in a blender and blend until smooth.

3. Peel the beetroot then thinly slice, ideally on a mandolin, and arrange on a platter in a thin layer.

4. Drizzle over the dressing, sprinkle over the thyme, toasted caraway seeds, walnuts and horseradish and serve.

THAI RICE PAPER ROLLS

 MAKES 8 ROLLS

85g thin **rice noodles**

8 **Thai rice paper spring roll wrappers**

200g **beansprouts**

5 **spring onions**, thinly sliced

1 **carrot**, coarsely grated

a large handful of **fresh coriander leaves**

a large handful of **fresh Thai basil leaves**

1 × quantity **lemongrass & chilli tofu** (see page 145), cut into 2cm cubes

PREP TIME: 30 MINS · COOK TIME: 10 MINS

Pretty, almost translucent rice paper rolls, stuffed with raw vegetables and lemongrass-scented tofu. (If you don't have time to make the lemongrass tofu on page 145 for this, you can use 280g ready-cooked tofu instead.)

1. Cook the rice noodles according to the packet instructions. Drain, then refresh under cold running water until cool. Prepare the rice paper wrappers according to the packet instructions.

2. Divide the noodles into 8 equal portions. Lay a wrapper out flat on a board in front of you. Lay a portion of the noodles in a vertical line in the middle of the wrapper, leaving about 3cm space at the top and bottom. Add an eighth of the beansprouts on top of the noodles, followed by an eighth of the spring onions, carrot, coriander and basil. Arrange an eighth of the tofu to one side of noodles.

3. Fold over both the top and bottom of the wrapper. Take one of the sides and fold over to snugly cover the filling. Starting from the side you've just folded, tightly roll over the filling, wrapping the loose edge firmly in as you roll. Arrange with the seam on the bottom. (If the roll looks a bit lumpy, roll it back and forth once or twice to help even it out.) Repeat with the rest of the wrappers and fillings.

> ### TIP
> Serve with nutty satay sauce (see page 80), sweet chilli sauce or the fish-sauce-style dressing from the Vietnamese pancakes on page 82.

SIGARA BOREK

175g **spinach**, stems removed

3 tablespoons **walnuts** or **unsalted pistachio nuts**

150ml **olive oil**, plus 2 tablespoons and extra for greasing

1 small **leek** or 3 **spring onions**, finely chopped

1 **onion**, finely chopped

2 cloves of **garlic**, crushed

4 tablespoons **pine nuts**

100g **marinated** or **grilled artichoke** or **artichoke hearts** from a jar, finely chopped

1 tablespoon finely chopped **fresh parsley**

1 teaspoon **lemon juice**, plus extra to taste

about 14 sheets of **filo pastry**, measuring 26cm × 30cm, or equivalent

salt and **freshly ground black pepper**

TIP

If you can, buy proper yufka pastry from a Middle Eastern supermarket or very good-quality filo – cheap filo often shatters as soon as you try and roll it.

PREP TIME: 35 MINS · COOK TIME: 40 MINS

Borek are stuffed filo parcels, made all over south-eastern Europe and the Middle East. Serve these cigar-shaped pastries with tzatziki (see page 230) as a starter, or as part of a mezze with babaganoush (see page 232), the tomato salad on page 156 and some falafel (see page 60). If you're making these ahead, freeze them before baking.

1. Steam the spinach with a little water in a large pan until wilted, or cook in the microwave, in a covered heatproof bowl, for 2 minutes. Allow to cool, then squeeze out thoroughly and finely chop. (Any excess liquid left in will make the pastry soggy.) Set aside.

2. Put the walnuts or pistachios in a food processor and blitz until they resemble rough sand, or pound in a pestle and mortar.

3. Heat the 2 tablespoons oil in a large heavy-based pan, add the leek or spring onions and onion and a large pinch of salt and sauté over a medium heat until translucent, about 10 minutes. Add the garlic and pine nuts and cook for 2 minutes, then add the artichoke and the walnuts or pistachios and cook, stirring, for another 2 minutes. Remove from the heat and add the parsley, spinach and lemon juice and season with pepper. Check the seasoning and add more salt or lemon juice, to taste.

4. Heat the oven to 180°C/350°F/gas mark 4. Pour the remaining oil into a bowl for brushing.

5. Take a sheet of filo and lay it out in front of you. Slice it into 2 or more long rectangles, each measuring about 12 × 26cm. Cover the rest of the filo with a clean damp tea towel to prevent it drying out and becoming very brittle. Brush the pastry rectangles with olive oil, then stack them together to form a double layer.

6. Place 1½ tablespoons of the filling at one of the short ends, and spread out slightly, leaving a 1cm gap of pastry on all 3 sides. Fold the long sides in by 1cm, just over the filling, then fold the short edge in by 2cm, so that the pastry begins to enclose the filling. Roll the pastry up into a tube, keeping the long edges folded inwards as you roll and brushing the newly exposed pastry with oil. Place, seam side down, on a large greased baking sheet (or 2 small ones). Repeat until you have used up all the filling.

7. Bake for 20–25 minutes, or until the pastries are golden and crisp. These are best served warm or at room temperature, but not straight from the oven as the filling will be extremely hot.

STUFFED FIGS

100g **walnuts**, chopped into
   small pieces

170g **vegan cream cheese**

2 tablespoons finely chopped
   fresh thyme

1 small clove of **garlic**, crushed to
   a paste

½ teaspoon **salt**

½ teaspoon **freshly ground
   black pepper**

16 fresh **figs**

60ml **maple syrup**

PREP TIME: 20 MINS · COOK TIME: 2 MINS

**There are some excellent vegan blue cheeses now available; if you find
one you like, swap a quarter of the cream cheese with blue cheese.
(Look out for cheese containing *Penicillium roqueforti*, as this gives
the blue-est flavour.)**

1. Toast the chopped walnuts in a hot dry frying pan over a high heat
   for a couple of minutes, tossing frequently, until slightly golden and
   fragrant. Tip out of the pan and allow to cool.

2. Place the cream cheese in a bowl and beat with a wooden spoon
   until smooth. Tip in half the cooled walnuts, half the thyme, the
   garlic, salt and pepper, and stir to combine.

3. Take a fig and using a small sharp knife, slice off the tip, then slice
   downwards in a cross shape, cutting only three-quarters of the way
   through to create space to stuff the fig. Push in a teaspoon of the
   cheese mixture. Repeat with remaining figs and cheese.

4. When ready to serve, arrange the figs on a platter and drizzle each
   one with a little maple syrup. Scatter over the remaining walnuts
   and thyme.

TIP
These can be served cold or
warmed up: to heat, place on
a baking tray under a hot grill
for 1–2 minutes.

CARROT 'GRAVLAX' ON RYE

FOR THE 'GRAVLAX':

2 large **carrots**, washed

2 tablespoons **salt**, plus extra to taste

1 tablespoon **neutral cooking oil**

2 tablespoons finely chopped
   fresh dill

3 **juniper berries**, crushed

2 teaspoons **vegan dry gin** (optional,
   choose gluten-free to keep this GF
   and WF)

zest of ⅛ **lemon**

2 teaspoons **lemon juice**

1 teaspoon **caster sugar**

a pinch of **kelp powder**

FOR THE SALAD:

1 teaspoon **lemon juice**, plus extra
   to taste

1 teaspoon freshly grated
   horseradish, **vegan
   horseradish mustard** or **vegan
   Dijon mustard**, plus extra to taste

1 tablespoon finely chopped
   fresh chives, plus extra to serve

4 tablespoons **vegan mayonnaise**
   (see page 224 for homemade)

¼ **cucumber**, deseeded and
   thinly sliced

½ head of **fennel**, thinly sliced

salt and **freshly ground
   black pepper**

TO SERVE:

vegan butter (see page 229 for
   homemade) or **vegan margarine**
   (optional)

4 thin slices of **rye bread**, cut into
   bite-sized pieces

PREP TIME: 35 MINS · COOK TIME: 50 MINS
MARINATING TIME: 1 HOUR

Whether it's the taste, a visual trick or a textural one, we were amazed to discover how close the humble carrot can get to traditional cured salmon gravlax.

1. Heat the oven to 200°C/400°F/gas mark 6.

2. Place the carrots on a sheet of foil and sprinkle with the salt. Fold the foil around the carrots to seal, then bake for 50 minutes. When cool enough to handle, rinse off the salt and pat dry. Rub or trim off the carrot skin. Slice the remaining flesh into long strips, as thinly as possible and no thicker than 1mm.

3. Place the strips in a bowl and add the remaining 'gravlax' ingredients. Toss gently but thoroughly, then leave at room temperature for an hour or so for the flavours to develop.

4. When ready to serve, make the salad. Whisk together the lemon juice, horseradish or mustard, chives and vegan mayo. Add a little pepper, then taste, add salt and more lemon juice or horseradish, if needed. (If it seems too thick, thin the dressing with a little water, but be sparing.) Put the cucumber and fennel in a bowl and pour over the dressing.

5. Taste the carrot gravlax – it may need a little more salt. If it seems at all wet, pat dry. Discard the juniper berries before serving.

6. Butter the bread pieces, if you like. Top each piece with a little salad, followed by the 'gravlax' and sprinkle with chopped chives to serve.

> **TIP**
>
> If you don't have homemade mayo, in a pinch you could use non-dairy plain yoghurt. For a simpler dish, omit the salad and serve with vegan cream cheese or vegan soured cream, on toasted bagels.

CELERIAC ROSTI WITH WILD MUSHROOMS

PREP TIME: 20 MINS · COOK TIME: 25 MINS

This is one of John's favourite party foods – he even likes eating it for breakfast. You can also make the mix into 6 large rosti and serve this as a main course.

FOR THE ROSTI:

1 tablespoon **chia seeds**

60ml **water**

1 small **celeriac**, peeled and grated

2 small **white onions**, thinly sliced or coarsely grated

3 cloves of **garlic**, crushed

20g **fresh chives**, finely chopped

1 teaspoon **salt**

3 tablespoons **ground almonds**

4 tablespoons **potato starch** or **ground arrowroot**

1 tablespoon finely chopped **fresh thyme**

neutral cooking oil, for frying

FOR THE WILD MUSHROOM TOPPING:

½ tablespoon **olive oil**

250g **wild mushrooms**, chopped

1 **leek**, thinly sliced into half-moons

4 cloves of **garlic**, minced

30ml **vegan Manzanilla** or other **dry sherry** (or **vegan white wine**)

1 tablespoon **vegan sherry vinegar**

200ml **unsweetened almond milk**

½ teaspoon **vegan butter** or **margarine** (choose soya-free to keep this SoF)

½ teaspoon **plain** or **gluten-free** (to be GF and WF) **plain flour**

1. To make the topping, heat the oil in a frying pan, add the mushrooms, leek and garlic and cook over a medium heat for about 15 minutes, until caramelized. Pour in the sherry and sherry vinegar and deglaze the pan, allowing it to bubble and evaporate for a couple of minutes.

2. Add the almond milk and bring to a vigorous simmer, then cook until the liquid has reduced by half. Mix the butter or margarine and flour together until smooth, then stir into the mushroom mixture. (Don't worry if the almond milk seems to split – the flour mixture should smooth it out.) Keep warm while you make the rosti.

3. Mix together the chia seeds and water in a small bowl and allow to soak for 5 minutes.

4. Put the thinly sliced or grated onion into a clean tea towel and squeeze out the juice. Mix the onion together with all the remaining rosti ingredients except the oil, then add the soaked chia and shape into 12 small patties.

5. Heat a drizzle of oil in a frying pan over a medium heat and cook the patties, in batches, for about 2 minutes on each side, or until golden and crispy. Top with the warm, creamy wild mushrooms.

> **TIP**
> If not serving immediately, the rosti reheat very well. Just place in a preheated oven at 180°C/350°F/gas mark 4 for 8–10 minutes.

PARSLEY & ALMOND TAPENADE

SERVES 4 *(ENOUGH TO TOP 20 CROSTINI)*

2–3 cloves of **garlic**, to taste

60g **blanched almonds**

60g **fresh parsley** (leaves and stalks)

zest and juice of 1 **lemon**

160g **green olives**, pitted

65ml **olive oil**

PREP TIME: 5 MINS

Use this to top crostini, or as a no-cook sauce for pasta, or dot it on top of avocado on toast, or loosen with a little more olive oil and drizzle over grilled courgettes.

1. If you prefer a milder flavour, blanch the garlic in a pan of boiling water for 3 minutes, then drain.

2. Meanwhile, toast the almonds in a hot dry frying pan for 2–3 minutes, tossing frequently, until golden and fragrant.

3. Place the blanched garlic in a mortar and pound with the pestle to a purée, then transfer to a food processor or blender with the toasted nuts and remaining ingredients and pulse to the texture of pesto.

4. Store in the fridge for up to 1 week, covered or in a jar and topped with a thin layer of oil.

> **TIP**
>
> To make crostini, cut a baguette into slices 1cm thick, brush with olive oil and bake in a preheated oven at 180°C/350°F/gas mark 4 for about 10 minutes, until crisp.

PARSNIP ROSTI WITH KALE & CHESTNUTS

PREP TIME: 25 MINS · COOK TIME: 15 MINS
SOAK TIME: 5 MINS

Instead of making this as a starter or nibble, you can make 4 big rosti and serve as a main course.

FOR THE ROSTI:

1 tablespoon **chia seeds**

60ml **water**

½–1 teaspoon **salt**

2 **parsnips**, grated

1 **onion**, thinly sliced

2 cloves of **garlic**, crushed

2 teaspoons **vegan Dijon mustard**

3 tablespoons **gram flour**

1 tablespoon finely chopped **fresh thyme**

1 teaspoon **freshly ground black pepper**

1 tablespoon **olive oil**

FOR THE KALE:

2 tablespoons **olive oil**

1 **onion**, finely chopped

4 cloves of **garlic**, minced

1 tablespoon finely chopped **fresh sage**

200g **kale**, stems removed, finely chopped

FOR THE CHESTNUT TOPPING:

100g **traditional** or **gluten-free breadcrumbs**

75g **cooked chestnuts**, finely chopped

4 cloves of **garlic**, minced

1 tablespoon finely chopped **fresh thyme**

3 tablespoons **olive oil**

salt and **freshly ground black pepper**

1. Mix the chia seeds and water and allow to soak for 5 minutes. To make the rosti, mix ½ teaspoon of the salt with the soaked chia seeds and the rest of the ingredients except the oil in a bowl. Taste and add the rest of the salt, if needed (ignore the bean flavour from the gram flour, this will cook away).

2. Shape the mixture into 5–6cm patties. Heat the oil in a large frying pan over a medium heat and fry the patties, in batches, for about 2 minutes on each side, until golden and firmed up. Keep warm while you cook the remaining patties.

3. Meanwhile, cook the kale. Heat the oil in a separate frying pan, add the onion, garlic and sage and fry for about 5 minutes over a medium-low heat, until beginning to caramelize. Add the kale and stir-fry for 4–5 minutes, until wilted and tender.

4. While the patties are cooking, toss the topping ingredients together, then tip into another pan and cook over a medium heat until golden. Alternatively, spread out in a baking tray and cook in a hot oven (220°C/425°F/gas mark 7) for about 10 minutes.

5. Serve the rosti topped with the warm kale and the chestnut crumb.

MALAYSIAN SWEETCORN FRITTERS

1 tablespoon **ground flaxseeds**

2 tablespoons **water**

300g **frozen sweetcorn**, defrosted

3 cloves of **garlic**, minced

2cm piece of **fresh ginger**,
   peeled and minced

2 ears of **corn on the cob**

2 small **red bird's eye chillies**,
   deseeded to taste and finely chopped

5 **spring onions**, thinly sliced

½ teaspoon **ground turmeric**

1 teaspoon **salt**

1 teaspoon **freshly ground
   black pepper**

4 tablespoons **plain** or **gluten-free
   plain flour**

1½ teaspoons **ordinary** or
   gluten-free baking powder

refined or **extra virgin coconut
oil** or **vegetable oil**, for frying

TO SERVE:
fresh coriander leaves
sweet chilli dipping sauce
lime wedges

*PREP TIME: 20 MINS · REST TIME: 30 MINS
COOK TIME: 25 MINS*

These sweet and spicy little fritters make an excellent party snack.

1. In a small bowl, mix together the ground flaxseeds and the water and allow to soak for at least 5 minutes.

2. Place the defrosted corn, garlic, ginger and soaked flaxseeds in a food processor or blender. Blitz until puréed, scraping the mixture down the sides of the bowl with a spatula a couple of times. When smooth, decant into a large bowl.

3. Using a sharp knife, strip the kernels from the ears of corn and add to the bowl with the remaining ingredients except for the oil. Mix well, then allow to rest for at least 30 minutes.

4. When ready to cook, heat about 6cm of oil in a deep heavy-based pan over a medium-high heat to 170°C/340°F, or until a cube of day-old bread browns in 30 seconds.

5. Use a teaspoon to scoop balls of the mixture and another spoon to carefully place the mixture into the oil. Cook 4 or 5 at a time. (Don't overcrowd the pan as this will lower the temperature of the oil and you will end up with soggy fritters. Allow the oil to come back to 170°C/340°F for a minute or two between batches.) When the fritters turn golden brown and rise to the surface of the oil, flip them over and continue to cook until golden all over. This should take 2–3 minutes per batch. Remove with a slotted spoon, allowing the excess oil to drain back into the pan. Drain on kitchen paper and keep warm while you cook the rest of the mixture.

6. Scatter the fritters with coriander. Serve with sweet chilli dipping sauce on the side and with lime wedges for squeezing over.

> *TIP*
> You can fry the fritters in advance and reheat in an oven heated to 180°C/350°F/gas mark 4 for about 10 minutes.

COURGETTE FRITTERS & LEMON CASHEW CREAM

MAKES
14

  (GF) (WF) (SoF)

PREP TIME: 15 MINS · SOAK TIME: 4½ HOURS
COOK TIME: 15 MINS

These are John's favourite fridge raiders.

FOR THE FRITTERS:

1 tablespoon **chia seeds**

60ml **water**

2 **courgettes**, coarsely grated

1 teaspoon **salt**

6 **spring onions**, finely chopped

4 tablespoons **gram flour**

1 tablespoon **nutritional yeast**

5 cloves of **garlic**, minced

½ teaspoon **freshly ground
black pepper**

1 tablespoon **vegan pesto** (see page
56 for homemade)

50g **plain** or **gluten-free
plain flour**

1 teaspoon **ordinary** or **gluten-
free baking powder**

neutral cooking oil, for frying

FOR THE LEMON
CASHEW CREAM:

125g **unroasted cashew nuts**

juice of ½ **lemon**

a generous pinch of **freshly ground
black pepper**

1 clove of **garlic**, crushed

zest of 1 **lemon**

125ml **water**

1 teaspoon **vegan Dijon mustard**

1 tablespoon **nutritional yeast**

a generous pinch of **salt**

1. First, soak the cashew nuts for the lemon cream in boiling water for 30 minutes, or cover with cold water and soak in the fridge for at least 4 hours or overnight. Mix the chia seeds and water and soak in the fridge for at least 4 hours too.

2. Toss the courgettes with the salt, then allow to drain in a colander over a bowl or the sink for 30 minutes.

3. Squeeze out any excess liquid from the courgettes in a clean tea towel, then mix together with the rest of the fritter ingredients except the oil.

4. Heat a drizzle of oil in a frying pan over medium heat. Using a tablespoon, scoop out portions of the fritter mixture and fry, in batches, for about 1–2 minutes on each side, until golden, puffed up slightly and set.

5. While the fritters are cooking, drain and rinse the cashew nuts, then blend in a high-powered blender with the remaining cashew cream ingredients until smooth.

6. Serve the fritters with the cream for dipping.

STUFFED AUBERGINE ROLLS

3 **aubergines**

2 tablespoons **olive oil**

340g **vegan cream cheese**

6 tablespoons **toasted pine nuts**

2 large handfuls of **fresh basil**,
   finely chopped

1 tablespoon chopped **fresh thyme**

1 bunch of **fresh chives**,
   finely chopped

125g **sun-blush tomatoes**,
   chopped

finely grated zest of 1 **lemon**

a generous pinch of **dried oregano**

2 cloves of **garlic**, crushed

a generous pinch of **salt**

½ teaspoon **freshly ground
   black pepper**

PREP TIME: 20 MINS · COOK TIME: 20 MINS

Griddled aubergine, wrapped around herby vegan cheese. These are made with sun-blush tomatoes, which are oven-roasted tomatoes in a jar, or you could use sun-dried tomatoes instead.

1. Slice the aubergines lengthways into long pieces about 5mm thick. Drizzle the slices with the oil.

2. Heat a griddle pan over a high heat. Cook the aubergine slices in the hot pan, in batches, for about 3 minutes on each side, until they have charred and are soft and cooked through. Repeat with the rest of the slices. Allow to cool.

3. Meanwhile, mix all the remaining ingredients together, reserving half the basil. Taste and add more salt, if needed.

4. Place about 1 tablespoon of the filling mixture on one end of a slice of aubergine, then roll up. Repeat with the remaining slices.

5. Sprinkle over the remaining basil before serving.

TIP
If you have any filling left over, it is great in sandwiches or on toast, or even stirred through hot pasta.

SPANISH CHICKPEA FRITTERS WITH ROMESCO

FOR THE FRITTERS:

I tablespoon **fennel seeds**

I teaspoon **cumin seeds**

I × 400g tin of **chickpeas**, drained

I tablespoon chopped **fresh thyme**
or I teaspoon **dried thyme**

I tablespoon **garlic powder**

I tablespoon **sweet
smoked paprika**

zest of I and juice of 2 **oranges**

I **red pepper**, roasted and finely
chopped (see Tip)

3 **spring onions**, finely chopped

I bunch of **fresh flat-leaf parsley**,
leaves chopped

100g **gram flour**

2 teaspoons **ordinary** or **gluten-
free baking powder**

½ teaspoon **salt**

neutral cooking oil, for frying

FOR THE ROMESCO SAUCE:

20g **blanched almonds**

5 cloves of **garlic**

120ml **extra virgin olive oil**

zest and juice of I **orange**

I tablespoon **vegan sherry vinegar**

I teaspoon **sweet smoked paprika**

I large **red pepper**, roasted (see Tip)

I tablespoon **fresh thyme leaves**

½ teaspoon **salt**, plus extra to taste

**PREP TIME: 25 MINS · STAND TIME: 30 MINS
COOK TIME: 25 MINS**

We love these fritters with their burst of orange zest. They make us
think of sitting by a swimming pool in the sunshine, sangria in hand.

---

1. First, make the fritter batter. Toast the fennel and cumin seeds in
   a hot dry pan over a medium heat for 30 seconds–1 minute, until
   fragrant, then tip on to a plate and allow to cool. Roughly mash the
   chickpeas with a potato masher, leaving some chickpeas whole. Add
   all the remaining ingredients and the toasted seeds to the chickpeas
   and mix until well combined. Allow to stand for at least 30 minutes.

2. Meanwhile, make the romesco. Toast the almonds in a hot dry pan
   for 2 minutes until golden. Tip into a food processor or blender with
   the rest of the ingredients and blend until completely smooth. Taste
   and add another ½ teaspoon salt, if needed.

3. Heat the oven to 200°C/400°F/gas mark 6.

4. Place a large frying pan over a medium heat and pour in enough
   oil to generously cover the base. Test a little nugget of the fritter
   mixture by frying it briefly to check the seasoning. Add more salt, if
   needed. Scoop heaped teaspoons of the mixture into the frying pan
   and flatten gently. Cook, in batches, for a couple of minutes on each
   side, until browned.

5. Transfer the fritters to a large baking sheet and bake for
   5–10 minutes. Serve warm with the romesco sauce for dipping.

> ### TIP
> Roast the red peppers for the fritters and sauce over a gas flame for
> 10–15 minutes, then peel and deseed. Or use roasted red peppers from
> a jar. Serve any leftover romesco sauce with croquetas (see page 178),
> over fried or boiled potatoes, steamed asparagus or broccoli, or with
> chargrilled spring onions.

AUBERGINE WEDGES WITH ALMOND & PARSLEY

4 **aubergines**, each cut into 6 wedges

1½ tablespoons **olive oil**

2 tablespoons **pomegranate molasses**

4 tablespoons **pomegranate seeds**

salt and **freshly ground black pepper**

FOR THE CRUMB:

50g chopped **almonds**

1 clove of **garlic**, minced

2 tablespoons finely chopped **fresh parsley**

½ teaspoon **fine salt**

½ teaspoon **freshly ground black pepper**

FOR THE HARISSA DRESSING:

1–2 teaspoons **salt**

1 tablespoon **cumin seeds**

1 tablespoon **coriander seeds**

1 teaspoon **caraway seeds**

2 tablespoons **dried edible rose petals**

1 **red chilli**

3 long **sweet red peppers** (or 4 **ready-roasted peppers**)

3 cloves of **garlic**

2 tablespoons **olive oil**

juice of 1 **lemon**

FOR THE TAHINI DRESSING:

2 tablespoons **tahini**

2 tablespoons **water**

juice of ½ **lemon**

1 small clove of **garlic**

½ teaspoon **ground cumin**

½ teaspoon **salt**

PREP TIME: 20 MINS · COOK TIME: 30 MINS

This recipe is a favourite of Chantal's daughter Tai and she would eat it every day if she could. The harissa dressing will make more than you need – keep leftovers in the fridge in a clean, sterilized jar with a lid, covered with a thin layer of olive oil.

1. Heat the oven to 200°C/400°F/gas mark 6. Place the aubergine wedges in a single layer in a baking tray, drizzle over the oil and season with a little salt and pepper. Roast for 30 minutes. Allow to cool, the aubergines can be served warm or at room temperature.

2. While the aubergines cook, make the dressings. Blitz 1 teaspoon of the salt with the rest of the harissa ingredients in a food processor or blender, then taste and add the remaining salt if needed. Scrape out and set aside until ready to use. In a separate bowl, whisk all the tahini dressing ingredients together.

3. Toast the almonds in a small dry pan over a low heat, tossing frequently, for 3 minutes (keep watch as they burn easily). Tip the almonds and all the crumb ingredients into a mortar, then bash together with the pestle until you get a crumby texture.

4. Place the cooked aubergine wedges on a serving plate and drizzle with the pomegranate molasses, 6 tablespoons of the harissa dressing and 4 tablespoons of the tahini dressing. (Any leftover tahini dressing will keep covered in the fridge for up to 4 days.) Sprinkle over the nutty crumb and top with the pomegranate seeds.

7

ON THE SIDE

CREARED SPINACH

SERVES 4

350g **baby spinach leaves**,
   tough stems removed

1 tablespoon **olive oil**

½ small **onion**, very finely diced

1 clove of **garlic**, crushed to a
   smooth paste

2 tablespoons **plain** or **gluten-free
   plain flour**

300ml **unsweetened plant milk**
   (use non-nut or non-soya to keep this
   NF or SoF)

a pinch of **freshly grated nutmeg**,
   plus extra to taste

2 teaspoons **lemon juice**, plus extra
   to taste

salt and **freshly ground
   black pepper**

PREP TIME: 10 MINS · COOK TIME: 30 MINS

A decadent way with greens.

1. Have ready a large bowl of cold water. Bring a large pan of water
    to the boil, add the spinach and blanch for 1 minute. Using tongs,
    immediately remove the spinach and plunge it into the cold water.
    Leave for a couple of minutes until completely cold, then drain and
    squeeze out thoroughly. Set aside.

2. Heat the oil in a large pan, add the onion and a pinch of salt and
    cook gently over a low heat, stirring often, for about 10 minutes, until
    soft and translucent, but not coloured. Add the garlic and cook for
    another minute.

3. Add the flour to the pan and stir well. Cook for 2 minutes, stirring.
    Gradually add the milk, whisking well after each addition to get rid of
    any lumps. Add the nutmeg and plenty of pepper.

4. Turn the heat down to low and cook, stirring, for about 5 minutes,
    until the sauce begins to thicken. Add the spinach and stir well until
    incorporated, then cook, stirring, until heated through and the
    spinach is not clumped together. Remove from the heat and add the
    lemon juice, then taste and season with more salt,
    pepper, nutmeg or lemon juice, if needed,
    and serve.

CREAMY POLENTA

GF WF NF SoF

500ml **boiling water**

100g **fine** or **coarse polenta**
(not quick cook) or **cornmeal**

½ teaspoon **salt**

1 tablespoon **refined coconut oil** or
vegan butter or **margarine**
(use non-nut or non-soya to keep this
NF or SoF, use less salt if using butter
or margarine)

TO SERVE: (OPTIONAL)

3 tablespoons **unsweetened
plant milk** (use non-nut or non-
soya to keep this NF or SoF)

1 tablespoon **nutritional yeast**

a generous pinch of **garlic powder**

PREP TIME: 5 MINS · COOK TIME: 35 MINS

Try this with mushrooms and shredded greens, both sautéed in garlic, black pepper and olive oil. Choose a coarse polenta for more texture, or fine polenta for a softer, smoother result.

1. Bring the water to the boil in a large pan over a medium heat. Gradually add the polenta, stirring well as you go to avoid lumps. When smooth, bring to a simmer, but beware: it can bubble up rather explosively.

2. Turn the heat down to low and cook for about 30 minutes, stirring frequently to prevent it sticking to the bottom of the pan. Add a splash more water if the mixture is too thick – a spoonful of the polenta should slowly slip off the spoon and back into the pan. When ready, the polenta should be creamy in texture and not at all gritty (exactly how long it takes will vary from brand to brand).

3. Add the salt and oil or butter. For really creamy polenta, add the milk and mix well. For really creamy and cheesy polenta, add the milk, yeast and garlic powder.

4. Check the seasoning and serve.

BOULANGÈRE POTATOES

650g **Maris Piper potatoes**,
  peeled or unpeeled

1 **onion**

60ml **olive oil**, plus extra for greasing

leaves from 1 sprig of **fresh
  rosemary** or 3 sprigs of **fresh
  thyme**, or a mixture

1 **bay leaf**, torn

300ml hot **vegan vegetable stock**
  (see page 140 for homemade)

salt and **freshly ground
  black pepper**

PREP TIME: 10 MINS · COOK TIME: 1 HOUR 10 MINS

The story goes that boulangère potatoes ('baker's potatoes') were
cooked in the village bakery's oven. As they cook, the thinly sliced
potatoes absorb all the rich flavour from the stock, onions and herbs.

1. Heat the oven to 180°C/350°F/gas mark 4. Slice the potatoes and
    onion as thinly as possible, ideally using a mandolin.

2. Line the bottom of a lightly greased medium gratin dish with a third
    of the potatoes, then arrange half the onion and herbs on top. Season
    well with salt and pepper and cover with another third of the potatoes
    and the remaining onion and herbs. Season well. Finish with a layer of
    potatoes. Press everything down firmly, using your hands.

3. Whisk together the hot stock and 2 tablespoons of the olive oil, then
    pour over the potatoes. It probably won't cover everything, but don't
    worry. Drizzle over the remaining oil.

4. Bake for about 10 minutes, then remove from the oven and gently
    press down again, using a spoon or spatula. The potatoes will have
    softened slightly and the stock will now cover more of them.

5. Return to the oven and bake for another 50–60 minutes, or until the
    top is deep golden and a sharp knife inserted into the centre meets no
    resistance. Allow to stand for 5 minutes before serving.

TIP
This recipe also works with other root vegetables – try adding carrots,
parsnips, celeriac or even beetroot. For a sweeter allium flavour, cook it
with thinly sliced leeks and garlic, as well as the onion. For a richer dish,
add a splash of vegan cream to the stock (as long as you know you have
found a brand that won't curdle when heated).

POLENTA CHEESY CHIPS

SERVES 4

GF WF NF SoF

PREP TIME: 10 MINS · CHILL TIME: 4 HOURS
COOK TIME: 55 MINS

100g **fine** or **coarse polenta**
(not quick cook) or **cornmeal**
500ml **boiling water**
½ teaspoon **salt**
1 tablespoon refined **coconut oil** or
vegan butter or **margarine**
(use non-nut or non-soya to keep this
NF or SoF, use less salt if using butter
or margarine)
3 tablespoons **unsweetened plant
milk** (use non-nut or non-soya to
keep this NF or SoF)
1 tablespoon **nutritional yeast**
a generous pinch of **garlic powder**
neutral cooking oil, for frying

Rebecca's kids love these 'cheesy' chips with their crunchy exterior and soft creamy centre. They dunk them in ketchup, but grown-ups might prefer to serve them with vegan salsa verde (see page 231) or garlicky aioli (see page 222)…or ketchup. Polenta and cornmeal are the same thing, but you might come across a number of options – yellow, white, fine and coarse. All will work in this recipe, with fine cornmeal giving a squidgier, smoother end result, and coarse cornmeal resulting in a crisper coating but more textured centre.

1. Cook the polenta in the boiling water following the method on page 211.

2. Add the remaining ingredients except the oil for frying and stir well, then check the seasoning.

3. Pour the polenta into a large 30 × 25cm baking tray lined with baking parchment. Smooth it over with a spatula until flat and about 1–1.5cm thick. Allow to cool, then place in the fridge to firm up for at least 4 hours, ideally overnight.

4. When set, slide the block of polenta on to a chopping board and slice into chunky chips, about 1.5 × 8cm.

5. Heat 5mm of cooking oil in a large frying pan over a medium heat until hot. Using a spatula, carefully slide a batch of chips into the hot oil and cook for 3–4 minutes, or until pale golden and crisp on the bottom. Gently turn over and cook on the other side. Remove with a slotted spoon, allowing any excess oil to drain back into the pan. Drain on kitchen paper and keep warm while you cook the rest of the chips.

TIP
You can also griddle or barbecue firm polenta. Once chilled and firmly set, cut into wedge shapes or triangles (smaller shapes might slip through the barbecue grill). Brush well with oil, then place on a hot barbecue or griddle pan and cook for 2–3 minutes on each side.

DOUBLE-COOKED SPICED PLANTAIN

SERVES 4

2 **green plantains**, unpeeled
½ teaspoon **salt**
a generous pinch of **freshly ground black pepper**
½ teaspoon **garlic powder**
½ teaspoon **chilli powder**
zest of 1 **lime**
about 200ml **vegetable oil**

PREP TIME: 15 MINS · COOK TIME: 1 HOUR

For scooping dips, as a side like fries, to use as crostini or just for snacking on. If you prefer these without spice, omit the garlic powder, chilli and lime and serve lightly coated in salt and pepper.

1. Make an incision into the peel of each plantain from top to bottom, then slice into 2cm rounds and peel the skin from each disc.

2. Place the plantain slices in a deep pan of boiling salted water and cook over a medium heat for 35–40 minutes, or until beginning to soften and become tender like parboiled potatoes. (The cooked pieces will need to be crushed, but they should not be too soft or they will fall apart.) Drain and allow to cool slightly.

3. Mix together the remaining ingredients except the oil in a large bowl and set aside.

4. Meanwhile, pour the oil into a large, fairly deep frying pan to a depth of about 1cm and heat. Place the plantain slices between 2 sheets of baking parchment. Using something heavy and flat (like the bottom of a tin or a heavy pan), crush each slice until about 5mm thick.

5. Fry the slices in the hot oil, in batches, for about 2 minutes on each side, or until golden. Remove with tongs or a slotted spoon, allowing the excess oil to drain back into the pan. Drain on kitchen paper.

6. When cooked, place the slices in the spice mixture and toss to coat each piece. Serve immediately.

TIP
These can be served with dips like guacamole (see page 234) and hummus (see page 60), or with chutney.

SMOKY POTATO WEDGES

SERVES
4

GF WF NF SoF

3 tablespoons **neutral cooking oil**
½ teaspoon **sweet
   smoked paprika**
a large pinch of **salt**
400g **sweet potatoes**, unpeeled
400g **white potatoes**, unpeeled

PREP TIME: 10 MINS · COOK TIME: 35 MINS

You can use all white potatoes or all sweet potatoes here, but we love a mixture for flavour and goodness – sweet potatoes are rich in vitamins A, C and B6.

1. Heat the oven to 200°C/400°F/gas mark 6. Whisk together the oil, paprika and salt.

2. Scrub the sweet potatoes and potatoes to remove any dirt, then pat dry. Cut into wedges about 8cm long and 1cm thick at their widest point. Toss in the oil mixture, then place in a baking dish and spread out in a single layer.

3. Bake for 15 minutes, then carefully turn each one. Return to the oven for another 20 minutes, or until each piece is golden all over and soft inside.

OLIVE OIL MASHED POTATOES

SERVES
4

 (GF) (WF) (NF) (SoF)

1kg **Maris Piper potatoes**, peeled
   and cut into chunks
3 cloves of **garlic**, unpeeled
25–50ml **mild-tasting olive oil**
50ml **unsweetened plant milk**
   (use non-nut or non-soya to keep this
   NF or SoF)
salt

PREP TIME: 10 MINS · COOK TIME: 20 MINS

Rich and silky mashed potatoes, made using an old Italian technique.

1. Bring a large deep pan of water to the boil, add a pinch of salt and the potatoes. Cook for 15–20 minutes, until very tender but not falling apart. Drain the potatoes, then return to the pan.

2. Meanwhile, cook the garlic cloves, still in their skins, in a hot dry pan over a medium heat for 10 minutes, turning often, until soft and sweet. Allow to cool slightly.

3. Mix 25ml of the oil and the milk together.

4. Pop the garlic cloves from their skins and crush into a smooth paste, then add to the drained potatoes and pour in the milk mixture. Mash the potatoes until completely smooth, ideally using a potato ricer. (Don't be tempted to blend the potatoes, though, as this can make them gluey.)

5. Taste and add salt and the rest of the oil, if needed. Serve immediately.

> **TIP**
> If you love cashew cream (see page 228) and don't need this to be nut free, or have found a good brand of vegan cream, stir a couple of tablespoons into the mash, just before serving.

LIME & CORIANDER CORN ON THE COB

SERVES

4

(GF) (WF) (NF) (SoF)

PREP TIME: 15 MINS · COOK TIME: 10 MINS

Chantal loves cooking this on the barbecue with her kids in the summer.

zest and juice of 1 **lime**

2 small bunches of **fresh coriander**,
  leaves finely chopped

2 teaspoons **olive oil**, plus extra for
  frying (optional)

5 **spring onions**, finely sliced

2 cloves of **garlic**, minced

½ teaspoon **fine salt**

4 ears of **corn on the cob**

freshly ground black pepper

1. Mix together the lime zest, coriander, oil, spring onions, garlic, salt and some pepper in a large shallow dish. Add the sweetcorn and massage the mixture into each cob. Remove from the marinade, reserving the marinade in the dish.

2. Barbecue the corn on a grill over white-hot coals, turning regularly, for 5–10 minutes, until cooked on all sides. Alternatively, heat a splash of oil in a large frying pan over a high heat, add the cobs and cook for 8–10 minutes, turning often until cooked all over.

3. Add the lime juice to the reserved marinade, then add the cooked sweetcorn and spoon it over. Serve immediately.

SIDE DISHES

COCONUT RICE & PEAS

1 tablespoon **refined** or **extra virgin coconut oil**

1 **onion**, finely diced

5 cloves of **garlic**, finely chopped

1 tablespoon chopped **fresh thyme**

1 **bay leaf**

250g **basmati rice**

250ml **water**

250ml **coconut milk**

1 × 400g tin of **kidney beans**, drained

salt and **freshly ground black pepper**

PREP TIME: 5 MINS · COOK TIME: 45 MINS

Serve this with the plantain curry on page 133 or with some cooked batched jackfruit (see page 50), seitan or firm tofu, tossed in jerk marinade from a jar and stir-fried or browned in a hot oven.

1. Heat the oil in a large pan over a medium-high heat. When hot, add the onion and garlic and cook for 4 minutes, then add the thyme and bay leaf and cook for another 4–6 minutes, until the vegetables are slightly caramelized.

2. Add the rice and toss in the onion mixture for 1–2 minutes, until slightly toasted. Stir in the water, coconut milk and kidney beans and season with salt and pepper.

3. Turn up the heat to high and bring to a steady simmer. Cover and cook for 10 minutes, then turn off the heat and allow to steam, covered, for 20 minutes. Check the seasoning and serve.

CARROT & RAISIN RICE

SERVES
4

(GF) (WF) (NF) (SoF)

2 tablespoons **olive oil**

I **onion**, finely diced

I clove of **garlic**, minced

½ teaspoon **ground turmeric**

I teaspoon **cumin seeds**

2 **cardamom pods**, bruised

I stick of **cinnamon**

2 **carrots**, coarsely grated

75g **raisins**

185g **basmati rice**

480ml **water**

½ teaspoon **salt**

freshly ground black pepper

PREP TIME: 10 MINS · COOK TIME: 45 MINS

A gently spiced golden-coloured rice.

1. Heat the oil in a heavy-based pan, add the onion and fry over a medium heat for about 10 minutes, until beginning to caramelize. Add the garlic, spices and cinnamon stick and cook for another minute, stirring, until fragrant.

2. Stir in the carrots and raisins and cook for another 5 minutes. Stir in the rice and toast in the carrot mixture for 2 minutes.

3. Add the water, salt and pepper and bring to the boil, then turn the heat down and simmer for 10 minutes, uncovered. Turn the heat off, cover and steam for 10–15 minutes, or until the rice is tender and fluffy.

SAUCES, MAYOS & DRESSINGS

GARLICKY AIOLI

Place 4 heaped tablespoons **vegan mayonnaise** (see page 224 for homemade) in a bowl. Add 1 clove of **garlic**, crushed to a paste, ½ teaspoon **vegan Dijon mustard** and 1 teaspoon **extra virgin olive oil** and whisk well to combine. Add more mustard or olive oil for a stronger flavour.

SPICY CHIPOTLE MAYO

Stir 1 teaspoon **vegan chipotle paste** into 4 heaped tablespoons **vegan mayonnaise** (see page 224 for homemade) until smooth, then taste and add more chipotle, if necessary – it should be smoky and spicy. If the paste causes the mayo to thin slightly, place in the fridge to thicken again. (Alternatively, using the same ratio of mayo to spice, add Korean gochujang chilli paste or sriracha hot sauce.)

TARTARE SAUCE

To serve with 'fish' and chips (see page 98) or in hot wraps (see page 103).

Mix 4 heaped tablespoons **vegan mayonnaise** (see page 224 for homemade) with 1 tablespoon rinsed and roughly chopped **capers**, 1 tablespoon finely chopped **gherkin** or **cucumber dill pickles**, 1 tablespoon finely chopped **shallot** (optional) and 1 tablespoon finely chopped **fresh parsley**. Add **salt** and **freshly ground black pepper**, to taste. Serve straight away or keep, covered, in the fridge for up to 4 days.

SMOKY SPANISH DRESSING

For salad leaves, cooked potatoes or roasted peppers.

Place the following in a sealable jar: 1 minced clove of **garlic**, 2 teaspoons **sweet smoked paprika**, 2 tablespoons **vegan sherry vinegar**, the zest and juice of 2½ **oranges**, 1 tablespoon chopped **fresh thyme**, 100ml **olive oil**, a generous pinch of **freshly ground black pepper** and ½ teaspoon **salt**. Shake together. Add more salt, if needed.

TAHINI YOGHURT DRESSING

 (GF) (WF) (NF) (SoF)

A rich nutty dressing that also goes with Middle Eastern lentil, couscous, freekeh or roasted vegetable-based salads, as well as green salads and slaws.

Whisk together 2 tablespoons **tahini** and 3 tablespoons **non-dairy plain yoghurt** (use non-nut or non-soya to keep this NF or SoF) until smooth. Add a pinch of **salt** and 1 teaspoon **lemon juice** or more to taste, then slowly add enough water to make the dressing thick but pourable. This will keep, covered, in the fridge for up to 4 days. (Try adding crushed **garlic** or very finely chopped herbs, like **dill**, **parsley** and **mint**.)

QUICK BARBECUE SAUCE

 (GF) (WF) (NF) (SoF)

For pulled jackfruit, for burgers, for mac-n-no-cheese (see page 114), to go with nachos, or for dunking fries, sweet potato wedges or cauliflower.

Blend the following together until smooth: 2 cloves of **garlic** and 2 **shallots**, both roughly chopped, 2 teaspoons **tomato purée**, 1 tablespoon **tamarind paste**, 1 teaspoon **mustard powder**, 2 teaspoons **black treacle**, 1 tablespoon **vegan cider vinegar**, 2 teaspoons **paprika**, 2 tablespoons **soft brown sugar**, 2 tablespoons **olive oil** (choose one with a mild flavour), 2 teaspoons **liquid smoke** (or the same of **sweet smoked paprika**), ½ teaspoon **cornflour**, 125ml **water**, ½ teaspoon **salt** and some **freshly ground black pepper**. Pour into a small, heavy-based pan and bring to the boil over a medium heat, then immediately turn the heat right down. Cook, stirring regularly, for 15 minutes, until the raw flavours have melded to create a sweet, tangy, smoky sauce. Add more smoke, sugar or salt, if needed. Cool before serving, or to store, pour the still-hot sauce into a clean, sterilized heatproof jar or bottle with a lid. Seal and keep in the fridge for up to 1 month. Once opened, eat within 5 days.

RANCH DRESSING

 (GF) (WF) (NF) (SoF)

Place 4 heaped tablespoons **vegan mayonnaise** (see page 224 for homemade), or for a very tangy dressing use 5 tablespoons **non-dairy plain yoghurt** (use non-nut or non-soya to keep this NF or SoF) instead, in a bowl. Add 2 teaspoons very finely chopped **dill**, 1½ tablespoons very finely chopped **fresh parsley**, 1½ tablespoons very finely chopped **fresh chives**, a generous pinch of **garlic powder**, 1 teaspoon **vegan cider vinegar** and 1 teaspoon **lemon juice**. Stir together. Add 2 tablespoons **unsweetened plant milk** (use non-nut or non-soya to keep this NF or SoF) and mix. Slowly add more milk as needed, until the dressing is as thick as syrup. Taste and add more vinegar, lemon, **salt** or **freshly ground black pepper**, as necessary. Use immediately or store, covered, in the fridge for a couple of days.

VEGAN MAYONNAISE

MAKES

1 × *250ml*

(GF) (WF) (NF) (SoF)

2 teaspoons **vegan cider vinegar**

1 teaspoon **lemon juice**

¾ teaspoon **mustard powder**

a generous pinch of **salt**

3 tablespoons **reduced aquafaba**
   (see Tip)

5 **chickpeas**, from a tin

150ml **neutral cooking oil**
   (not coconut oil)

PREP TIME: 10 MINS

Maybe we shouldn't say so, but we prefer our homemade mayo to most of the ones sold in jars. It is creamy, tangy, rich and almost impossible to tell the difference from the traditional version. Adding a tiny pinch of black salt (see page 38) will add an even more authentic eggy flavour to this. Use a stick blender for this recipe.

We got the idea for including a few chickpeas from the Serious Eats Vegan Experience food blog – every year food-science writer J. Kenji López-Alt has a vegan month where he explores the science of vegan cookery, and we can't recommend it enough. He suggests using chickpeas to help stabilize the mayo's emulsion, and he's right.

1. Place the vinegar, lemon juice, mustard powder, salt, aquafaba and chickpeas in a tall, thin container big enough for a stick blender (or use the stick blender jug) and whizz until smooth, pale and completely combined.

2. Very slowly drizzle the oil into the container, whizzing constantly on the highest setting possible. It may take up to 5 minutes, but the mixture should start to thicken and turn white as you gradually add the oil.

3. The mayo will keep, covered or in a glass jar with a lid, in the fridge for up to 5 days.

TIP
You need aquafaba (tinned chickpea water, see page 12) that is quite thick for this recipe. Different brands of chickpeas can behave differently – so if your aquafaba is watery, rather than gloopy, simmer it on the hob to reduce it by half, then cool before using. If the mayo blends but doesn't thicken, don't despair – you probably need to try a different brand of chickpea. Keep the resulting milky mixture and use it as a base for ranch or Caesar salad dressing (see pages 223 and 173).

STRINGY 'CHEESE' SAUCE

SERVES 8 **AS A MAIN**

(GF) (WF) (SoF)

75g **unroasted cashew nuts**

500ml **cold water**

4 tablespoons **tapioca flour**

1 clove of **garlic**, crushed to a
    smooth paste

juice of ½ **lemon**

1 teaspoon **nutritional yeast**

a pinch of **black salt** (see page 38)

½ teaspoon **salt**, plus extra to taste

PREP TIME: 10 MINS · SOAK TIME: 30 MINS
COOK TIME: 15 MINS

Use this to top pizzas, in hot sandwiches, as cheese on toast, on top of
pasta bakes or in lasagne or moussaka.

1. Soak the cashew nuts in boiling water for at least 30 minutes, or cover
   with cold water and soak in the fridge for at least 4 hours or overnight.

2. Drain and rinse the cashew nuts, then place in a high-powered
   blender with the remaining ingredients and blend on high until
   smooth. Taste and add more salt, if needed.

3. Pour the cashew mixture into a hot pan over a medium heat and cook
   gently for about 15 minutes, stirring constantly, until the mixture
   becomes thick and stringy like melted mozzarella.

4. Allow to cool before using. Wrap well and store in the fridge for up to
   4 days.

VARIATION: SMOKY SPICED STRINGY 'CHEESE'

When blending the soaked cashew nuts and other ingredients, add
1 tablespoon vegan chipotle paste, zest of ½ lime, ½ teaspoon ground
cumin, 1 teaspoon garlic powder and 1 teaspoon smoked sweet paprika.
When the cashew mixture has started to thicken in the pan, add 2 finely
chopped spring onions, a handful of finely chopped fresh coriander and
2 tablespoons finely chopped pickled jalapeños. Stir to combine and cook
as above until thick and stringy.

SAUCES, MAYOS & DRESSINGS

CASHEW CREAM

MAKES

1 × 350ml

150g **unroasted cashew nuts**

100ml **cold water**, plus more
   as needed

FOR SOURED CREAM:

¼ teaspoon **lemon juice**,
   plus extra to taste

¼ teaspoon **vegan cider vinegar**,
   plus extra to taste

a pinch of **nutritional yeast**
   (optional)

a pinch of **salt**

FOR SWEETENED CREAM:

½ teaspoon **vanilla extract**

1 teaspoon **maple syrup**, or to taste

a pinch of **salt**

PREP TIME: 5 MINS · SOAK TIME: 30 MINS

Whether you are vegan or just embracing a more plant-based way of eating, cashew nuts are your new best friend. They are relatively bland, but rich, and so make excellent creams and yoghurts.

1. Soak the cashew nuts in boiling water for 30 minutes, or cover with cold water and soak in the fridge for at least 4 hours or overnight.

2. When ready to make the cream, drain and rinse the cashew nuts. Tip into a high-powered blender and add the cold water. Blend on high until completely smooth, gradually adding more water as necessary to get the texture you want.

3. Leave as it is, or add the extra soured or sweetened cream ingredients. Store, covered, in the fridge for up to 5 days.

TIP

Adding more water to the cashew cream can leave you with something closer to single dairy cream, so add water very gradually if you want a thicker cream or plan to use this as a base for yoghurt, as soured cream or as a whipped pudding topping.

SAUCES, MAYOS & DRESSINGS

MAKES

1 × 125ml

PREP TIME: 5 MINS

VEGAN BUTTERS

It's hard to find a vegan margarine or butter on the market that doesn't contain palm oil and does the job of traditional butter when it comes to melting on a hot piece of toast, so we set out to create one. We have two methods – one involving white miso and one using pickle brine – and you should experiment with both to see which one you like best. Both taste buttery, rather than of pickle or miso.

Traditional butter is cultured, which gives it its flavour. Both miso and pickles are fermented, too, and pickle brine in particular is rich in lactic acid, which is found in butter. (We use it in mac and 'cheese' sauce, for the same reason.) However, because miso and pickle brine vary in both their punch and saltiness, you should treat this as a guide and add salt to suit your taste.

Choose a natural pickle brine from a jar of pickled vegetables that isn't full of other herbs or flavourings, and which doesn't contain vinegar – cabbage is good.

Sunflower lecithin is sold in health food shops as a supplement, but it is also a brilliant natural emulsifier. You can buy it as a powder or liquid (halve the quantities below if you use a liquid). Without it, the chilled butter will have a grainy texture, as the fats and liquids separate.

Once you find a balance that works for you, you can make this 'butter' in bulk and freeze it. It keeps for up to 4 days in the fridge, so we tend to make small quantities more often.

Both butters are a pale creamy colour. If you want yellow butter, add a pinch of turmeric, but be sparing – we accidentally made neon, glow-in-the-dark butter... and no one would eat it. The method is the same for both the butters.

MISO BUTTER

40ml **unsweetened plant milk** (use non-nut or non-soya to keep this NF or SoF)

2 teaspoons **sunflower lecithin powder**

1 tablespoon **neutral vegetable oil** (sunflower is good)

½ teaspoon **white** or **yellow miso paste** (use non-soya to keep this SoF)

¼ teaspoon **vegan cider vinegar**

80g **refined coconut oil**, melted until liquid

good-quality **sea salt**

PICKLE BUTTER

   SoF

40ml **unsweetened plant milk** (use non-nut or non-soya to keep this NF or SoF)

2 teaspoons **sunflower lecithin powder**

2 teaspoons **pickle brine**

1 tablespoon **neutral vegetable oil** (sunflower is good)

80g **refined coconut oil**, melted until liquid

good-quality **sea salt**

1. Place all the ingredients except the melted coconut oil and salt in a tall, thin container big enough for a stick blender (or use the stick blender jug) and whizz until smooth. Add the melted coconut oil and whizz again. Taste and add salt, if needed, then whizz one more time.

2. Pour into a clean jar or tub with a lid and refrigerate until firm before using as a spread. Store in the fridge for up to 4 days.

DIPS & RELISHES

SERVE 4

RED PEPPER & WALNUT DIP

 (GF) (WF) (SoF)

Although this is a dip, it can also be served as a relish with grilled vegetables, like aubergines, courgettes, charred spring onions or roasted roots.

Gently toast 100g **walnuts** in a small, hot, dry pan over a medium heat, stirring frequently, for a couple of minutes. Add 1 tablespoon **cumin seeds** and toast for 30 seconds until fragrant. Blend in a food processor with 2 roasted **red peppers** (see Tip, page 204), 3 tablespoons **extra virgin olive oil**, ½ teaspoon **salt**, 6 cloves of **garlic** and 1 tablespoon **pomegranate molasses** until it forms a smooth paste.

NUT CHEESE & CHIVE DIP

 (GF) (WF) (SoF)

Soak 200g **unroasted cashew nuts** in boiling water for 30 minutes, or cover with cold water and soak in the fridge for 4 hours or overnight. Drain and rinse. Blend in a high-powered blender with 215ml **cold water**, 1 tablespoon **vegan cider vinegar**, 2 tablespoons **nutritional yeast**, 3 cloves of **garlic**, 2 tablespoons **non-dairy plain yoghurt** (we use **coconut yoghurt** or **cashew yoghurt**), ½ teaspoon **salt** and ½ teaspoon **black pepper**. Add 3 tablespoons each of finely chopped **fresh chives** and **parsley**, mix, then taste and add more salt, if needed.

TZATZIKI

 (GF) (WF) (NF) (SoF)

A cooling mint and garlic sauce, to go with Middle Eastern dishes or curries, in sandwiches or as a dip.

Grate 1 **cucumber** and sprinkle with 1 tablespoon **salt**. Allow to stand in a seive for about 20 minutes to draw out the moisture. Tip the cucumber onto a clean tea towel and squeeze out the excess water. In a clean bowl, mix the cucumber with 200ml **non-dairy plain yoghurt** (use non-nut or non-soya to keep this NF or SoF), the juice of ½ **lemon**, 1 minced clove of **garlic**, 1 small bunch of **fresh mint**, finely chopped, and a generous pinch of **freshly ground black pepper**. Taste and add extra salt, pepper or lemon juice, as necessary.

SMOKY CASHEW QUESO SAUCE

 (GF) (WF)

To use on top of nachos, over chilli cheese dogs (see page 118), or as a dip.

Blitz 6 tablespoons **cashew cream** (see page 228), 3 tablespoons **nutritional yeast**, a scant ½ teaspoon **sweet smoked paprika**, 1 tablespoon **lime juice**, 1 teaspoon **tomato purée**, 1 teaspoon **white** or **yellow miso paste** (optional), 1 tablespoon **neutral cooking oil** (not coconut oil; the oil is optional, but it gives a smoother, creamier texture) and a large pinch of **salt** in a food processor or blender until smooth. Taste and add more salt, if needed. The end result should be salty, smoky, creamy, cheesy and very moreish.

DATE & PRESERVED LEMON CHUTNEY

   (GF) (WF) (NF) (SoF)

This is fabulous with the spiced Moroccan tofu on page 76, or with couscous or quinoa, steamed and mixed with pulses and roasted vegetables.

Gently toast ⅛ teaspoon **cumin** seeds in a small, hot dry pan over a medium heat, stirring frequently, for 30 seconds–1 minute. Halve 2 **preserved lemons**, remove the flesh and pips and discard. Finely dice the skin and 100g **pitted dates**. Pummel 1 clove of **garlic** with ½ teaspoon **salt** to form a purée. Mix with the cumin, diced dates and lemons, 50g finely chopped **fresh coriander**, 1 bunch of finely chopped **fresh parsley**, a peeled and grated 3cm piece of **fresh ginger**, the juice of ¼ **lemon** and 3 tablespoons **extra virgin olive oil**. Use immediately, or to store, place in a jar with a lid, cover the surface with a layer of oil and keep in the fridge for up to a week.

SALSA VERDE

   (GF) (WF) (NF) (SoF)

This tart green sauce can be diluted with more oil and used as salad dressing for lentil or gram-based salads, or is delicious drizzled over warm new potatoes, roasted vegetables (especially sweet roots like carrots) or squash and even whole cobs of corn. It is really good dolloped on top of risotto, as well.

Strip the leaves from 8 sprigs of **fresh parsley**, 5 sprigs of **fresh basil** and 1 sprig of **fresh mint**, then place in a bowl. Add 1 tablespoon **rinsed capers**, 2 teaspoons **vegan red wine vinegar**, 1 crushed clove of **garlic**, 2 teaspoons **vegan Dijon mustard**, a pinch of **kelp powder** (optional) and 8 tablespoons **extra virgin olive oil**. Blitz with a stick blender to a rough pesto-like purée (or pummel using a pestle and mortar). Add **salt**, if needed, and a dose of **freshly ground black pepper**. (If the kelp powder or capers are salty, you may not need any salt at all.) Depending on what you're serving this with, you could also add **tarragon** or diced **shallot**.

PICO DE GALLO

    (GF) (WF) (NF) (SoF)

Use this raw salsa in tacos or alongside any Mexican-style dish.

Mix 2 finely diced **shallots** with 450g deseeded and finely chopped **tomatoes**. Add the juice of ½ **lime**, 1–2 teaspoons finely chopped **red chilli**, 2 tablespoons finely chopped **fresh coriander** and a pinch of **salt**. Taste and add more salt, if needed.

COCONUT CHUTNEY

    (GF) (WF) (NF) (SoF)

Heat 1 tablespoon **vegetable oil** in a small pan. When hot, add 2 teaspoons **mustard seeds** and a large pinch of **cumin seeds** and toast, just until they begin to crackle. Remove from the heat and add 1 teaspoon grated **fresh ginger**. Stir and let sizzle.

Tip 8 tablespoons **desiccated coconut** into a heatproof bowl and add 100ml **boiling water**, the toasted spices and a good pinch of **salt**. Mix together and add more boiling water until you get a good consistency – it should be thick rather than watery, but not stiff. Allow to cool before serving.

BABAGANOUSH

SERVES 8 WITH OTHER DISHES

(GF) (WF) (NF) (SoF)

3 large **aubergines**

2–3 tablespoons **lemon juice**

2 cloves of **garlic**, crushed to a paste

1 tablespoon **tahini** (optional)

3 tablespoons **olive oil**

1 tablespoon finely chopped **fresh parsley**

salt

PREP TIME: 10 MINS · COOK TIME: 15 MINS

Dip crudités, hunks of bread or strips of toasted pitta into this, or use in sandwiches or to top crostini as a party nibble or snack. It's best to cook the aubergines over a gas flame or on a barbecue, but you can also use the grill. (Protect the hob top with aluminium foil to make cleaning up easier.)

1. Place each aubergine directly over a gas flame on the hob, or place all three on a grill over a hot barbecue (the coals should be white). Cook, turning often, until blackened, blistered and charred. Each aubergine will take about 15 minutes. This is quite a smoky process, so open a window or use an extractor fan. Alternatively, heat the grill to its highest setting, place the aubergines underneath and cook until charred all over and completely collapsed.

2. Transfer the cooked aubergines to a sieve set over a bowl or the sink and allow to drain and cool. When cool enough to handle, place on a board and slice open lengthways, so they open like a book. Scoop out the soft flesh with a spoon, discarding any very seedy bits.

3. Place the flesh in a bowl with 2 tablespoons of the lemon juice and the garlic and mash roughly. Next add the tahini, if using, and olive oil, then mix and mash until you have a textured, creamy purée. Stir in the chopped parsley. Taste and add the rest of the lemon juice, and salt, if needed. The finished dip should be smoky, sharp from the lemon and garlicky.

4. The dip will keep, covered, in the fridge for a couple of days, but is best served at room temperature.

TIP

If you love mint, it works really well here, so add 1 tablespoon finely chopped fresh mint at the same time as the parsley.

GUACAMOLE

4 OR MAKES 200g

(GF) (WF) (NF) (SoF)

1 clove of **garlic**

2 ripe **avocados**

2 **spring onions**, finely chopped

2 tablespoons finely chopped
fresh coriander

zest and juice of ½ **lime**

a generous pinch each of **salt** and
freshly ground black pepper

PREP TIME: 5 MINS · COOK TIME: 3 MINS (OPTIONAL)

Avocados are stuffed with healthy fats, as well vitamins K, C, all the Bs, E and lots of fibre.

1. If you prefer a milder flavour, blanch the garlic in a pan of boiling water for 3 minutes, then drain and mince.

2. In a bowl, mash the avocados with a fork. We like some texture to our guac, but mash it as smooth as you like. Mix in the garlic and remaining ingredients, then check the seasoning.

3. Guacamole is best eaten soon after making, but if you need to store it, keep in the fridge for up to 24 hours with a layer of clingfilm or kitchen paper pressed on to the surface to stop it from going brown.

AVOCADO CREMA

4 WITH TACOS

(GF) (WF) (SoF)

60g **cashew cream** (see page 228)

60g **avocado** (about 1 avocado)

1 tablespoon **lime juice**, plus extra
to taste

1 tablespoon finely chopped
fresh coriander

a pinch of **ground cumin**

a large pinch of **salt**

PREP TIME: 5 MINS

This guacamole alternative is especially good with 'fish'-style tacos (see page 63). If you don't have cashew cream, you could use non-dairy plain yoghurt (but not coconut yoghurt). If serving a large group, double up the recipe.

1. Put all the ingredients in a food processor or blender and process until completely smooth. Taste and add more salt or lime, if needed.

FRESH MANGO CHUTNEY

MAKES

1 × 500ML

   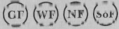

1 tablespoon **refined** or **extra virgin coconut oil**

1 **onion**, finely diced

4 cloves of **garlic**, minced

6cm piece of **fresh ginger**, peeled and minced or grated

1 **red chilli** (less if you're serving to little ones), deseeded if you prefer a milder chutney and finely chopped

2 teaspoons **nigella seeds**

1 teaspoon **coriander seeds**

1 teaspoon **cumin seeds**

1 teaspoon **yellow** (or **white**) **mustard seeds**

2 **green cardamom pods**, bruised

3 **fresh** or **frozen mangoes**, peeled and cut into 2cm chunks

250ml **water**

squeeze of **lime juice** (optional)

salt

PREP TIME: 20 MINS · COOK TIME: 1 HOUR 5 MINS

Serve this spiced fresh fruit chutney with curry. Leftovers should be frozen, since this chutney isn't made with lots of sugar.

1. Heat the oil in a heavy-based pan over a medium-high heat. When hot, add the onion and cook for about 10 minutes, until translucent and starting to brown. Add the garlic, ginger and chilli and cook for another 4 minutes.

2. Add all the spices and cook for about a minute, then add the mangoes and the water. Bring to the boil, then turn down to a low simmer, cover and cook for about 45 minutes, stirring regularly, until the mango begins to break down. The chutney should be lumpy with a good bit of texture, but exactly how long it takes for the chutney to cook will depend on how ripe the mango is.

3. When cooked, season with salt to taste and the lime juice, if you think it needs a little tartness. Fish out the cardamom pods and allow to cool before serving.

4. Store in the fridge, covered, or in a tub or jar, for a couple of days, or freeze.

TAMARIND YOGHURT

MAKES

1 × 125ml

2 teaspoons **tamarind paste**

125ml **non-dairy plain yoghurt** (use non-nut or non-soya to keep this NF or SoF)

2 teaspoons finely chopped **fresh mint**

a pinch of **ground cumin**

a pinch of **salt**

PREP TIME: 5 MINS

This works well with lots of curries and Asian dishes. Serve it with the vegetable samosas on page 182.

1. Stir together all the tamarind yoghurt ingredients. Taste and add more salt, if needed.

CASHEW YOGHURT

MAKES
1 × 300ml

(GF) (WF) (SoF)

300ml **cashew cream** (see page 228)
1½ teaspoons **probiotic powder***

*The probiotic powder should
include some or all of the following:
lactobacillus acidophilus, bifidobacterium
lactis, streptococcus thermophilus,
bifidobacterium bifidum*

PREP TIME: 5 MINS · FERMENTING TIME: 8 HOURS

There are some good non-dairy yoghurts available, but nothing beats
the homemade stuff. It's easy, promise. Use it anywhere you would use
traditional yoghurt.

1. Stand the cashew cream in a jar inside a jug of hot water, until it is just
   warm to the touch. Then add the probiotic powder and stir well.

2. Pour the cream into a sterilized jar with a lid. Loosely cover with the lid,
   but don't do it up tightly, then wrap in a clean towel or place in a small
   fabric coolbag. Leave in a warmish place with a steady temperature (an
   airing cupboard or on top of the fridge) for 8–24 hours.

3. Taste it after 8 hours. When it's tangy enough for you, remove the
   jar from its warm wrappings and place in the fridge to halt the
   fermentation. This will keep, in the fridge, covered, for up to 5 days.

MUSHROOM ANCHOVIES

MAKES
200g

(GF) (WF) (NF) (SoF)

200g large firm **mushrooms**, stalks
   and caps separated and both sliced
   into 3mm-thick slices
2 tablespoons **olive oil**
½ teaspoon **kelp powder**
½ teaspoon **tamarind paste**
1 teaspoon **sea salt**, plus extra to taste
½ teaspoon **vegan cider vinegar**
2 teaspoons **brine** from a jar of
   capers

**PREP TIME: 15 MINS · MARINATING TIME: OVERNIGHT
COOK TIME: 8 MINS**

Any mushrooms will work in this recipe. Use these umami-packed
'anchovies' on top of pizzas (see page 110), or chopped into pasta sauces.

1. Heat 1 tablespoon of the oil in a large frying pan, add the mushroom
   stalks and caps and sauté over a medium heat for 6–8 minutes, until
   just beginning to brown, but not dry out or crisp up.

2. Meanwhile, in a bowl large enough for all the mushrooms, mix the
   remaining oil with the rest of the ingredients.

3. Tip the mushrooms into the marinade and toss to coat. The
   mushrooms should taste briny and very salty, so add a pinch more
   salt if needed. Allow to cool and leave for at least 1 hour so that
   the flavours can penetrate the mushrooms, or ideally refrigerate
   overnight.

4. Drain off the marinade before use. The mushrooms will keep in the
   fridge, covered and in the marinade, for up to 4 days.

QUICK PICKLED RADISHES, CUCUMBER & GINGER

MAKES

1 × **400ml**

6cm piece of **fresh ginger**, peeled

20 small **radishes**, about 100g

10cm chunk of **cucumber**, halved lengthways

80ml **vegan rice vinegar** or **vegan cider vinegar**

80ml **water**

½–1 teaspoon **fine salt**

3 teaspoons **maple syrup**

PREP TIME: 10 MINS • COOK TIME: 5 MINS

Choose small pink or purple radishes for this, or those labelled as spring, summer or European radishes. If you'd rather have either cucumbers or radishes, but not both, just increase the quantities of whichever vegetables you prefer.

1. Slice the ginger, radishes and cucumber very thinly, using a mandolin, if possible.

2. Bring the vinegar, water, ½ teaspoon of the salt and maple syrup to the boil in a small non-reactive pan. Stir until the salt has dissolved, then carefully taste and add the rest of the salt, if needed.

3. Remove from the heat and immediately add the sliced vegetables. Stir again to ensure everything is covered in the liquor. The pickles will be ready to eat as soon as they are cool enough to handle.

4. If you want to store the pickles, pour the pickling liquor and vegetables while still very hot into a clean, dry, sterilized and heatproof jar with a lid. Seal immediately and keep in a cool dark place for up to 3 months.

5. Once open, they will keep in the fridge for a week or two (although they've never lasted that long in our houses…).

> *TIP*
> Tangy, sweet, crunchy and peppery, these pickles are perfect for noodle soups or salads, and go beautifully with sushi (see pages 180–1) or poke (see page 160).

SPICED GRAM FLOUR FLAT BREAD

SERVES
4

   (GF) (WF) (NF) (SoF)

PREP TIME: 15 MINS · REST TIME: 20 MINS
COOK TIME: 10 MINS

A high-protein and low-carb side for curries or dal, this also works as a
wrap for kebabs.

80g **gram flour**

150ml **water**

2 finely chopped **spring onions**

1 small bunch of **fresh coriander**,
   finely chopped

1 **red chilli** (less if you're serving to
   little ones), deseeded and finely
   chopped

1 teaspoon **garam masala**

½ teaspoon **salt**

a generous pinch of **freshly ground
   black pepper**

neutral oil, for cooking

1. Whisk the gram flour and water together in a large bowl. Add the
    remaining ingredients except the oil and whisk again. Allow to rest
    for about 20 minutes.

2. Heat a little oil in a heavy-based frying pan over a medium-high heat.
    When hot, spoon in a ladleful of the batter and tilt the pan to spread
    it out. Cook for 1–2 minutes, then flip over and cook on the other side
    until golden.

3. Remove from the pan and keep warm while you cook the rest of the
    flat breads.

> **TIP**
> Turn into thepla-style flat breads by adding a handful of finely chopped
> fresh fenugreek (we get ours frozen in the supermarket), or a tablespoon
> of dried fenugreek and a spoonful of turmeric – gorgeous with lentils.

CAROLE'S EASY GLUTEN-FREE FLAT BREADS

125g **ground arrowroot**

100g **ground almonds**

2 tablespoons **olive oil**, **coconut oil**
   or **avocado oil**, plus extra for frying

220ml **water**

a pinch of **salt**

PREP TIME: 5 MINS · COOK TIME: 4 MINS

Chantal's mum Carole has these for breakfast every single morning – plain or with anything from peanut butter and jam, coconut oil, avocado and spring onion, or vegan smoked 'salmon' and avocado. She also uses them to make hot wraps (for wrap filling ideas, see page 103).

1. Whizz all the ingredients in a food processor or blender until smooth.

2. Place a heavy cast-iron or non-stick pan, frying pan over a high heat and add a little drizzle of oil, swirling to coat the base of the pan.

3. Use a ladle to scoop out a portion of the batter and pour into the hot pan. Swirl the pan again to spread out the batter. Cook for 1–2 minutes, or until it starts to set on the top, then gently flip over. Repeat, until both sides are golden. Serve immediately, as these flat breads don't keep well once cooked.

4. Repeat with the remaining batter, or if you only need 1 or 2 flat breads, it can be stored in the fridge for up to 4 days.

VEGAN BRIOCHE-STYLE BUNS

250ml **unsweetened plant milk**
(use non-nut or non-soya to keep this NF or SoF), plus 1 tablespoon for glazing

1 tablespoon **dried active yeast**

3 tablespoons **caster sugar**

150g **vegan butter** or **margarine**
(use non-nut or non-soya to keep this NF or SoF), melted and cooled

600g **strong white bread flour**, plus extra for dusting

½ teaspoon **fine salt**

2 teaspoons **golden syrup** or **agave nectar**

1 teaspoon **vegetable oil**, plus extra for greasing

**PREP TIME: 30 MINS · RISE TIME: 2 HOURS
COOK TIME: 25 MINS**

These are excellent with burgers (see pages 92, 102 and 104) or split, toasted and slathered with jam.

1. Warm the milk very gently in a pan until just lukewarm. Stir in the yeast and sugar. Take off the heat and allow to stand for 5–10 minutes, until beginning to froth and smell distinctively yeasty. When it has a good bubbly head, add the cooled melted butter or margarine and mix again.

2. Sift the flour and salt into a large bowl. Mix in the yeasty milk with a wooden spoon until the mixture comes together, then use your hands to form into a soft, slightly sticky dough. Turn on to a clean work surface dusted with flour.

3. Knead the dough, pulling it towards you, then back over itself, using your knuckles to press it down, for 5–10 minutes, until the dough is smooth and elastic. (Alternatively, use a stand mixer fitted with a dough hook.) If the dough is really sticky, add a handful of flour. Place in a clean bowl, cover with clingfilm or a clean damp tea towel to stop it drying out and allow to rise in a warm place for at least 1 hour, until doubled in size.

4. Knock the dough back, using your knuckles to gently press it back to more or less its original size. Using a sharp knife, divide into 8 equal-sized pieces, then shape into neat balls. Place on 2 lightly greased large baking sheets, cover with a clean damp tea towel and allow to rise for another 30–60 minutes, until doubled in size.

5. Heat the oven to 190°C/375°F/gas mark 5.

6. When the buns have risen, mix the syrup or agave, the oil and the remaining 1 tablespoon milk together. Gently brush the buns with the glaze, then bake for 15 minutes. Brush again with the glaze, then return to the oven, spinning the trays around to ensure even cooking. Bake for another 8–10 minutes, until the glaze is shiny and golden, the bread is evenly browned and the buns sound hollow when tapped on the base.

7. Allow to cool on a wire rack (if you break into the buns while still hot, the moisture inside will escape as steam and make them dry).

TIP
Turn these buns into cardamom brioche by adding 1 tablespoon ground cardamom, or into saffron brioche, by adding 1 teaspoon saffron strands mixed with 2 tablespoons boiling water and soaked for at least 10 minutes – add when you mix the wet and dry ingredients together. Or try adding chopped dairy-free chocolate, chopped nuts or dried fruit – dried sour cherries are especially good.

CRUNCHY BITS

ROASTED CHICKPEAS

This is a good way to use up leftover chickpeas after draining the liquid to use as aquafaba (see page 12). They also make a healthy pre-dinner snack (chilled glass of vegan wine optional, but recommended).

Heat the oven to 200°C/400°F/gas mark 6. Tip 2 × 400g tins of drained **chickpeas** into 1 or 2 baking trays in a single layer. Use kitchen paper or a clean tea towel to blot away as much liquid as possible, then roast for 5 minutes, or until the chickpeas are completely dry. Pour 2 tablespoons **neutral cooking oil** into the tray and toss to coat. Return to the oven and roast for another 20 minutes, giving the tray a jiggle halfway through. Tip the chickpeas into a bowl. Add a good pinch of **salt**, a pinch of **chilli powder**, ½ teaspoon **ground cumin**, ½ teaspoon **sweet smoked paprika** and 2 teaspoons **toasted sesame oil**. Toss well, then check the seasoning. Serve immediately or allow to cool completely and store in an airtight container for up to 24 hours (although they are crunchiest eaten straight after cooking).

ROASTED NUTS

Chuck a handful of these into sweet or savoury dishes for texture and extra goodness. All nuts contain healthy fats, B vitamins, calcium, protein and fibre, while Brazils contain selenium, almonds contain vitamin E, macadamias are rich in thiamin and manganese, and walnuts contain omega 3.

Heat the oven to 180°C/350°F/gas mark 4. Spread out 100g mixed **raw unsalted nuts** (chopped into pieces, if necessary) on a baking tray and roast for 5–7 minutes, until golden (or toast in a hot dry pan over a low heat, tossing frequently, for 2–4 minutes, until brown). If you want to coat the nuts with spices, use **water** or **neutral cooking oil** to help the spices stick – mix 2 tablespoons oil with your chosen flavourings (**paprika**, **sugar**, **salt**, **cumin**, **za'atar**, **chilli**) and then toss the nuts thoroughly before roasting in the oven.

CROUTONS

Heat the oven to 160°C/325°F/gas mark 3. Cut 400g slightly **stale sourdough bread** into slices and trim off the crusts (or use a **baguette**, cut into thin slices on an angle). Brush both sides of each slice with **olive oil**, then cut into 2cm squares (if using sourdough).

Rub the bread with a halved clove of raw **garlic** before baking for garlicky croutons. Bake for 10–15 minutes, turning once, or until crisp and golden. Allow to cool completely if storing. They will keep for up to 3 days in an airtight container. The croutons can also be frozen – crisp up in a warm oven for 5 minutes before using.

DUKKAH

This addictive Egyptian nut seed and spice mix is an incredibly versatile (as well as nutritious) condiment. Scatter it on salads, over soups, on top of dips like hummus or tzatziki, over grilled vegetables after cooking, over nut cheeses spread on crackers, or mix with a little oil and brush over hot non-dairy flat breads...

Place the following in a hot dry pan set over a medium heat: 50g **unsalted pistachios**, 75g **blanched hazelnuts**, 25g **blanched almonds**, 1 teaspoon **fennel seeds**, 1 teaspoon **cumin seeds**, 2 tablespoons **sesame seeds**, 10 **whole black peppercorns**, 2 teaspoons **coriander seeds**, ½ teaspoon **paprika**, 1 teaspoon **sumac** and a generous pinch of **salt**. Toast gently, tossing often, until the spices are fragrant and the nuts are beginning to turn brown. Tip into a blender, spice grinder or food processor. Process until the texture of rough sand. It will keep in an airtight container for several weeks. (Try adding **pumpkin**, **nigella**, **caraway** or **sunflower seeds**, or a pinch of good-quality **dried thyme**.)

PANGRATTATO

We put this in our previous book, *Happy Soups*, because it makes a brilliant crunchy topping, but we wanted to include it here, too, because it is so good at adding flavour and texture to salads, gratins and bakes. You can even throw a handful of it with some olive oil into a bowl of freshly cooked pasta and eat it as a scrunchy, flavourful sauce.

Heat the oven to 180°C/350°F/gas mark 4. Toss together 150g **fresh breadcrumbs**, made from slightly stale bread, 1 crushed clove of **garlic**, the zest of ½ **lemon** and some **freshly ground black pepper**, making sure the garlic doesn't clump together in one place. Add 2 tablespoons **olive oil** and toss again. Spread the crumbs out in a single layer on a baking sheet and bake for 5–8 minutes, until the crumbs are golden brown and fragrant, turning once halfway through. Allow to cool slightly, add **salt**, if needed, then stir in 2 tablespoons very finely chopped **fresh parsley**. Use straight away, keep in a sealed box for a day or two, or freeze. If making in advance, don't add the parsley until serving and, if frozen, crisp up again in the oven before using.

TOASTED SEEDS

Toast 40g **pumpkin seeds** and 1–2 tablespoons **mixed sesame seeds** and **flaxseeds** in a hot dry frying pan over a medium heat for 2–3 minutes, until the pumpkin seeds begin to pop and puff up. Allow to slightly brown, giving them a nutty flavour, but ensure they don't burn. Remove immediately from the pan and add any spices (**cumin**, **smoked chilli** or **paprika**, or **ground coriander**, and a pinch of **sea salt**) while the seeds are still piping hot. They will keep for a week or so in a sealed container.

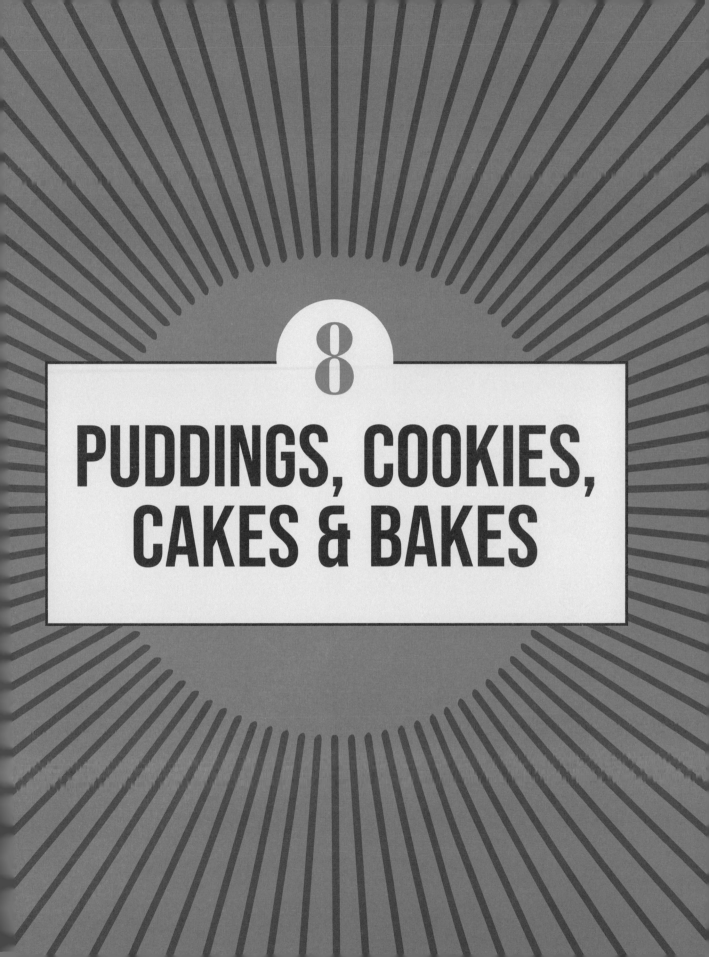

8

PUDDINGS, COOKIES, CAKES & BAKES

CHOCOLATE CARAMEL TART

375g **ready-made vegan shortcrust pastry**

125ml **unsweetened plant milk**, plus 1 tablespoon (use non-soya to keep this SoF), plus extra if needed

½ teaspoon **neutral cooking oil**, such as **sunflower**

½ teaspoon **golden syrup** or **agave nectar**

400g **dairy-free dark chocolate** (72% cocoa solids), broken into pieces

2 teaspoons **vanilla extract**

2 tablespoons **caster sugar**

150ml **vegan caramel**, **date caramel** or **salt caramel sauce** (see page 248 for homemade, cooled until fairly firm)

1 teaspoon **unsweetened cocoa powder**

50g **toasted flaked almonds**

PREP TIME: 20 MINS · CHILL TIME: 2 HOURS 15 MINS COOK TIME: 40 MINS

If ready-made pastry doesn't say it's made with 'all-butter' then chances are it is vegan, making posh puddings like this very achievable (but check the label). Ready-made shortcrust pastry usually comes in 375g blocks or ready-rolled sheets. You will only need about half this much, but you can freeze the leftovers. Most dark chocolate is dairy free, but, again, check the label and watch out for soya, too, if necessary.

1. Heat the oven to 200°C/400°F/gas mark 6.

2. Roll out the pastry to about 2mm thick and so it fits a 25cm loose-bottomed tart tin. Line the tin with the pastry, trimming the overhanging edges to form a neat edge (save the trimmings for another recipe). Chill for 15 minutes in the freezer.

3. Cut out a large sheet of baking parchment to fit the tart tin, then gently press it into the corners, pleating the paper so it sticks upwards over the edges. Fill with ceramic baking beans (or dried beans that you don't intend to cook) and bake for 15 minutes.

4. Meanwhile, mix together the 1 tablespoon milk, the oil and golden syrup or agave nectar.

5. Remove the pastry case from the oven and carefully lift out the paper and beans. Reduce the oven to 170°C/340°F/gas mark 3½. Prick the base all over with a fork, then lightly brush all over with the milk wash. Bake for a further 15–20 minutes, spinning the tart tin around halfway through for even baking, until the case is golden brown and quite crisp. Set aside while you make the filling.

6. Melt the chocolate, milk, vanilla and sugar in a heatproof bowl set over a pan of just simmering water until the chocolate is melted and the mixture thickens (if it becomes fudgy or grainy, add a couple more tablespoons milk and beat until smooth and silky). Remove from the heat and allow to cool slightly.

7. Spread the caramel sauce smoothly over the bottom of the cooled pastry case. Spoon over the warm chocolate ganache, disturbing the caramel layer as little as possible. Use a spatula to gently spread the filling out. Chill for 2 hours until set. (Don't worry if it looks like it has separated slightly.)

8. When ready to serve, transfer from the tin to a serving plate, dust with the cocoa and sprinkle the almonds on top.

TIP
The tart can also be decorated with fresh berries. Serve on its own, or with vegan cream or whipped cashew cream (see page 257), vegan ice cream (see pages 284–89), chocolate sorbet (see page 290) or whipped coconut cream (see page 257).

CARAMEL SAUCE

MAKES 200 ml

PREP TIME: 5 MINS · COOK TIME: 25 MINS

Use this in desserts, over ice cream, in coffee, hot chocolate or even cocktails. The cream of tartar is optional, but it helps prevent the sauce crystallizing.

200g **white caster sugar**

75ml **unsweetened plant milk** (use non-nut or non-soya to keep this NF or SoF)

2 heaped tablespoons **vegan butter** or **margarine** (use non-nut or non-soya to keep this NF or SoF), melted

a pinch of **cream of tartar** (optional)

sea salt

1. Pour the sugar into a scrupulously clean and dry, deep heavy-based pan and cook over a medium-low heat for about 10 minutes, until it begins to melt. Do not stir it.

2. Meanwhile, warm the milk in the microwave or in a pan. Mix it with the melted butter or margarine in a jug. Whisk in the cream of tartar, if using.

3. When about a third of the sugar is melted, remove from the heat and stir gently with a clean, dry wooden spoon to incorporate the unmelted sugar. Continue to stir for about a minute until all the sugar has melted and no graininess remains.

4. Carefully pour in 1–2 tablespoons of the milk mixture, but beware as the caramel will bubble and splutter. Stir to combine, then carefully add the rest of liquid and salt, to taste (add more for a salted caramel sauce). If it has split or is lumpy, return to a low heat and melt again, but only very briefly or it may become more like bitter toffee than caramel.

5. Allow to cool slightly. Use immediately or pour into a clean, heatproof jar with a lid while still hot; it will thicken considerably as it cools. Store in the fridge for up to 2 weeks. Bring up to room temperature to soften.

DATE CARAMEL SAUCE

MAKES 300 ml

**PREP TIME: 10 MINS · SOAK TIME: 20 MINS
COOK TIME: 1 MIN**

A fudgy sauce for puddings, pancakes, ice cream sundaes, chocolate sorbet (see page 290), or to use in our banoffee pie or chocolate & raspberry torte (see pages 250 and 258).

250g **dates**, pitted

5 tablespoons **refined coconut oil**

1 tablespoon **maple syrup**

1 teaspoon **vanilla bean paste**

a pinch of **salt**

1. Soak the dates in boiling water for at least 20 minutes, or overnight in the fridge. Drain, then blitz with the coconut oil in a food processor or blender (or use a stick blender). If any bits remain (and it's hard to get this absolutely smooth, even in a high-powered blender), then press the sauce through a sieve with the back of a spoon.

2. Place the sauce in the microwave to melt the oil (or heat very briefly on the hob). Stir in the maple syrup, vanilla and salt and mix until smooth.

3. The sauce will thicken and become fudgy as it cools. To use as a thick caramel in our banoffee pie or chocolate tart, allow to cool completely. This will keep for up to a week in the fridge.

> **TIP**
>
> For a thinner, more pourable date caramel, blend the sieved sauce with a little plant milk or water until you achieve the desired consistency. You can also chill the caramel, then dip balls of it in melted chocolate or roll it in cacao, to make truffles.

PUDDINGS, COOKIES, CAKES & BAKES

CUSTARD

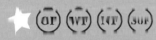

250ml **unsweetened plant milk**
(use non-nut or non-soya to keep this
NF or SoF)

2 tablespoons **cornflour**

2 tablespoons **caster sugar**

1 teaspoon **refined coconut oil**

1 teaspoon **vanilla extract** or
vanilla bean paste

a tiny pinch of **ground turmeric**
(optional)

a tiny pinch of **salt**

zest of ½ **unwaxed lemon**

PREP TIME: 5 MINS · COOK TIME: 20 MINS

The lemon zest doesn't turn this into a lemon custard, it's just a subtle flavour enhancer. The turmeric is for colour – add as little as you can, or you will taste it. Serve with poached fruit, or the fruity crumbles on page 44.

1. Pour 2 tablespoons of the milk into a small bowl and whisk in the cornflour until completely smooth, then add the sugar.

2. Warm the remaining milk and the coconut oil in a small pan over a low heat without boiling it. Add the cornflour mixture in a steady stream, whisking as you go. Turn up the heat to the medium and gradually bring the custard to a simmer, stirring frequently to prevent the bottom of the pan catching and burning.

3. Turn the heat down to low and cook for 10–15 minutes to cook away the flavour of the cornflour. Add the vanilla, turmeric, if using, salt and lemon zest, and continue to cook for 2 minutes, until you can't taste the cornflour. Cook for a little longer, if needed.

4. Serve hot or warm. If not using immediately, cover the surface with a layer of clingfilm or baking parchment to prevent a skin from forming.

BANOFFEE PIE

SoF

PREP TIME: 30 MINS · SOAK TIME: 30 MINS
CHILL TIME: 40 + 20 MINS · COOK TIME: 45 MINS

We were missing sticky, sweet and over-the-top puddings. So we invented our own. We use gluten-free or ordinary Hobnobs for the pie base, but you can use any firm, crunchy vegan biscuit.

Coconut caramel is a bit tricksy and unpredictable, depending on the brand of milk used – we have turned our failures into fudge and toffee. It is worth persevering, but equally, we fully respect an easy shortcut. You can use the date caramel sauce on page 248 or shop-bought vegan caramel sauce from a jar instead. You will need about 350ml.

FOR THE BASE:
250g **vegan biscuits**
½ teaspoon **ground cinnamon**
110g **refined coconut oil**, melted, plus extra for greasing

FOR THE CARAMEL:
800ml **coconut milk**
200g **caster sugar**

FOR THE CREAM FILLING:
200g **unroasted cashew nuts**
60–90ml **unsweetened almond milk**
juice of ½ **lemon**
2 ripe **bananas**
1 teaspoon **vanilla bean paste**

FOR THE TOPPING:
2 **bananas**
20g **dairy-free dark chocolate**

1. Soak the cashew nuts for the cream filling in boiling water for 30 minutes, or cover in cold water and soak in the fridge for at least 4 hours or overnight.

2. Blitz all the base ingredients in a food processor or blender until the texture of fine sand. Tip out into a greased deep 23cm loose-bottomed springform cake tin. Spread out across the tin and about 4cm up the sides, patting to smooth out and help fill up. Chill while you make the caramel.

3. Heat the coconut milk and sugar in a heavy-based pan over a low heat for about 5 minutes, stirring often, until the sugar is dissolved and the mixture reaches simmering point. Turn up the heat slightly and simmer gently for 35–40 minutes, stirring frequently and scraping down the sides of the pan, to prevent the sauce splitting and becoming oily. (If the sauce does split, you may be able to bring it back together by stirring it off the heat, briskly.)

4. When the caramel is a pale gold, thick and creamy, remove from the heat and pour over the biscuit base in the tin, then spread out evenly. Chill in the fridge for 20 minutes.

5. To make the cream, drain and rinse the cashew nuts, then blitz in a high-powered blender with 60ml of the almond milk and the remaining ingredients until completely smooth, thick and creamy. If too thick, add the rest of the almond milk and blitz again. Spoon on top of the caramel and smooth over.

6. Slice the bananas for the topping into 1cm-slices, cutting on an angle, then arrange on top of the cream. Grate or shave the chocolate over the top.

7. Chill the pie for at least 30 minutes before serving, then transfer to a serving plate.

TIP
For easy removal from the tin, run a large clean cloth or tea towel under hot water. Squeeze out, then wrap the sides of the tin in the cloth for 30 seconds to loosen the base and stop it sticking. Balance the tin on a mug or jar, undo the catch and allow the sides of the tin to drop down, releasing the pie.

MERINGUE MESS

1 × 400g tin of unsalted chickpea liquid (**aquafaba**) reserved and chilled for at least 1 hour

caster sugar

a generous pinch of **cream of tartar**

½ teaspoon **rosewater**

1 teaspoon **vanilla extract** (be sure to choose one that is alcohol-based)

FOR THE TOPPING:

1 × quantity **whipped coconut cream** or **cashew cream** (see page 257)

400g **fresh fruit** (quartered figs and a handful of **pomegranate seeds**, or sliced ripe **peaches**, ripe **strawberries**, **raspberries**, **blueberries**, or any other in-season **berries**)

2 tablespoons **dried edible rose petals** (optional)

2 tablespoons **toasted flaked almonds** or **unsalted pistachio nuts**, toasted and chopped, or a mixture (optional)

PREP TIME: 40 MINS · CHILL TIME: 1 HOUR
COOK TIME: 6 HOURS

This recipe uses aquafaba (see page 12). Some brands produce meringues that don't have any bean flavour at all, but others are not so dependable, which is why we add both vanilla and rosewater to this dish. Aquafaba meringues take a bit of practice, so we made this recipe a mess rather than a pavlova– it is the perfect way to hone your skills, and if you end up with hollow or cracked meringues, nobody will notice! If you find aquafaba tricky, see our troubleshooting tips on page 224. When you have practised and are confident – and for a really extravagant dessert – double the meringue and cream recipes, and cook two large meringues, baking as below. Stack them like a sandwich, with some cream and fruit in the middle and on top, to make a double-height pavlova.

1. Heat the oven to 100°C/225°F/gas mark ¼. Weigh the chilled aquafaba, then weigh out the same amount of caster sugar (you need a 1:1 ratio of aquafaba to sugar). Set aside the sugar.

2. Pour the aquafaba into the spotlessly clean bowl of a stand mixer fitted with the whisk attachment (or a large mixing bowl if using an electric hand whisk). Add the cream of tartar. Whisk vigorously for at least 5 minutes, or until very firm, stiff peaks form (you should be able to turn the bowl upside down without the mixture moving).

3. Gradually add the sugar, 1 tablespoon at a time, whisking for at least 2 minutes between each addition (this will take about 15 minutes, which is why a stand mixer is useful).

4. When all the sugar is incorporated, add the rosewater and vanilla. The meringue will have lost some of its height and look wetter and shinier. Continue to whisk for at least 5 minutes, or until the meringue forms stiff, glossy and dense peaks.

5. Spoon the meringue in 4–6 large dollops on to a baking sheet lined with a large piece of baking parchment. Bake for 2 hours, or until the meringues are crisp. Turn the oven off and leave the meringues in the oven for about 4 hours, to completely dry out.

6. When ready to serve, peel away the baking parchment from the cooled meringues. Break into chunks and place on pretty dessert plates. Spoon the whipped cream around the meringue, then arrange your choice of fruit, petals and nuts on top. Add the toppings only when ready to serve, as the cream will soak into the meringue – fine for an hour or so, but not much longer.

PUDDINGS, COOKIES, CAKES & BAKES

CHOCOLATE CAKE WITH CHOCOLATE ICING

× 24CM CAKE

125g **refined coconut oil**, melted, plus extra for greasing

3 tablespoons **ground flaxseeds**

250ml **boiling water**

100g **unsweetened cocoa powder**

125ml **unsweetened plant milk** (use non-nut or non-soya to keep this NF or SoF)

¾ teaspoon **fine salt**

½ **banana**, mashed until completely smooth

1 tablespoon **vegan cider vinegar**

1 tablespoon **vanilla extract** or **vanilla bean paste**

75ml **agave nectar** or **golden syrup**

3 tablespoons **freshly brewed strong black coffee** (optional)

275g **plain flour**

1 tablespoon **bicarbonate of soda**

1 tablespoon **baking powder**

125g **caster sugar**

TO SERVE:

2–3 tablespoons **jam** (**cherry**, **blueberry**, **blackberry** and **raspberry** all work well)

1 × quantity **glossy chocolate icing** (see page 256) or **avocado chocolate frosting** (see Tip on page 256)

vegan sprinkles

100g **vegan dark chocolate** (optional)

vegan edible lustre (optional)

PREP TIME: 25 MINS · STAND TIME: OVERNIGHT
COOK TIME: 35 MINS

This cake is dark and deeply flavoured, and is best slathered in chocolate icing or even avocado chocolate frosting. If you're not planning to ice it, add an extra 50g caster sugar to the cake mix. The texture of the cake is best the next day, as it firms up, so make the cakes in advance.

1. Heat the oven to 180°C/350°F/gas mark 4. Grease 2 loose-bottomed 24cm cake tins and line with baking parchment.

2. Mix the ground flaxseeds and 75ml of the boiling water together in a small heatproof bowl and allow to soak for 5 minutes.

3. In a large heatproof bowl, whisk together the cocoa powder and the rest of the boiling water to form a smooth paste. Add the soaked flaxseeds, the milk, salt, mashed banana, cider vinegar, vanilla, agave nectar or golden syrup, melted oil and coffee and stir together.

4. Sift the flour, bicarbonate of soda and baking powder into a separate large bowl. Stir in the sugar until well mixed.

5. Mix the wet and dry ingredients together until just combined. Immediately divide the mixture between the prepared tins, tapping once or twice on the side to remove any big bubbles.

6. Bake for 30–35 minutes, or until the cakes are just pulling away from the sides of the tin and a skewer comes out clean. Allow to cool in the tins for 10 minutes, then carefully transfer to a wire rack and allow to cool completely. Store in an airtight container overnight.

7. The next day, trim the tops of the cakes flat, if necessary, so that they stack neatly. Sandwich together with a little jam, before spreading the top and sides with the chocolate icing or avocado chocolate frosting and scattering with vegan sprinkles. Melt the dark chocolate, if using, and pour a thin layer on to a sheet of baking parchment. Allow to cool, then dust with edible lustre. Crack into pieces and arrange the shards on top of the cake.

GLOSSY CHOCOLATE ICING

300g **refined** or **extra virgin coconut oil**

8 tablespoons **unsweetened cocoa powder** or **cacao powder**, sifted

1 teaspoon **vanilla bean paste** or **vanilla extract**

90ml **golden syrup** or **agave nectar**

PREP TIME: 5 MINS · COOK TIME: 3 MINS

Makes enough to ice the top of 2 individual cakes, or the top and sides of 1 double-layered cake.

1. Melt the coconut oil. Cool slightly, if it's very hot, then stir in the remaining ingredients, mixing until completely smooth.

2. For a liquid-like, glazed glossy icing, allow the mixture to cool very slightly, then spoon over the cake(s), allowing the icing to drizzle down the sides.

3. For a fudgier icing, allow the mixture to cool until soft and spreadable, rather than liquid, and use a palette knife to spread it over the cake(s).

TIP

To make avocado chocolate frosting, mix 2 mashed avocados with 4 tablespoons sifted icing sugar, 4 tablespoons sifted unsweetened cocoa powder and 2 teaspoons vanilla extract or vanilla bean paste. Add more sugar or cocoa powder to taste, then beat until smooth before using.

WHIPPED COCONUT CREAM

SERVES
2

(GF) (WF) (NF) (SoF)

400ml **full-fat coconut milk**, tin
   chilled overnight

1 tablespoon **icing sugar**, plus extra
   to taste

1 teaspoon **vanilla extract**

1 teaspoon **vegan cider vinegar** or
   lemon juice

a pinch of **salt**

PREP TIME: 5 MINS · CHILL TIME: OVERNIGHT

This is wonderful dolloped on to tropical fruit, as a topping for meringues, with crumbles, cakes, or spread on to vegan scones with jam.

1. Open the chilled tin of coconut milk without shaking it and carefully remove the thicker coconut cream that has risen to the top, leaving behind the coconut water (save it for smoothies).

2. Spoon the coconut cream into a chilled bowl. Sift in the icing sugar and add the vanilla. Using an electric hand whisk or a stand mixer fitted with the whisk attachment, whisk for about 30–60 seconds, until soft peaks form. Add the cider vinegar or lemon juice and salt and beat again to combine. Add a little more sugar, if you like.

WHIPPED CASHEW CREAM

SERVES
4

(GF) (WF) (SoF)

300ml thick **cashew cream**
   (see page 228), chilled

a generous pinch of **cream of tartar**

1 teaspoon **icing sugar**, plus extra
   to taste

PREP TIME: 3 MINS

A rich cream, but lighter and more delicate in flavour than the whipped coconut above, this is great with almost any pudding. Cashew nuts happen to be an excellent source of dietary copper too.

1. Spoon the chilled cashew cream into a chilled bowl (see Tip). Sift in the cream of tartar and icing sugar and beat for about 30–60 seconds, until soft peaks form. Add a little more sugar, if you like.

TIP

If your kitchen is warm, chill the bowl you are going to whisk the cream in for 10 minutes before using.

CHOCOLATE & RASPBERRY TORTE

115g **unroasted cashew nuts**

60g **refined coconut oil**

300g **vegan plain biscuits**

250ml **cold water**

1 teaspoon **vanilla bean paste**

juice of 1 **lemon**

1 teaspoon **icing sugar**
(you can use unrefined icing sugar)

a pinch of **salt**

400g **dairy-free dark chocolate**,
broken into pieces

135g **raspberries**

PREP TIME: 20 MINS · SOAK TIME: 30 MINS
COOK TIME: 5 MINS · CHILL TIME: 1 HOUR

Thom Malley, at the LEON Borough (head) office, makes a delicious tart with chocolate and raspberries, but his isn't vegan, so Chantal was inspired to create her own version. Use vegan biscuits like digestives or rich tea to make the base.

1. Soak the cashew nuts in boiling water for at least 30 minutes, or cover with cold water and soak in the fridge for at least 4 hours or overnight. Drain and rinse.

2. Melt the coconut oil in a small pan or the microwave. Crush the biscuits using a food processor or wrap them in a clean tea towel and bash with a rolling pin. Mix the melted oil and biscuits together.

3. Cover the base of a loose-bottomed 23cm cake tin with the biscuit mixture, pressing it down until even and smooth, and about 2cm thick.

4. Blend the drained cashew nuts in a high-powered blender with the water, vanilla, lemon juice, icing sugar and salt until smooth.

5. Melt the chocolate in a heatproof bowl over a pan of just simmering water, stirring frequently, until smooth (don't allow it to overheat or it will be become gritty). Mix into the cashew mixture.

6. Arrange the raspberries in a layer on the biscuit base, then pour over the chocolate mixture. Tap the tin firmly on the worktop to release any bubbles, then smooth the top with a spatula or palette knife. Chill for at least 1 hour, or until completely firm. Serve at room temperature.

ALMOND, ORANGE & CARDAMOM CAKE

23CM CAKE

PREP TIME: 20 MINS · COOK TIME: 40 MINS

Cardamom gives this almond cake a gorgeous, delicate perfume.

125ml **neutral cooking oil**, plus
  extra for greasing
12 **cardamom pods** or ½ teaspoon
  ground cardamom
200g **plain flour**
150g **ground almonds**
150g **caster sugar**
2 teaspoons **baking powder**
a pinch of **salt**
zest and juice of 1 **orange**, plus curls of
  peel from 1 **orange**, to serve
125ml **non-dairy plain yoghurt**
  (use non-soya to keep this SoF),
  plus 1 heaped tablespoon per person,
  to serve (optional)
75ml **unsweetened plant milk**
  (use non-soya to keep this SoF)
2 teaspoons **vegan cider vinegar**

1. Heat the oven to 180°C/350°F/gas mark 4. Grease the sides of a loose-bottomed 23cm cake tin and line the base with baking parchment.

2. If using cardamom pods, bash each one to split and release the seeds, then grind to a powder using a pestle and mortar. Place the ground cardamom in a large bowl with the flour, almonds, sugar, baking powder and salt and mix well.

3. Reserve 1 teaspoon of the orange zest, then whisk together the remaining zest, the orange juice, 125ml of the yoghurt, the milk and vinegar, then pour into the dry ingredients. Mix just until combined (over-mixing can make cakes chewy).

4. Pour the mixture into the prepared tin and bake for 40 minutes, or until risen, firm and deep golden, and a skewer comes out clean. Allow to cool in the tin for 10 minutes, then turn out on to a wire rack and cool completely.

5. If using, whisk the remaining zest into the remaining yoghurt and serve with slices of the cake.

CHOCOLATE MOUSSE

150ml **aquafaba** (tinned chickpea water, see page 12)

1 teaspoon **lemon juice**

200g **dairy-free dark chocolate** (minimum 70% cocoa solids), broken into pieces

2 tablespoons **unsweetened plant milk** (use non-soya to keep this SoF), plus extra 2–3 tablespoons, if needed

1 tablespoon **caster sugar**

1 teaspoon **vanilla extract**

fresh seasonal fruit, **nuts** or **toasted coconut flakes**, or a mixture, to decorate

PREP TIME: 18 MINS · CHILL TIME: 3 HOURS COOK TIME: 10 MINS

This is our favourite way to use the mysterious, egg-white-like properties of aquafaba (see page 12). It makes this chocolate mousse silky, creamy and fluffy. Save the chickpeas for another dish – there are loads of options in this book, including crunchy roasted chickpeas (see page 242) for snacking.

1. Pour the aquafaba into the spotlessly clean bowl of a stand mixer fitted with the whisk attachment (or a large mixing bowl if using an electric hand whisk). Add the lemon juice and whisk vigorously for at least 5 minutes, until the mixture forms stiff peaks (you should be able to turn the bowl upside down without the mixture moving). Set aside.

2. Melt the chocolate, the 2 tablespoons plant milk, the sugar and vanilla in a heatproof bowl set over a pan of just simmering water, stirring frequently, so that the bottom doesn't start to cook and become gritty. If the mixture starts to look fudgy, very thick or grainy, gradually add more milk, mixing thoroughly each time, until the mix is silky smooth. It will be quite thick, but should be glossy and easy to stir. Remove from the heat and allow to cool until just warm to the touch.

3. Using a metal spoon, gently fold the chocolate mixture into the whisked aquafaba until incorporated, scraping up the chocolate from the bottom of the bowl (it will sink below the aquafaba). This will take a few minutes, but be patient and don't rush – the mixture will gradually turn from pale brown to a rich chocolate brown.

4. Gently pour into a large serving bowl, or divide between individual bowls or glasses. Chill for at least 3 hours to firm up.

5. Remove from the fridge about 15 minutes before serving and decorate with fruit, nuts or toasted coconut.

> **TIP**
> Fold the chocolate mixture into the whisked aquafaba rather than stirring it in, to prevent knocking all the air out and turning the mixture to liquid.

PUDDINGS, COOKIES, CAKES & BAKES

NEW YORK-STYLE BAKED CHEESECAKE

FOR THE TOPPING:

125g **unroasted cashew nuts**

2 × 270g tubs of **vegan
cream cheese**

250g **vanilla soya yoghurt**

1 teaspoon **vanilla bean paste**

150ml **maple syrup** or
agave nectar

zest of 1 **lemon**

4 tablespoons **tapioca flour** or
ground arrowroot

1 tablespoon **gram flour**

1 tablespoon **tahini**

FOR THE BASE:

125g **ground almonds**

110g **ordinary oat flour**
or **gluten-free oat flour**

50g **coconut sugar**
(or **soft brown sugar**)

60ml **refined** or **extra virgin
coconut oil**, melted

*PREP TIME: 15 MINS • SOAK TIME: 30 MINS
CHILL TIME: 2 HOURS • COOK TIME: 55 MINS*

This can be served as it is, or with a fruit coulis, chocolate sauce or caramel sauce (see pages 290 and 248), or with fresh berries.

1. Soak the cashew nuts in boiling water for 30 minutes, or cover with cold water and soak in the fridge for at least 4 hours or overnight.

2. Heat the oven to 200°C/400°F/gas mark 6.

3. Mix all the base ingredients together to form a sandy, loose-textured dough. Press firmly into the base of a 23cm springform loose-bottomed tin. Bake for 15 minutes.

4. Meanwhile, drain and rinse the cashew nuts, then blend in a high-powered blender with the remaining topping ingredients until smooth.

5. Remove the base from the oven and turn the oven down to 180°C/350°F/gas mark 4. Pour the topping on to the base and bake for another 35–40 minutes, or until golden and almost firm to the touch. Allow to cool in the tin, then chill for 2 hours.

6. Bring the cheesecake to room temperature, then remove from the tin and serve.

SCONES

MAKES
10

  (NF) (SoF)

300g **plain flour**, plus extra for dusting

3 teaspoons **baking powder**

2 tablespoons **caster sugar**

scant ½ teaspoon **salt**

75g **refined coconut oil**, chilled
until firm, if necessary

150ml **unsweetened plant milk**
(use non-nut or non-soya to keep this
NF or SoF), plus 1 tablespoon for
glazing

1 teaspoon **agave nectar** or
golden syrup

½ teaspoon **neutral cooking oil**

PREP TIME: 20 MINS · COOK TIME: 14 MINS

Serve these warm, with vegan butter (see page 229) or whipped coconut cream (see page 257) and jam. Just add cucumber sandwiches for a vegan afternoon tea. If your coconut oil is at all soft, place it in the freezer while you measure out the rest of the ingredients.

1. Heat the oven to 200°C/400°F/gas mark 6.

2. In a large bowl, sift together the flour and baking powder, then add the sugar and salt. Tip into a food processor, add the chilled coconut oil and blitz briefly until the mixture looks like sand.

3. Tip back into the bowl and gradually add the milk until you have a craggy, sticky dough (you may not need all of the milk). Press it together rather than kneading it to avoid over-working the dough (this makes scones tough and brittle).

4. Turn the dough out on to a clean work surface dusted with flour. Pat it out (don't roll it) until about 2cm thick. Using a 6cm pastry cutter, cut out rounds, pressing down firmly without twisting the cutter. (Twisting makes the dough rise in different directions in the oven and leads to Leaning-Tower-of-Pisa scones.) Gather up the trimmings and press together, then pat out again to make 10 scones.

5. Transfer the scones to a baking sheet lined with baking parchment. Mix together the 1 tablespoon plant milk, the agave nectar or golden syrup and neutral cooking oil, then gently brush the tops of the scones with the glaze. Bake for 12–14 minutes, until risen and light golden on top.

> **TIP**
> For fruit scones, add 50g sultanas and 50g raisins, along with the milk. For crunch, add a pinch of golden granulated sugar to the tops, after glazing.

CHOCOLATE, RAISIN OR COCONUT COOKIES

PREP TIME: 20 MINS · COOK TIME: 16 MINS

Quick, crunchy and completely impossible to resist.

75g **refined coconut oil**, solid and at room temperature

50g **muscovado sugar**

50g **caster sugar**

60ml **aquafaba** (tinned chickpea water, see page 12)

a pinch of **salt**

½ teaspoon **vanilla extract**

½ teaspoon **vegan cider vinegar**

½ teaspoon **baking powder**

175g **plain flour**

2 tablespoons **ground almonds**

FOR CHOCOLATE CHIP COOKIES:

100g **dairy-free dark chocolate**, cut into 5mm pieces, or **dairy-free chocolate chips**

FOR RAISIN COOKIES:

75g **raisins**

FOR COCONUT & CHIA SEED COOKIES:

2 tablespoons **desiccated coconut**

1 tablespoon **chia seeds**

1. Heat the oven to 180°C/350°F/gas mark 4.

2. Using an electric hand whisk or a stand mixer fitted with the whisk attachment, beat together the oil, sugars, aquafaba, salt, vanilla and vinegar until creamy. Scrape down the sides of the bowl, then sift in the baking powder and flour and add the almonds. Run the mixer slowly until all the ingredients are incorporated and come together to form a soft dough.

3. Add the chocolate, raisins or coconut and chia, as liked, and stir in with a spoon.

4. Divide the mixture into 16–18 equal-sized 3cm balls. Arrange on 2 non-stick baking sheets or silicone baking mats, leaving at least 5cm between each one as they will spread out. Press the balls lightly to flatten slightly.

5. Bake for 14–16 minutes, or until golden brown all over. Allow to cool on the sheets or mats for 5 minutes. Using a spatula or palette knife, lift on to a wire rack to cool, or eat warm.

TIP

If you don't have any aquafaba to hand, you can use flaxseeds to bind these cookies. Soak 2 tablespoons ground flaxseeds in 60ml water for 5 minutes and use in place of the aquafaba. The cookies may take 18 minutes to bake if made with flaxseeds instead of chickpea water. Try adding 50g chopped hazelnuts or chopped almonds to the cookie dough, in addition to or instead of the other flavourings. For double chocolate chip cookies, cut back the flour to 150g and add 25g unsweetened cocoa powder, sifted in at the same time.

PUDDINGS, COOKIES, CAKES & BAKES

NUT BUTTER JAM COOKIES

PREP TIME: 10 MINS · COOK TIME: 15 MINS

100g **gluten-free oat flour**

125g **light soft brown sugar**
  or **coconut sugar**

120g **peanut butter**

40g **almond butter**

40g **tahini**

60ml **unsweetened almond milk**

60g **chopped almonds**

1 teaspoon **gluten-free
  baking powder**

a pinch of **salt**

oil, for greasing

4 tablespoons **jam** (we use St Dalfour
  strawberry, made with no
  added sugar)

Crisp, high in protein and…dangerous to be around. These don't last long near us. If your nut butters are very oily then these cookies might spread quite a bit in the oven – try draining a bit of the oil that floats on the top of nut butters off before using the more solid butter underneath.

1. Heat the oven to 190°C/375°F/gas mark 5.

2. Place all the ingredients except the oil and jam in a bowl. Mix together to form a thick paste.

3. Arrange 6 spoonfuls of the mixture on each of 2 greased large baking sheets, keeping the mix in rounds as much as possible. Press each dollop lightly to flatten slightly.

4. Bake for 12–14 minutes, or until the cookies begin to colour slightly.

5. Remove from the oven and use the back of a small spoon to make a small well in the centre of each cookie. Place a teaspoonful of the jam in each well. Return to the oven for 1 minute to allow the jam to melt and for the cookies to finish cooking.

6. Allow to cool before eating (as molten jam can be painful!).

OAT COOKIES

MAKES
12

PREP TIME: 15 MINS · CHILL TIME: 1 HOUR
COOK TIME: 10 MINS

If you can't find oat flour, blitz ordinary oats to a fine powder in a food processor or blender.

1 tablespoon **chia seeds**

3 tablespoons **water**

130g **vegan butter** or **margarine**
(use non-nut or non-soya to keep this NF or SoF)

125g **soft brown sugar**

95g **ordinary** or **gluten-free oat flour**

120g **ordinary** or **gluten-free rolled oats**

120g **raisins**

1 teaspoon **vanilla bean paste**

1 teaspoon **ground cinnamon**

1 teaspoon **ordinary** or **gluten-free baking powder**

a pinch of **salt**

oil, for greasing

1. In a small bowl, mix together the chia seeds and water and allow to soak for at least 5 minutes.

2. Cream the butter and sugar together until pale and fluffy. Add the soaked chia seeds and the rest of the ingredients and mix together. Chill for 1 hour, covered.

3. Heat the oven to 190°C/375°F/gas mark 5.

4. Remove the dough from the fridge and roll into walnut-sized balls. Squash into cookie shapes and place on a greased baking sheet (they don't spread that much).

5. Bake for 8–10 minutes. Don't allow the cookies to colour too much and remove from the oven to firm up – they will be soft when you take them out.

6. Allow to cool completely on the baking sheet, then store in an airtight container for up to 2 days.

LEMON POLENTA CAKE WITH BLACKBERRIES

SERVES
2

   (GF) (WF) (SoF)

PREP TIME: 15 MINS · COOK TIME: 35 MINS

A pretty cake with summer berries. Serve as it is, or with whipped cashew cream or coconut cream (see page 257), or non-dairy yoghurt.

FOR THE CAKE:

100g **ground almonds**

100g **fine polenta** or **cornmeal**

150g **caster sugar**
  (it can be unrefined)

zest and juice of 3 **lemons**

100ml **mild-tasting olive oil**, plus
  extra for greasing

50g **plain** or **gluten-free
  plain flour**

½ teaspoon **ordinary** or
  gluten-free baking powder

1 tablespoon **chia seeds**

1 teaspoon **vanilla bean paste**

a pinch of **salt**

FOR THE TOPPING:

450g **blackberries**

3 tablespoons **agave nectar**
  or **maple syrup**

80ml **water**

zest and juice of 1 **lemon**

1. Heat the oven to 180°C/350°F/gas mark 4.

2. Stir together all the cake ingredients in a large bowl until you have a thick smooth batter. Pour into a greased 23cm springform cake tin and bake for 25–30 minutes, until pale golden, slightly caramelizing around the edges and pulling away from the sides of the tin.

3. Meanwhile, make the topping. Place all the ingredients in a pan and bring to a simmer. Cook for 30 minutes, until the blackberries are still whole but very soft and the liquid forms a syrup. Allow to cool slightly.

4. Allow the cake to cool in the tin for 10 minutes, then remove and set on a plate. Pour over the blackberry topping and serve, warm or at room temperature.

GINGERBREAD

MAKES

(10) **PEOPLE OR 20–30 BISCUITS**

(NF) (SoF)

75g **refined coconut oil**

3 tablespoons **agave nectar** or **golden syrup**

1 tablespoon **black treacle**

50g **muscovado sugar**

225g **plain flour**, plus extra for dusting

½ teaspoon **bicarbonate of soda**

2 teaspoons **ground ginger**

1 teaspoon **ground cinnamon**

a generous pinch of **ground cloves**

a pinch of **freshly grated nutmeg**

a pinch of **salt**

2 tablespoons **water**

FOR VEGAN ROYAL ICING:

180–200g **icing sugar**

2 tablespoons **aquafaba** (tinned chickpea water, see page 12)

a generous pinch of **cream of tartar**

½ teaspoon **vanilla extract**

PREP TIME: 35 MINS · CHILL TIME: 30 MINS
SETTING TIME: 24 HOURS · COOK TIME: 17 MINS

Make gingerbread people, or cut the dough into stars and press small holes in before baking for Christmas decorations. The exact ratio of sugar to liquid needed to make vegan royal icing varies between brands of chickpeas, so you may have to tweak how much sugar you use.

1. Gently melt the oil, agave nectar or golden syrup, treacle and brown sugar in a pan over a low heat. Allow to cool slightly.

2. In a large bowl, sift together the flour, bicarbonate of soda, ginger, cinnamon, cloves and nutmeg. Add the salt and mix well.

3. Pour the oil mixture and water into the dry ingredients. Mix together, then form into a dough using your hands (when cool enough to handle). It will be quite crumbly, but press and pat the mixture together to form a firm ball. Wrap in clingfilm and chill for at least 30 minutes to firm up.

4. Heat the oven to 180°C/350°F/gas mark 4. Remove the dough from the fridge and set aside for 10 minutes.

5. Using a rolling pin dusted with flour, gently roll out the dough on a clean work surface dusted with flour until about 3mm thick. Use gingerbread or cookie cutters to cut out your chosen shapes. Re-roll the trimmings and cut more out – you may need to flour the surface again, but be sparing, as excess flour will make the cooked biscuits look dusty. Transfer carefully on to 2 baking trays lined with baking parchment.

6. Bake for 12 minutes. The biscuits will feel slightly soft when they come out of the oven, but will harden as they cool (be careful not to over-bake as they will become tooth-shatteringly crisp when cooled).

7. To make the icing, sift 180g of the icing sugar into a large bowl. Add the aquafaba, cream of tartar and vanilla. Use a fork to whisk together, then use an electric hand whisk and beat until smooth and thick. If the mixture seems runny, or if you want to use the icing to pipe small flowers or frills for a cake, sift in some or all of the remaining icing sugar, then mix well again and test in a piping bag to see if the mixture is firm enough. For flowers, you want a mixture that is almost fudgy in texture.

8. Using a piping bag fitted with the narrowest nozzle, pipe designs on to the gingerbread. Set aside to harden; this can take up to 24 hours (make sure not to stack them until the icing is completely hard). The gingerbread will keep in a sealed container for up to 5 days.

MISO BUTTER CARAMEL POPCORN

SERVES 4

2 tablespoons **neutral cooking oil**

75g **popping corn**

90ml **maple syrup**

1 tablespoon **vegan butter**
or **margarine** (use non-nut or non-soya to keep this NF or SoF)

2 teaspoons **white** or **yellow miso paste** (use soya-free to keep this SoF)

a pinch of **sea salt** (optional)

PREP TIME: 10 MINS · COOK TIME: 25 MINS

Crunchy, buttery, golden, sweet and salty popcorn. If you really love salted caramel, you may want to add a pinch of sea salt, but bear in mind that miso can be salty, especially if making this for kids.

1. Pour half the oil into a large pan, add the popping corn and toss until each kernel is coated in oil. Place over a medium heat, cover and wait until you hear popping sounds inside the pan. Regularly shake the pan, using one hand (covered with a tea towel or oven glove if necessary) to keep the lid in place. When the popping subsides, remove from the heat. Set aside.

2. Heat the oven to 140°C/275°F/gas mark 1.

3. Bring the maple syrup to the boil in a small pan over a high heat, then remove from the heat and immediately add the butter and miso paste. Melt together and mix well to remove any lumps of miso.

4. Grease a large baking tray with the remaining oil. Tip the cooked popcorn into the tray and spread it out. Drizzle over the maple mixture, then use 2 wooden spoons or tongs to toss the popcorn well, making sure each piece is lightly coated. Spread the popcorn out.

5. Bake for 15 minutes. The popcorn will still be slightly soft, but the caramel will firm up quickly as it cools. Run a wooden spoon or spatula under the popcorn, so none of it sticks to the sheet as it cools. Sprinkle with the salt, if using.

6. This can be kept for a day or two in an airtight container, but it is best eaten the day it is made (and you will find it hard to stop that happening, in any case!).

TIP
You can make this addictively sweet-and-spicy by adding hot sauce or hot smoked paprika to the maple mixture – add ½ teaspoon at a time, tasting as you go. Alternatively, toss 1–2 teaspoons white or black sesame seeds through the toasted popcorn.

PUDDINGS, COOKIES, CAKES & BAKES

CHOCOLATE BROWNIE CAKES

75ml **neutral cooking oil**, plus
extra for greasing

2 tablespoons **ground flaxseeds**

75ml **water**

200g **dairy-free dark chocolate**
(minimum 70% cocoa solids)

150ml **unsweetened plant milk**
(use non-soya to keep this SoF)

1 teaspoon **vanilla extract**

75g **plain flour**

50g **gram flour**

2 tablespoons **unsweetened
cocoa powder**

½ teaspoon **baking powder**

150g **caster sugar**

1 tablespoon **strong black coffee**
(optional)

2 large pinches of **sea salt**

100g **mixed nuts** (**walnuts,
pecans, blanched almonds** or
blanched hazelnuts), chopped

**fresh berries, coconut sorbet,
vegan ice cream** (see pages
286–9) or **vegan cream** or
coconut yoghurt, to
serve (optional)

PREP TIME: 20 MINS · COOK TIME: 20 MINS

Squidgy, fudgy, melt-in-the-middle chocolate brownie cakes. The gram flour, along with the ground flaxseeds (available in supermarkets), acts to bind and moisten them. You can replace it with more plain flour, but the brownies will be more crumbly. You can use melted extra virgin coconut oil for these, but it will give the brownies a slight coconut flavour. If making for children, omit the second pinch of salt.

1. Heat the oven to 180°C/350°F/gas mark 4. Line a 12-hole muffin tin with greased silicone cases (or brush paper cases with oil) or line with baking parchment. (The brownies will stick to an unlined tin.)

2. In a small bowl, mix together the ground flaxseeds and water and allow to soak for at least 5 minutes.

3. Break 150g of the chocolate into chunks, then melt in a heatproof bowl with the milk, oil and vanilla over a pan of just simmering water, stirring frequently (don't overheat or the chocolate will split and become grainy). Remove from the heat and allow to cool slightly.

4. Chop the remaining chocolate into small pieces.

5. Sift the flours, cocoa powder and baking powder into a large bowl. Stir in the melted chocolate, the chocolate pieces, sugar, flaxseed mixture, coffee, if using, 1 pinch of the salt and the nuts until just combined.

6. Spoon the mixture into the prepared tin, dividing evenly between the 12 holes. Sprinkle the remaining salt, if using, over the tops of the brownies.

7. Bake for 13–15 minutes, until the tops are firm and cracking, but the centres are still very obviously runny (they will firm up considerably as they cool). Allow to cool in the tin for 5 minutes, then transfer to a wire rack to cool completely.

8. Carefully remove any lining paper as the brownies will be fragile. Serve the brownies, warm or cold, on their own, or with fresh berries, coconut sorbet, vegan ice cream or cream, or coconut yoghurt. They are best eaten within 24 hours of being made. Store in an airtight container at room temperature and, if you like, reheat for 20–30 seconds in the microwave.

LAUREN'S MAPLE & VANILLA GLAZED DOUGHNUTS

MAKES
10

250ml **unsweetened plant milk** (use non-nut or non-soya to keep this NF or SoF)

50g **caster sugar**

½ teaspoon **vanilla bean paste** (or seeds from ½ **vanilla pod**, scraped out)

2 teaspoons **dried active yeast**

400g **strong white bread flour**, plus extra for dusting

1 teaspoon **salt**

1 teaspoon **ground cinnamon**

3 tablespoons **vegan butter** or **margarine** (use non-nut or non-soya to keep this NF or SoF)

neutral cooking oil, for greasing and frying

FOR THE GLAZE:

200g **icing sugar**, plus extra if needed

75ml **unsweetened plant milk** (use non-nut or non-soya to keep this NF or SoF)

1 tablespoon **maple syrup**

1 teaspoon **vanilla extract** or ¼ teaspoon **vanilla bean paste**

PREP TIME: 35 MINS · RISE TIME: 1½ HOURS
COOK TIME: 20 MINS

Lauren Watts is the founder of Dough Society, a vegan doughnut and coffee shop in Hackney, London, selling 20 – yes you read that right! – different kinds of vegan doughnut and they are all incredible. Lauren adapted the shop's recipe for home cooking, just for us.

1. Warm the milk very gently until just lukewarm. Whisk in the sugar, vanilla and yeast. Allow to stand for 5 minutes until foamy.

2. In the bowl of a stand mixer fitted with a dough hook, mix together the flour, salt and cinnamon and knead for 4–5 minutes, until well incorporated and smooth. Add the butter or margarine a tablespoon at a time, kneading until incorporated and smooth before adding the next tablespoon. When it has all been added, put the dough in a clean, lightly oiled bowl, cover with a clean damp tea towel or clingfilm and allow to rise in a warm place for about an hour, or until doubled in size.

3. Using a floured rolling pin, roll out the dough on a clean work surface dusted with flour until about 1.5cm thick. Cut into rounds using an 8cm pastry cutter, then use a smaller 3.5cm cutter to create holes in the middles. Place the rings on 2 baking sheets lined with baking parchment. Knead together the dough trimmings and re-roll. When the dough has all been used, cover loosely with the clean tea towel or clingfilm and allow to prove in a warm place for 30 minutes.

4. Once proved (they'll be fluffy looking and will have increased in size), heat about 6cm of oil in a deep heavy-based pan over a medium heat to 170°C/340°F, or until a cube of day-old bread browns in 30 seconds.

5. Meanwhile, make the glaze. Sift the icing sugar into a bowl, then add the rest of the ingredients and mix well, ensuring there are no lumps. The glaze should be opaque and about as thick as golden syrup – if it seems too thin, sift in a little more icing sugar and blend until smooth again.

6. Using a spatula, carefully lower 2 doughnuts at a time into the hot oil and cook for 2 minutes on each side, or until golden all over. Remove with tongs, allowing the excess oil to drain back into the pan. Drain on kitchen paper while you cook the rest of the doughnuts.

7. When all the doughnuts are cooked, dip each one in the glaze, turning to coat, then place on a wire rack set over a tray (to catch the drips) to cool. These are best eaten while warm, or at least on the day they are made.

TIP
You need to work the gluten in the dough, so we recommend using a stand mixer to prevent tired arms. Try and keep the cooking oil at a steady temperature – too hot and the doughnuts will become hard and brown on the outside while being raw inside, too cool and the doughnuts will be greasy and flabby.

9
DRINKS, SORBETS & ICES

AFFOGATO WITH AMARETTI BISCUITS

1 shot of freshly made **hot espresso**

2 scoops of **cashew vanilla ice cream** (see below) or shop-bought

2–3 **amaretti biscuits** (see opposite, choose gluten-free to keep this GF and WF)

PREP TIME: 10 MINS

Rebecca often serves affogato when friends come for dinner – made with vanilla ice cream, espresso and amaretti biscuits, it's easy, but tastes wonderful. It takes her back to a holiday in Levanto, Italy, and eating affogato on warm summer evenings.

1. To assemble the affogato, make the espresso shot and don't allow it to cool. Place 2 scoops of the ice cream into a small wine glass, small sundae glass or coffee cup. Immediately pour over the hot espresso. Break each biscuit into 2–3 chunks and scatter on top. Serve immediately.

CASHEW VANILLA ICE CREAM

100g **dates**, pitted

500g **cashew cream** (see page 228), chilled

a generous pinch of **cream of tartar**

6 tablespoons **refined coconut oil**

90ml **maple syrup**

2 teaspoons **vanilla bean paste**

1 teaspoon **vegan cider vinegar**

a pinch of **salt**

PREP TIME: 20 MINS · SOAK TIME: 15 MINS
FREEZE TIME: 7½ HOURS

1. Soak the dates in boiling water for 15 minutes. Whisk the cashew cream and cream of tartar using an electric whisk until it forms soft peaks.

2. Drain the dates, then place with the coconut oil in a blender and blend to a smooth purée. If any bits of fruit remain, press through a sieve. Transfer to a microwave-proof bowl and melt in the microwave for 30 seconds. Add the remaining ingredients and mix until smooth.

3. Gradually pour the date mixture into the whipped cashew cream, whisking again, and occasionally scraping down the sides of the bowl.

4. Pour the mixture into a freezer-proof bowl and place in the freezer for 30 minutes. Remove from the freezer and stir, using a fork to break up any lumps as much as possible without mashing it. (If it seems to be freezing very fast, don't worry, as you can blend again before serving.) Repeat this process twice more, then freeze completely for 6 hours or overnight. (Alternatively, if you have an ice cream maker, churn according to the manufacturer's instructions.)

5. About an hour before you want to serve, remove from the freezer. If it is really hard, scrape it into a blender. If your blender has a tamper, use it to press the ice cream down towards the blades. Use a spatula to scrape down the sides. Try not to blitz for too long, as the heat of the blades and motor will start to melt the ice cream after about 1 minute.

6. Scrape back into the bowl, or a tub with a lid if you want to store it, and return to the freezer. Remove 15 minutes before serving, to soften.

AMARETTI BISCUITS

MAKES
12

   (GF) (WF) (SoF)

oil, for greasing

60ml **aquafaba** (tinned chickpea
water, see page 12)

150g **ground almonds**

85g **caster sugar**, plus extra for rolling

½ teaspoon **ordinary** or
   gluten-free baking powder

½ teaspoon **almond extract**
   (optional)

25g **chopped** or **flaked almonds**

a pinch of **salt**

PREP TIME: 10 MINS · COOK TIME: 18 MINS

**Our amaretti are crisp on the outside and squidgy within. Store in
airtight container for up to 4 days or freeze after baking and cooling.**

1. Heat the oven to 180°C/350°F/gas mark 4. Line a baking sheet with baking
    parchment and brush lightly with oil.

2. Mix everything together, stirring to form a sticky paste.

3. Pour a little extra sugar into a small bowl, for rolling the biscuits. Using your
    hands, roll tablespoon-sized pieces of the dough into neat balls. Roll in the
    sugar until well coated, then place on the baking sheet, leaving about 3cm
    between each one as they will spread out. Press gently to flatten slightly.

4. Bake for 15–18 minutes, until light golden. Keep an eye on them towards
    the end of cooking so they don't scorch at the edges or on the bottom. Allow
    to cool and firm up on the baking sheet.

DRINKS, SORBETS & ICES

CASHEW ICE CREAM

SERVES 4

Use the cashew vanilla ice cream recipe on page 284 as the base for these icy treats.

DARK & RICH CHOCOLATE ICE CREAM

PREP TIME: 25 MINS · SOAK TIME: 15 MINS
FREEZE TIME: 7½ HOURS

1 × quantity **cashew vanilla ice cream** (see page 284)
150g **dairy-free dark chocolate**, broken into pieces
1 teaspoon instant **espresso powder** (or **instant coffee granules**, ground to a powder)
50g **dairy-free chocolate chips** or **chopped block chocolate**

1. Make the cashew ice cream following the method on page 284.

2. Two hours or so before you want to serve, melt the chocolate in a heatproof bowl over a pan of just simmering water (don't overheat or it will split and become grainy). Remove from the heat and mix in the espresso powder. Allow to cool.

3. Stir the cooled melted chocolate and the chocolate chips into the ice cream after it is blended for the final time, then allow to freeze completely. Remove from the freezer about 15 minutes before serving to soften slightly.

MAPLE PECAN ICE CREAM

PREP TIME: 25 MINS · SOAK TIME: 15 MINS
COOK TIME: 10 MINS · FREEZE TIME: 7½ HOURS

125g **pecan nuts**
1 tablespoon **refined coconut oil**
1 tablespoon **maple syrup**
1 tablespoon **unrefined caster sugar**
1 × quantity **cashew vanilla ice cream** (see page 284)

1. Heat the oven to 180°C/350°F/gas mark 4. Grease a baking sheet. Tip the pecan nuts into a heatproof bowl.

2. Place the oil, syrup and sugar in a small pan over a high heat and carefully bring to the boil, then immediately take off the heat and pour the mixture over the pecan nuts. Stir to coat.

3. Place the pecans in a single layer on a greased baking sheet. Bake for about 6 minutes, or until golden, turning once halfway through the cooking time. Allow to cool, then finely chop.

4. Make the cashew ice cream following the method on page 284. Fold through the candied pecans after the ice cream is blended for the final time, then allow to freeze completely.

BANANA CARAMEL ICE CREAM

PREP TIME: 25 MINS
SOAK TIME: 15 MINS
COOK TIME: 15 MINS
FREEZE TIME: 7½ HOURS

1 tablespoon **refined coconut oil**

4 **bananas**, thinly sliced

2 tablespoons **maple syrup**

60ml **coconut cream** (from the top of an unshaken tin)

1 teaspoon **vanilla bean paste**

1 × quantity **cashew vanilla ice cream** (see page 284)

1. Melt the oil in a large frying pan over a high heat. When hot, add the bananas and cook for 2–3 minutes on each side, until golden and sticky. Add the maple syrup and when bubbling, add the coconut cream and vanilla paste. Cook, stirring frequently, until the mixture is thick and the bananas have melted into the sauce. Allow to cool slightly, then blend to purée in a blender (or use a stick blender).

2. Make the cashew ice cream following the method on page 284.

3. Ripple through the banana mixture after the ice cream is blended for the final time, then allow to freeze completely. Remove from the freezer about 15 minutes before serving to soften slightly.

Clockwise from top left: maple pecan ice cream, dark & rich chocolate ice cream and avocado coconut gelato (recipe overleaf)

AVOCADO COCONUT GELATO

SERVES
6

  (GF) (WF) (NF) (SoF)

2 × 400ml tins of **full-fat coconut milk**, chilled overnight in the fridge

8–10 tablespoons **icing sugar**, sifted

4 **avocados**, chopped

zest of 2 **limes** and juice of 1 **lime**

PREP TIME: 20 MINS · CHILL TIME: OVERNIGHT
FREEZE TIME: 4 HOURS

This isn't a vegan invention – sweet avocado ice cream made with a traditional custard has been around for a long time, and is common in South America. Kids and adults alike will love this version, with its vivid colour and incredibly creamy texture set off by the zing of lime.

1. Remove the coconut milk from the fridge without shaking the tins. Carefully scoop the white cream from the top of the tins, leaving the clear liquid behind (use this in smoothies or porridge).

2. Place the cream in a large bowl or the bowl of a stand mixer fitted with the whisk attachment. Beat until fluffy, then gradually add 8 tablespoons of the sugar, beating after each addition.

3. Using a stick blender (or food processor or blender), purée the avocados with the lime zest and juice until absolutely smooth, then spoon into the whipped cream. Beat again until completely incorporated and the mixture is pale green and fluffy. The beaters should leave a firm ribbon-like trail on top of the gelato mixture when lifted out of the bowl. Taste, and add more icing sugar if needed. Then pour into a freezer-proof bowl or tub and place in the freezer for 30 minutes.

4. Remove the gelato and give it a good stir (don't worry if it's beginning to seem lumpy – it will get a quick whizz in the blender to smooth it out before serving). Repeat 3 times, then leave for 2 hours to freeze completely. (Alternatively, if you have an ice cream maker, churn the mixture according to the manufacturer's instructions and freeze.)

5. About 20 minutes before you want to serve the gelato, remove it from the freezer and allow to soften for 10 minutes. Transfer to a blender, then blitz for about 1 minute, scraping the sides down and/ or using the tamper to press the gelato down towards the blades while blending (try not to run the blender for more than a minute as the heat of the blades will start to melt the gelato).

6. Using a spatula, scrape into a freezer-proof bowl or tub and return to the freezer for 5–10 minutes, then scoop into bowls, tubs, cones or sundae glasses to serve.

DRINKS, SORBETS & ICES

BANANA CHOCOLATE HAZELNUT ICE CREAM

SERVES
2

   (GF) (WF) (SoF)

4 **bananas**, sliced and frozen overnight

2 tablespoons **unsweetened cocoa powder**

2 tablespoons **maple syrup**

½ teaspoon **vanilla bean paste**

2 tablespoons **hazelnut butter**

PREP TIME: 15 MINS · FREEZE TIME: OVERNIGHT + 30 MINS

Easy-peasy ice cream, no milk or cream required, just bananas and nuts. Frozen bananas make excellent ice cream, and with minimal added sugar but maximum taste, this recipe is particularly good for kids.

1. Place the bananas, cocoa powder, half the maple syrup and the vanilla in a blender (preferably a high-powered one). Blend on the highest setting until smooth, then decant into a freezer-proof dish or tub.

2. In a small bowl, mix together the hazelnut butter and remaining maple syrup until combined. Swirl through the ice cream, but don't let it mix too thoroughly.

3. Eat straight away, or if it seems melted, return to the freezer for 30 minutes to firm up.

CHOCOLATE SORBET

500ml **boiling water**

200g **caster sugar**

60g good-quality **cacao powder** or **unsweetened cocoa powder**

250g **dairy-free dark chocolate**, broken into small chunks

1 teaspoon **vanilla extract**

a pinch of **salt**

75g **frozen berries**, to serve (optional)

PREP TIME: 20 MINS · COOK TIME: 5 MINS
FREEZE TIME: 3 HOURS 20 MINS

Rebecca is obsessed with chocolate ice cream, and as soon as she stopped eating dairy, became equally obsessed with finding a way to make a vegan version. Although this is technically a sorbet, it is incredibly creamy despite containing no milk of any kind. It is loosely based on David Lebovitz's recipe for chocolate sorbet, from his book *The Perfect Scoop*, but our version doesn't require an ice cream maker.

The cooled but unfrozen chocolate mixture can be used as chocolate sauce for puddings or sundaes. Or just eaten with a spoon, straight from the jug. We won't judge you.

1. Pour the water into a large deep pan with the sugar and cacao or cocoa powder. Bring to the boil and boil for 1 minute, whisking carefully and steadily. Remove from the heat and add the chocolate, whisking to encourage it to melt. Add the vanilla and salt and whisk until completely smooth. Pour into a blender and blend for at least 1 minute until foamy. Allow to cool and thicken.

2. When cool, place the blender jug in the freezer for 20 minutes (set a timer). Remove and use a spatula to scrape down the sorbet closest to the edge and mix in, then blend for about 20 seconds. Repeat this process of freezing, scraping and blending 3 more times, then freeze the mixture, still in the jug, for 2 hours.

3. Remove from the freezer, scrape down the sides and blend for 30 seconds, or until completely smooth, then transfer the mixture to a freezer-proof tub, cover with a lid and allow to freeze completely.

4. Remove from the freezer about 10 minutes before you want to serve.

5. If serving with frozen berries, place in the blender and blitz into tiny pieces, then scatter them over the sorbet.

ALL THE MILKS

Although we love making our own milks on occasion, it's worth remembering that commercial plant milks almost all have added calcium and vitamins like D or B12, which can be hard to find in a vegan or plant-based diet, and are especially important for children.

OAT MILK

PREP TIME: 10 MINS · SOAK TIME: 4 HOURS

Adding lemon juice to the soaking liquid may help reduce the amount of phytic acid in the milk (see page 24 for more information). This is best for using on cereal or in cold drinks, as it doesn't contain any stabilizers or emulsifiers, and doesn't respond well to heat.

250g **oats** (use gluten-free to keep this GF and WF)

3 teaspoons **lemon juice**, plus extra to taste

750ml **cold water**

1–3 teaspoons **agave nectar**, to taste

salt

1. Place the oats and half the lemon juice in a non-reactive bowl or tub with a lid and cover with cold water. Allow to soak for 4 hours or overnight.

2. Drain the oats and rinse thoroughly, to get rid of any slimy gloop. Place in a blender with the cold water, the rest of the lemon juice, 1 teaspoon of the agave nectar and a pinch of salt. Blend on high for about 30 seconds.

3. Pour the oat mixture into a muslin-lined sieve and strain out the solids, squeezing out the last of the liquid with your hands. Add extra lemon juice, salt or agave nectar to taste.

4. Store in the fridge, in a container with a lid, for up to 4 days. Stir before use.

HEMP MILK

PREP TIME: 5 MINS

Hemp seeds are available from health food stores or large supermarkets, or online. This is best made in a high-powered blender.

100g **shelled hemp seeds**

250g **creamed coconut**

2 **dates**, pitted

½ teaspoon **vanilla bean paste**

400ml **cold water**

a pinch of **salt**

1. Blend all the ingredients together in a high-powered blender until smooth. Chill before serving.

CASHEW MILK

MAKES **1** litre

(GF) (WF) (SoF)

PREP TIME: 5 MINS · SOAK TIME: 30 MINS

225g **unroasted cashew nuts**

800ml **cold water**

1-2 **dates**, pitted

1 teaspoon **vanilla extract** or **vanilla bean paste** (optional)

a pinch of **salt**

1. Soak the cashew nuts in boiling water for 30 minutes, or cover with cold water and soak in the fridge for at least 4 hours or overnight.

2. Drain and rinse the cashew nuts, then blend in a high-powered blender with the remaining ingredients until completely smooth (if your blender is up to the task, this won't need straining).

3. This will keep in a bottle in the fridge for up to 4 days, but remember to shake or whisk it well before use, as it will separate.

CHOCOLATE MILK

MAKES **1** litre

(GF) (WF) (SoF)

PREP TIME: 5 MINS · SOAK TIME: 30 MINS

225g **unroasted cashew nuts**

800ml **cold water**

5–7 **dates**, pitted, to taste

1 teaspoon **vanilla extract** or **vanilla bean paste**

20g **unsweetened cocoa powder**

a pinch of **salt**

1. Soak the cashew nuts in boiling water for 30 minutes, or cover with cold water and soak in the fridge for at least 4 hours or overnight.

2. Drain and rinse the cashew nuts, then blend in a high-powered blender with the remaining ingredients until completely smooth (if your blender is up to the task, this won't need straining).

3. This will keep in a bottle in the fridge for up to 4 days, but remember to shake or whisk it well before use, as it will separate.

TIP

For a strawberry version of our chocolate milk, omit the dates and cocoa, and add 15 hulled strawberries and up to a tablespoon of maple syrup.

ALMOND MILK

MAKES **1** litre

(GF) (WF) (SoF)

PREP TIME: 5 MINS · SOAK TIME: 8 HOURS

125g **blanched raw almonds**

950ml **cold water**

a pinch of **salt**

2 **dates**, pitted

1. Cover the almonds in cold water and soak in the fridge for at least 8 hours, ideally overnight.

2. Drain and rinse the almonds, then blend in a high-powered blender with the remaining ingredients until completely smooth. Strain through a nut bag or sieve lined with muslin.

3. This will keep in a bottle in the fridge for up to 4 days, but remember to shake or whisk before use, as it will separate.

SMOOTHIES

Treat these two recipes as the basis for your smoothie experiments – add turmeric, non-dairy yoghurt, vegan kefir, spinach, pear, avocado, cayenne, berries, mango, passion fruit or orange...

CARROT, APPLE, GINGER & PINEAPPLE

PREP TIME: 10 MINS

½ small **pineapple**, peeled and diced

1 **apple**, cored and cut into chunks

1 **carrot**, cut into chunks

2cm piece of **fresh ginger**, peeled

zest and juice of 1 **lime**

ice cubes, to serve

1. Stack the ingredients in a high-powered blender so that the pineapple and apple are closest to the blade, as their juice will help the blending process. Add the remaining ingredients and blend until smooth.

2. Pour into 2 glasses over ice.

KALE, CUCUMBER & MINT

PREP TIME: 10 MINS

1 **apple**, cored and cut into chunks

½ **cucumber**, cut into chunks

100g **kale**, thick stems removed, roughly chopped

a small handful of **fresh mint leaves**

3cm piece of **fresh ginger**, peeled

zest and juice of 2 **limes**

ice cubes, to serve

1. Stack the ingredients in a high-powered blender so that the apple and cucumber are closest to the blade. Add the remaining ingredients and blend until smooth.

2. Pour into 2 glasses over ice.

WHISKY SOUR

   (GF) (WF) (NF) (SoF)

PREP TIME: 10 MINS

This aquafaba sour follows the traditional recipe, and works just as well with gin, for a gin sour, or pisco, for a pisco sour (use the bitters to decorate the top of the drink, rather than shaking them with everything else). For an amaretto sour, mix 50:50 amaretto and whisky, and reduce or leave out the sugar.

60ml **bourbon** (or **whisky** of your choice)

5 teaspoons **lemon juice**

2 tablespoons **simple sugar syrup**

2 tablespoons **aquafaba**
 (tinned chickpea water, see page 12)

3 dashes of **Angostura bitters**

ice cubes

maraschino cherry and a **lemon slice**, to garnish

1. Place all the ingredients except the ice and garnish in a cocktail shaker (or a tempered glass jar with a lid). Shake for 10 seconds, to whip and mix the ingredients. Add ice cubes to fill the shaker by about two-thirds and shake again for 10 seconds.

2. Using a fine cocktail strainer or sieve, strain the cocktail into a glass (preferably, a pretty coupe glass or a rocks glass), leaving the ice behind.

3. Arrange the lemon slice around the cherry on a cocktail stick to resemble a 'sail', then add to the drink and serve immediately.

> **TIP**
> Aquafaba has been used instead of raw egg white by enlightened bartenders for a few years – as well as being vegan, it works better because it stays fresh for longer, doesn't smell eggy and there are no worries about tummy bugs.

VEGAN CREAM LIQUEUR

 (GF) (WF) (NF) (SoF)

PREP TIME: 5 MINS

Sweet, creamy and devilishly easy to drink. Double or triple this and store in the fridge for a couple of days. It works very well with bourbon or Irish whisky.

60ml **vegan brandy** or **vegan whisky**

2 tablespoons **freshly brewed espresso** or
 very strong coffee

30ml **Kahlua coffee liqueur**

1 teaspoon **maple syrup**, **agave nectar** or
 simple sugar syrup

3 tablespoons **coconut cream** (from the top of
 an unshaken tin)

2 tablespoons **unsweetened plant milk** (use non-nut or
 non-soya to keep this NF or SoF)

½ teaspoon **vanilla extract**

3 dashes of **vegan chocolate bitters** (optional)

a pinch of **salt**

ice cubes, to serve

1. Place all the ingredients except the ice in a cocktail shaker or blender. Shake or blend until mixture is completely smooth.

2. Pour into 2 glasses over ice cubes.

INDEX

LEON TEAM

Margo Herda
Rute Barreiros
Ben Iredale
Tom Green
Cristina Cirican
Claire Didier
Anderson
Martyn Trigg
Istban Szep "Pisti"
John Corrigan
Thom Malley
Nina Amaniampong
Kristina Dabkeviciene
Rui
Claudinei DS
Thiago Turibio Da Silva
Mariana
Lukasz Kubiak
Avy Visockis
Ewan Milne
Beth Emmens
Marco Berardi
Radoslaw Zemsta
Gabor Salai
Manuela Crivellari
Mahbuby Rabbani
Kristen Rego
Benjamin B
Alan Mcniven
Nichola Norton
Kashmira John
Lee Dunning
Erika Garcia
Katie Jones
Adriano Paduano
Hannah A
Lena Cumacenko
Ana Sobrinho
Johanne Rakotoarisolo
Orsolya Lazar-Erdelyi
Anna K
Matthew Ali
Jade Ebejer
Luca Galvanelli
Gary Marriott
Alessandro Perleonardi
Andrea Gil
Liliya Georgieva
Kelly Coakley
Alisson Grossi
Stacey Strachan
Ana María Nóbrega
    Quijano
Viviane Bogdanov
    Simao
Lob Tang
Severina Pascale
John Vincent
Nacho Curtolo
Corey Douglas
Dimi Dimitrov
Lidia Budkowska
Cameron Essam
John Brooks
Beatrice Gessa
Dovy
Arti Dhrona
David Del Rio Dos
    Santos
Katalin Szabo
Simona Donato
Marta Sedano Vera
Katarzyna
Niki Vrtiskova

Emily Hawkley
Simone Florian
Andreia Ivascu
Andras Klug
Alana
Bence Kovacs
Clara Ballesteros
Rebecca Di Mambro
Giovanna Fuentes
Antony Perring
Chris Burford
Fabio Soliman
Andrea Bulgarelli
Roberta Adamo
Ylenia Bermudez
    Sanchez
Carolyn Prieur
Csaba Borsos
Luca Berardi
Marcos DD
Enioluwa
Ottie
Valeria Colesanti
Ania Swietlicka
Ioannis
Elsayed Mohamed
Jenny Di Nunzio
Cengiz Rahmioglu
Adam Blaker
Izabela Kaniuk
Clara Iudica
Ramona A
Csaba Lukacs
Sam McIntyre
Daniela-Claudia
    Varvarei
Andrea Bassi
Arthur Toso
Filippo Ciarla
Oluwatobiloba Olutayo
Tierney Fauche
David John O'Leary
Gemma Kearney
Kayanda Besa
Ignas
Saffron Cann
Andreea Tudor
Dmitrijs Cumacenko
Natasha Cowdrey
Anto
Kamila Kilian
Russell Simpson
Zoe
Paul Farmer
Albie
Rabbil
Claudia Costea
Pablo Olalla Vilches
Vanessza
Amir
Hannah T
Loui
Ruth JN
Debbie Thorpe
Gabriele K
Tanya
Ana Nicoleta Lisman
Mary
Justyna S
Shewit
Emin Cheese
Nirav Desai
Enrico Bonetti
Alberto Biasi

Merche Martin
Magdalena S
Mehdichaouqi
Miguel M
Rafa Rafiki
Lina Lazarova
Zydrune
Sabrina Stefan
Sensa Madonna
Joanne
Salvatore
Lynda-Sabah Elbounabi
Adrian Pompey
Maciej "Magic" Meyza
Erika Kupfer
Ednvinas
Vanessa Valadao
Silvia Zuccarino
Maria D
Melissa Wilson
Yasmin M
Nundi Parsons
Valeira A
Hector Itachi
Frederique Anctil
Vaiva
Giacomo
Adam Nagy
Andrea Franchi
Nicholas Scovell
Alaina
Desisisisisi
Patrick McKenny
Peter Meszaros
Bruna Lise De Moura
Michaela
Sexy Ozzy
Giada
Elizangela
Alex Maj
Ali Delaney
Charlotte McCarter
Kendra Guerrero
Charlene H
Erika P
Jada Kennedy-Mark
Paul Casey
Shanti
Tammy
Nomsa
Adam Klosowski
Alina L
Suada Fetahu
Oskar Z
Patricia R
Gianluca Marletta
Vendella Oppenheimer
Agnes
Peter B
Luca L
Sara
Jimena CV
Chineye
Hector Morillo Aguilera
Yasmine
Philippa D
Marcin Kaminski
Engila Saidy
Rabson Mwale
Youcef
Federica Cicero
Kelly LG
Alexandra K
Anastasie Etoundi

Valerii Subaci
Gioele
Rosie E
Aisha
Klaudia Baran
Srijana Bantawa-Doman
Lautaro Curtolo
Aleksandra D
Caroline Gabrielle
    Jacqueline Marty
Dywain
Lenia
Carolanne C
Aurora Minuto
Mala Gurung
Giulia Archetti
Joanna S
Kamau Pink
Kevin Freitas Silva
Elizabete
Rosario
Valentina S
Aleksandra Z
GintareKi
Mizhgan
Sam (Bush)
Amilton de Sousa
Sam Velvet
John-Alex
Katalin E
Leticia
Aleksandra M
Cato Tønnessen
Diana B
Felix Rivas
Kassius Lipko
Cindy Veeren
Danielle
Geoffrey Osei-Kofi
Yasmina
Georgios
Wided
Federica G
Mohammed Z
Bilal Hussain
Nacho Arroyo
Marco Reick
Anna CS
Magdalena M
Claudia VF
Raquel Binelli Campos
Mar
Jade O'Mahoney
Jade Richter
Erik
Denis Krastev
Hubert
Djafar Ouahchia
Katie Harris
Dora T
Neeraj Gangurde
AmandaGiatti
Anthony O
Ines Eshak
Katrina
Rosie Bayliss
Yassien Hamza
Ayanna A
Nasteho Elmi
Daniela GA
Valentina SP
Tomoko Klosowski
Ashleigh VDH
Cristiano Sequeira

Gouveia
Vida
Magdalena M
Juliana António De
    Almeida Cardoso
Delice
Shipon
Annastacia Crooks
Kasia
Agata Cyminska
    Thomas
Joao A
Sandra Silva
Thomas Hopper
Cameron Love
Iraman
Lidija
Poppy Kitcher
Angelika G
Lucy IM
Olakunle
Sebastian Puchalski
Shelby Davey
Vincenzo
Ainara
Aaron Rahn
Paulo T
Louise Wells
Sal
Simran Jandu
Virgilia Ianotaro
Ginte
Kristina M
Zoltan Almasi
Matteo Leschiera
Chun C
Emin Ho Van
Hannah Driscoll
Magdalena Szpytma
Gabriela
Hristina
Joan Oltra
Chris Frame
Klaudia
Ollie Cooney
Gabriele S
Manuela O
Maria V
Nicola Loveday
Michael F
Vladareanu Andreea
Michelle Nkedi
Sean Matthews
Wojciech L
Harry Harrison
Joana AS
Mathilde Perrais
Rodrigo Bettiol Ribeiro
Daniela I
Patrik
Anna Kormos
Charlotte Wilkinson
Ian
kara
Kobe Clerc
Megan
Carolina FH
Diana Ibrion
Suzanne
Isidor
Tamas C
Erica Molyneaux
Ioana Gavrila
Justina Cesnauskyte

Rapha Gomez
Carlos B
Helen
Viktor
Ami Wilkins
Franchesca S
Carlos AS
Giuseppe Fallucchi
Jesus
Jana B
Łukasz Ludowich
Iulia Tat
Angelika O
Mei
Sakinah
Shereen Ritchie
Jennifer
Yordan
Irene
Michele C
Sarela MM
Lakshmi
Carla A
Patrycja Lipinska
Renata Taylor
Joshna Aloor
Karolina N
Benjamin H
Emmanuel Sule
Haissatou
John Jordan
Sana
Maya Gordon
Eva Zacharia
Seval
Ellsys Mélanos'
Lorna
Rosa
Tim Smalley
Alessandro Straccia
Benedict W
Viktoria Raj
Tamara
Nezliya Muhara
Dorinda
Valentina OH
Lorenzo
Raj
Priscilla
Alexander King
Aida Morer Caba
Gissell
Manoela Groh
Mauricio PG
Stephen C
Wojtek Wujcikowski
Alina
Delphine Hille
Galina
Saico
Saskia Harrison
Emma AC
Asha Folkes
Joao S
Tazar
Anna K
Daniel H
Rebeca Calugareanu
Curtis HW
Eddy
Hope
Izabela M
Elzie Coakley
Matthina C
Aashutosh
Aldona Lis
Edwar
Enoch Bugyei
Nadia Furno

Gemma Holroyd
Sarah Davies
Faith Ajamogha
Jonay Gutierrez Rodriguez
Mansour
Mirella
Victor Ayoze Campos Benitez
Domante Putnaite
Carla P
Arnold A
Sophie Hudson
Zaenab Popoola
Kinda Rama
Luiz LDM
Carlos PM
Gabriela GO
Kai S
Zeinab
Judit Comas Ginebra
Borislav L
Marco Cadel
Nycola Buttress
Sindy Reyes
Sukunya
Martha Dougma
Pasquale
Frederick
Justyna C
Alexander S
Gkioka
Alise Jugbarde
Didi
Edmundas
Rebecca C
Vika Kapustina
Ashleigh C
Jean F
Hildah
Judit Lara
Eliza Ward
Anna Addis
Elisabetta
Emily G
Josh M
Oliver Pope
Vanessa Chiarolla
Meseret
Viktorija
Kieran Finch
Omar Ammar
Aishat Seriki
Eloise
Toluwani
Alberto-Mihai Ilies
Attila Gereb
Chloé Suffell
Eashan
Lara Eyre
Nana
Valentin
Henry Nice
Martina Rossi
Randa
Alexandra B
Francesco P
Gregory
Indre
Robin Auld
Sofia Macedo
Lara Willson
Zarah
Adjoa
Flora Brazuelo Millán
Jana S
Shani
Tianna
Andrew G

Eduardo
Fran Cherpin
Mauricio LA
Liuba Marchionne
Millie Geldard
Beatriz RC
Habiba
Liliana
Milena
Dow Panyawong
Yuliyan
Alejandra
Jonathan Lau
Julian Antonio
Crawford
Simona M
Yewande
Aleksandra M
Ryen
Peter Bosze
Keelan Gervis
Ibrahima
Ivaylo Mitev
Jamane Barrett
Manuel
Manuela L
Morena
Pablo A
Phili Alexander
Rickeisha
Grzegorz
Lucila
Niccolo
Jimmy
Narja
Anca Ghitescu
Andrè "Sexual Chocolate" Taylor
Dadi Velichkov
Ilyes
Olivia Lajos
Alfred R
Ayhan H
Jessica Z
Myumyun
Sergio Jerez
Syed
Anthony GV
Emitinan
Dalia Torres Sánchez
Sebastian BO
Roxana
Serena Bersani
Valerio C
Lucy P
Trevor
Alba
Amarae
Mason
Andres HB
Dorota
Elisa Pompa
Joseph C
Kotryna
Oscar Drowley
Oluwatofunmi
Elisa
Damian Wiban
Greg Stolowski
Charlotte Wells
Jean K
Nikki McHale
Grazvile Dragunaite
Ina Kozemiakina
Kazam Tatlases
Mark Tyler
Mateusz Z
Chelsea Burns
Serena

Jahdarae
Ali H
Ana P
Dawn Hackett
Francesco Condemi
Saenuri Kim
Ruth Ventura
Emerson
Katarzyna W
Ayan H
Alessia Stabile
Paulo Monteiro
W. Wal Zygadlo
Mohammad ali
Iqra
Javier
Miguel JA
Charlotte C
Mouad
Yuliana
Elaine
Beato R
Ben W
Claudia HM
Karolina M
Lopes
Rukshana
Ellie Holder
David R
Adarsha
Ramona L
Marco R
Orlan Masilu Lokubike
Awil W
Leone
Lyubov
Maike
Irena Cashman
Gabriel Bastos-Vankirk
Maria Oaches
Maymuna Ali
Vivien
Ilona
Amia
Jean L
Salvija
Karolina Ciepal
Kevin S
Alberto L
Jasmine
Ainhoa
Amal Ishaq
Petya
Catia Santos
Claire Richford
Marianna
Yozkan
Karin
Ali EH
Nathan DS
Alexandros K
Karen Stone
Veronica DS
Giovanny B
Mariyah
Alessio
Edward Wells
Jose
Mohit Panchal
Salome
Juan LA
Monia
Arvids P
Charles C
Daniele MS
Marc
Sigita
Veronica D
Adrian M

Enrique P
Francesco De Stasio
Davide C
Sergio Lasa
Ludo Romagnoli
Edison
Viviane CB
Zakery
Clarice R
Sebastian F
Asmin H
Donat
Carla T
Fruzsina
Charlie B
Cristina PI
Nikolay
Yherson
Michael G
Nathan Franklin
Dragos
Richárd Cseh
Simona M
Anowar M
Jack Cooper
Nsimba
Luchiano Blackett
Juan G
Katya
Melissa St.Clair-Braudé
Valentina V
Zelie
Guste
Miriam
Elaiza Endziulaityte
Armani L
Carlos ST
Michele D
Yenis
Annie P
Mario O
Cynthia BT
Florencia
Keli
Mario DCS
Mateusz K
Nedas Sirutis
Annie Lo
Patricia SR
Jorge
Kelin
Emma S
Alicia M
Andres AP
Beatrice Griffanti
Eloína
Riccardo
Giovanni
Jonathan Simao (Jonny)
Mark N
Andre Wesley Barbosa
Chiara L
Diego Andrés Gómes Teixeira
Emeline M
Gabriele S
Leopold
Michael A
Michela Bosco
Saoussane
Andreea G
Angus L
Jordan
Tom Wellingham
Andrea Hamrova
Eugene
Madalina G
Savio
Victor S

Anastasia S
Claudia Esposito
Claudia HA
Marco Mundo
Marjorie
Patricia F
rachel
Isaura
Carlo S
Ana Maria Zamfir
Brandon S
Claudia PA
Dario G
Fernando
Gaija
Hilal
Jonatan
Massimiliano
Patrick J
Rimaldo
Shela Begum
William
Eilidh
Ashik M
Katy Carrington
Noora Kippola
Simone Liggi
Simona I
Szymon
Donus Sarican
George
Kiaro Saulter
Krisztofer
Nemesio
Severine
Stephen M
Desislava Avramova
Dylan Faulds
Erfan
Jacqueline Mierez
Hudo
Ondrej
Enrico N
Lloyd
Holly Blake
Oussama Izem
Anna L
Damian L
Erica DM
Rita Tumaite
Toma Ezulike
Edyta Diakowicz
Gabriel SDA
Alexandra S
Corynne K
Dennis M
Filipe
Dora B
Luis DPC
Allaine N
Gabriel Bilal Annouka
Debora
Dublin
Leo McIntosh
Tatiana
Guilherme
Alessia Miani
Christopher K
Quinn Durlston-Powell
Yesha Patel
Cristina S
Marcin K
River Manning
Alex
Alyisha Isabella Pillai
Dominik Erdei
Jamey Collier
Marcos MG

Natasha R
Omojiade
Rebecca J
Sorina
Tamla Tyrell
Jacob
Jamela
Ladislav Novák
Michal Frankiewicz
Petar
Andrea Kyei
Ruben B
Billy C
Celina HR
Gabriela K
Genevieve
Daniel Scalabrino
Mihaela S
Regan
Yasmin A
Liliane Castro
Kia
Mahima
Shea
Trischia Joyce
M Saberon
Valerio S
Amber
Andrea US
Anisoara Burlacu
Jusdian Harkinto
Sukaina
Vee Williams
Zachary Caparanga
Francess
Joselyn
Gabriele M
Ayretin R
Carlos TM
Emilio
Evie Lythgoe-Cheetham
Saarah Hussain
Eva ES
Timonth L
Becky
Bree Faucher
Claudia MA
Danillo Rezende
Dom Carter
Gabriel I
Giorgia
Vinicius
Callum C
Harley
Rhiannon
Calvin H
Joweria
Sarah WQ
Easmund Lau
Fabio VP
Pauline
Alp Watmough
Anil S
Anna B
Antonio P
Gary Chan
Jessica AC
Lucas Gobbo
Luis M Cortes
Whitney Abayomi
Catalina G
Saffa Abdi
Tamas Babarczi
Malika Barry
Joseph C
Agata Michniewicz
Ivan
Ruben MV

Carlo M
Ifeoma
Jessica LM
Sophie M
Artemios
Callum W
Chloe W
Cristian C
Dace R
Dominika
Freya Scott Broomfield
Gustavo
Hish
Junita A
Maryam
Maryan
Matej Ludvik
Simone A
Sona Ivanovicova
Xavier
Adam ElBounabi
Tabassum
Toms Krauklis
Egle
Lydia Vale
Richard C
Vladislav
Maria L
Abraham
Onik Akhid Zavaed Rahman
Alexander H
Nadda Arbullami
Paula Cortes
Sirem
Sumer Saleh
Thomas F
Whitneyanne Ideh
Zubair Ben Rais
Matias CEM
Vitor
Noelia
Petra
Adonnis Gilhodes
Clyde IO
Daniel D
Hannah O
Juan BG
Lauren Brooker
Marcin N
Maria Rosa
Migle
Paola
Samanta
Samson
AmriT
Erden
Htut Khaung
Lewis
Lohloh
Lindsay
Marzena
Mel
Nada
Omari
Saeed
Wiam
Zunezo Sadiq
Brandon P
Lucky Abat
Ναταλία Τσερνίσεβα
Sergio MJ
Bartosz Z
Panera Izaura
Natalia Wyzycka
Nicole Olutayo
Patrycja Dworak
Andrew Reid - Duncan

Despoina
Mariam
Mohammed F
Sofia V
Ciarán Linehan
David SR
Edna
Karissa Govender
Oshinbori
Pio
Susmita
Alexander C
Aminat
Andres Yunda
Cheryl B
Oskar K
Mihaela R
Pavel
Cherise A
Jean D
Juceleyde
Karolina S
Khadijah
Ranjith Nair
Aviva T
Carlos SG
Hesham
Rosheen
Teja
Yasmin Ali
Aleksandra W
Aleshandro L
Andreya RD
Eunice Goncalves Furtado
Giorgos Polykarpou
Klaudia G
Mishelle Leiva
Moez Abdu
Pinky
Rafael
Silvija Vaiciunaite
Sophia
Tom Binnie
Valerija
Aydan J
Dimitris
Gabriela Mavrichi
Joshua
Katia
Sarah A
Yasmin I
Fazira Naraju
Lesly
Peiheng
Salma Azad
Allison J
Hana
Krystian Starczewski
Raluca Lazarescu
Olivia O
Antal Babarczi
Emiliya
Fatin C
Fern
Ilhan Ali
Lewis Daws
Sam Arojo
Sam MA
Luke Anokhin
Toca Mela
Jimmy Allen
Jane Melvin
Steve Head
Julian Hitch
David Bulbrook
Victoria Coyne
Simon Kelsey

Nick Evans
Brad Blum
Spencer Skinner
Fersen Lambranho
Rodrigo Boscolo
Maryte (Maria)
Paul Butcher
Howard Lockwood
Liza Nicol
Gijs van der Wilk
Koen Huiskes
James Powell
Stuart FitzGerald
Brian McIntyre
Donna Doyle
Aileen Cummins
Nickie Bartsch
Glenn Edwards
Marcelo Butron Arnez
Ashley Thornton
Ryan Bell
Steph Gaspar
Carlen Dickerson
Lucy Knowles
Simon Ward-Nicholson
James Turner
Natalia DiPalma
Kayley Van Dijk
Walter Seib
Natalie Ward
Meera Chohan
Andie Dickens
Grace Brown
Ayo Aderibigbe
Nicole Delafuente
Macey Brown
Aliyah Zaman
Jake Hawkshaw
Jakob Addo
Lena Pusey
Kimberley Hanson
Jessie Smith
Joshua Jackson
Verinda Sohal
Jacob Townson
Stuart Martin
Betsy Hyacinthe
Emi Kano-Binch
Melanie Egdell
James Wallace
Vanessa Robinson
Emily Scott
Melanie Le Roy Accra
Muhammad Rouf
Minelva Bartley
Stephanie Corr-Amajo
Thania Halima
Shetu Rahman
Kayleigh Lythgoe
Md Azizur Rahman
Alexandra Vasilescu
Laura Zamfir
Wanda Perretta
Cosmin Mociornita
Maria De Los Angeles
Sadjo Camara
Karolina Goralska
Mohammed Hadi
Elena Segovia Donoso
Madalina Stancioiu
Nicolas Atzeni
Suzan Hassen
Marius Enache
Georgi Mladenov
Alexia Plegnon
Stephane Grant
Wojciech Sokolowski
Malgorzata Pasierb

Sarah Middleton Johns
Jaydene Webley
Maria Turcu
Zatim Amada
Lakeisha Langford
Sonia Cuellar
Alexandru Coman
Alexandru Vasilescu
Adetayo Agoro
Reece Bartley
Liliana Busnosu
Yasmin Christian
Louise Kamau
Safiya Simmonds
Chioma Opara
Parth Lakhisarani
Tatiana Muruaga
Mihaela Brinzea
Dominik AmIahowicz
Juan Schlitter
Daisy De Melo
Anna Maria Tsamasfyr
Michael Nunoo
Crina Muresan
Erika Lozano Chaparro
Lois Nyamekye
Jessica Lakay
Rudy Awaga
Feven Woldemariam
Lucinda Langford
Magdalena Lasota
Cinzia Oliviero
William Abe
Madeleine Zehetner
Princess Adebiyi
Markiyan Mitchyn
Priscilla Agyare
Joel Owusu-Ansah
Nii Dowuona-Ocran
Asad Jamil
Antonio Cimmino
Sivanyaa Sivanayagam
Villane Walcott
Deborah Zonzolo
Renee King
Dalia Samuel
Cassie Cooney-Gordan
Khalid Hassan
Conrad Omari
Yusuf Dawood
Maria Pena Montano
Asheka Jones
Chijioke Ude
Aini Abdulah
Naomi Estrela
Cherno Bmai
Nathalia Henao
Oliver Reeves
Kristianne Punzalan
Sara Hassan
Dimitrinka Pandova
Anum Khan
Choi Cheung
Mollie Martin
Ndabane Makukula
Jacob Udnæs
Adrienne Lough
Alit Dewa
Amalie Vorren
 Søndergaard
Anna Stefansen
Ariel Baeña
Beñat Elortza Larrea
Reibild Vermes
Christina Young
 Shpukha
Diana Fernandes
Elliott Bowen

Emil Hugnell
Hans Rabben
Helene Skjenneberg
Hojattullah Hassani
Hyojung Son
Julie Eikaas
Katrina Tania Locsin
Kristian Shishmanov
Lisa Helena Andersson
Louise Lindeberg
Lucrecia Amante Dalog
Lulu Gakunju
Maya Jamal
Milad Shadadi
Milos Djoric
Miodrag Krajnovic
Nadin Louelf
Nawraj Sapkota
Nilana Salawati
Oriane Jolly
Orthon Leer Madengue
Paulina Tarnowska
Ramon Gimenez Rius
Rebekah Solomon
Rumman Chowdhury
Sebastian Torres
Seonmi Mun
Shamsah Luswata
Sondre Skjenneberg
Souzana Leontidou
Thomas Nanos
Traci Milimo
Vigdis Eygló
 Einarsdóttir
Zoitsa Gorgou
Anne-Katrine
 Ertesvåg Aa
Sara Werselius
Marianne Galleberg
Marianne Lund
Evelina Söderholm
Jessica Van Der Zee
Islam Bashir
Richard Vieira Rijo
Ghylène Dam
Ayla Meijer
Sebas van Loon
Ritika Nowlakha
Naomi de Haas
Loeka
AM Trawicka
Garry
Tatiana
Aram
Rochelle
Marika
Viktoria
Emanuela
Christine
Hussain
Mohammed
Timea
Giovanni
Sherifat
Annaka
David
Roxana
Jeremy
Gabriela
Paula
Daniela
Arlene
Antzel
Issa
Mohamed
Anastasija
Mohammed
Naomi

Natasha
Iqra
Joyce
Meshach
Maria
Edrissa
Miriam
Fatou
Kwame
Lis Morina
Nicola Tidu
Nicola
Goran
Peter
Rashny
Merveil
Peter
Yenis
Tamas
Erykah
Christian
Anwer
Amy
Craig
Byron
Dominika
Agnieszka
Magdalena
Malgorzata
Kamil
Mariola
Patrjcja
Elizabeth
Helen
Chloe
Iliana
Magdalena
Andrzej
Tiffany
Izabela
Harry
Mario
Erika
Marianela
Maria
Martin
Mariusz
Rafael
Fernande
Joanne
Hocine
Misrraldo
Anabela
Ruvimbo
Ildiko
Luz
Milena
Kazia
Luis
Tania
Luis
Andreia
Antonio
Jack
Anna
Niamh
Anna
Lucy
Lin
Morven
Justine
Jasmine
Emilia
Cecilia
Aniko
Robert
Stanislava
Kristina Aleknaviciute

Andre
Emilia
Anthony
Prem
Rosy
Stanley
Manuel
Maria
Joe
Dorothy
Livina
Milroy
Sam
Perpetua
Joylon
Sarbjit
Nikita
Lucia
Vclison
Wilton
Anita
Nikita
Manuela
Mateusz
Asley
Franky
Janefa
Yatin
Tariro
Aaron
Bartosz
Ahmed
Joycelynn
Jasdeep
Madonna
Rochelle
Amandia
Calen
Laila
Teanne
Ananya
Maryam
Sonam
Robert
Rosary
Nasser
Sylwia
Celestina
Valentina
Renato
Aston
Shannon
Gloria
Martynas
Annamaria
Rita
Alyssa
Roselyn
Giorgia
Flory
Nikita
Johnny
Cheyyenne
Prokash
Abdulqadir
Maya
Veruska
Laurentine
Migle
Bijoux
Valentino
Ana
Ayyaz
Abdurahman
Mirko
Giovanni
Ionela
Annabella

Raphael
Hamraj
Matthew
Stefan
Ayesha
Mahima
Beatrice
Anamaria
Hodan
Anna
Andra'
Belnela
Esa
Olsen
Dilaver
Bohdan
Iyaniwura
Cameron
Marvin
Semhar
Mariam
Cameron
Grace
Nicos
Emilian
Charlotte
David
Helga Jonas
Petrina
Sarah
Richard
David
Megan
pratima
Joe
Eleisha
Georgia
Emily
Jay
Ellie
Caris
ryan
James
Jacob
Leanne
Eleanor Bentley
Emily
Annabelle
Eleanor
Melissa
Ryan
Liam
Ben
Gabrielle
Hannah
Ana
Emily
Liam
Nadine
Jessica
Charlotte
Jack
Jemmima
Shaunie
Jeremy
Ellie
Rob Woowal
Patriciaa
Rosalle Horsman
Andrea Tomkinson
George Newens
Connor James Smith
Gemma Roberts
Bethany Bate
Alex Hunt
Matt Job
Lucy Priest
Keeley McCandless

ACKNOWLEDGEMENTS

FROM REBECCA

I was excited, but not a little daunted, when I was asked to help create a vegan book with the team at LEON. So, I was very happy indeed to learn I would be co-authoring *Fast Vegan* with Chantal, as well as John – Chantal is a hugely imaginative cook and brought so many brilliant ideas to the kitchen. Plus, we had such a good, gossipy time cooking together.

As ever, working with John was a pleasure – I have so much admiration for what he does with LEON, and the principles by which he and the business stand.

I would like to thank my wonderful little girls, Isla and Coralie, for once again putting up with their house being turned into a development kitchen and photography studio.

We were so lucky to feature recipes from some of our favourite chefs and cooks. Thank you to Meriel Armitage at Club Mexicana (clubmexicana.com), David Clack and Frank Yeung at Mr Bao (mrbao.co.uk), Maisie Williams at Burger Garden (facebook.com@ burgerlolz), Lauren Watts at Dough Society, Rinku Dutt at Raastawala (Twitter @raastawala), Cem Yildiz at What the Pitta (whatthepitta.com), Vida Scannell from LEON and Jemima Grant, who generously allowed us to use their recipes here.

Sian Henley and my husband Steven Joyce were a dream team when it came to making the recipes look delicious in the photos, with Jo Ormiston sourcing the most gorgeous places to shoot in and beautiful things to shoot on. Thank you to Tom Groves, Holly Triggs, Lauren Law, Stephanie Howard, Libby Silbermann, Anna Hiddlepit and Seonid Bulmer for being such excellent assistants, and to Lee Oliver, Anamika Singh and Sean Matthews for providing the party vibes. The whole shoot went so smoothly, all thanks to a great team. (Thanks for making short work of the 'excess' doughnuts, chocolate cake and cookies, too!) Sian and chef/food stylist Iain Graham also gave invaluable feedback on the recipes, helping to improve them no end, for which we are very grateful. (Although any mistakes remain our own.)

Thanks to Alison Starling, Pauline Bache and Jonathan Christie at Octopus for celebrating the good bits and easing us through the trickier bits of creating such a big book! Thanks again to my agent, Antony Topping, for bringing us all together in the first place.

FROM CHANTAL

I'd like to thank John and his family, plus Marion, my children Tai and Ethan, and my mum for trying all my food, again and again. Extra thanks also to my family for washing up after me too! Thanks also to Rebecca, for steering me through, to everyone who worked on the book and the team at Octopus.

FROM JOHN

Rebecca and Chantal are two of my fave peeps. I have worked with Rebecca on two previous books and this time the whole adventure was just as brilliant and just as fun. So, thank you Rebecca for the dedication you have and the joy you bring. You bring so much love and easy authority to your work. This is Chantal's first book ever and surely has to be the first of many. I have known Chantal for seven years as a private cook and also as an important part of our LEON food development team. Chantal is one of the most creative and curious chefs that I have met. Chantal you are a special person, so deal with it.

Thank you to Jo Sidey, who has been very important to the development of graphic design at LEON and to our culture more broadly. Thank you to Sean Matthews who gave the book an added bit of graphic magic. Thanks also to photographer Steven Joyce, for making the food look as good as it tastes.

We rely on the nutritional expertise of a wide range of people including Robert Verkerk, Mel Aldridge, Megan Rossi, Carole Symons and Lucie Jansen, and I am very grateful for your advice.

To my wife, Katie, and Natasha and Eleanor, you have to enjoy and endure the LEON rollercoaster without knowing whether there is a corkscrew or loop the loop coming up next. I am grateful for your love, support and counsel

What LEON is today, and therefore the values in this cookbook, have been influenced very much by Mum and Dad. Mum, you are the best human being that anyone

will ever meet. Thank you for teaching me positivity and resilience. And for being here so much for all the family. We love you.

Dad, I miss you. You were so gentle and funny and clever and loving. And you showed me how to have fun too. LEON has your name. I hope I can make sure it keeps your values too.

We have great publishers who have become part of the LEON family. Alison Starling, Jonathan Christie and Pauline Bache in particular deserve our thanks for their professionalism and dedication.

Everything we do relies on my colleagues who work in the restaurants every day, making sure that each guest gets a big welcome and perfect food every time. Thank you to all of you. I am so grateful.

To Borough support team: wow! I could not ask to work with a more dedicated group of people. You are family. Thank you, too, to the LEON Board (Tim, Brad, Spencer, Nick, Fersen and Rodrigo and Antony) for putting up with me, for now. You give me so much of your time, and I am so grateful for that. We need to take LEON to more people and places together.

And thank you to to our franchisees. You have chosen to invest in us and we take the responsibility very seriously.

Lastly to the mums and dads (managers) who run all the LEON restaurants. You are the heart of the company. And also the brains and the guts. Thank you.

An Hachette UK Company
www.hachette.co.uk

First published in Great Britain in 2018 by Conran, an imprint of
Octopus Publishing Group Ltd
Carmelite House
50 Victoria Embankment
London EC4Y 0DZ
www.octopusbooks.co.uk

Photography by Steven Joyce
Design, art direction and styling: Jo Sidey (Ormiston)
LEON designer: Sean Matthews
Food styling: Sian Henley

Publisher: Alison Starling
Creative director: Jonathan Christie
Senior editor: Pauline Bache
Copyeditor: Jo Murray
Senior production manager: Katherine Hockley

We have endeavoured to be as accurate as possible in all the
preparation and cooking times listed in the recipes in this book.
However they are an estimate based on our own timings during recipe
testing, and should be taken as a guide only, not as the literal truth.

Nutrition advice is not absolute. If you feel you require consultation
with a nutritionist, consult your GP for a recommendation.

Standard level spoon measurements are used in all recipes.
1 tablespoon = one 15ml spoon
1 teaspoon = one 5ml spoon

Fresh herbs should be used unless otherwise stated. If unavailable
use dried herbs as an alternative but halve the quantities stated.

Ovens should be preheated to the specific temperature
– if using a fan-assisted oven, follow manufacturer's
instructions for adjusting the time and the temperature.

This book includes dishes made with nuts and nut derivatives. It
is advisable for customers with known allergic reactions to nuts
and nut derivatives and those who may be potentially vulnerable
to these allergies, such as pregnant and nursing mothers, invalids,
the elderly, babies and children, to avoid dishes made with nuts
and nut oils. It is also prudent to check the labels of pre-prepared
ingredients for the possible inclusion of nut derivatives.